CONTENTS

CAMBRIDGE LECTURES

SIR ARTHUR QUILLER-COUCH,
born in 1863 in Cornwall. Educated at
Clifton and Trinity College, Oxford, and
adopted a literary career. Knighted in 1910;
and in 1912 appointed Edward VII Professor
of English Literature at the University of
Cambridge, being elected a fellow of Jesus
College.

CAMBRIDGE LECTURES

BY

SIR ARTHUR QUILLER-COUCH

Essay Index Reprint Series

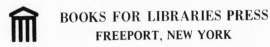
BOOKS FOR LIBRARIES PRESS
FREEPORT, NEW YORK

First Published 1943
Reprinted 1972

Library of Congress Cataloging in Publication Data

Quiller-Couch, Sir Arthur Thomas, 1863-1944.
   Cambridge lectures.

   (Essay index reprint series)
   Reprint of the 1943 ed., which was issued as no. 974
of Everyman's library: essays & belles-lettres.
   CONTENTS: Inaugural lecture.--On the lineage of
English literature.--The art of reading. [etc.]
   1. English literature--Addresses, essays, lectures.
2. Literature--Addresses, essays, lectures. I. Title.
II. Series: Everyman's library, no. 974.
PR99.Q57 1972   820'.9   72-4723
ISBN 0-8369-2970-5

PRINTED IN THE UNITED STATES OF AMERICA

INAUGURAL LECTURE

WEDNESDAY, JANUARY 29, 1913

IN all the long quarrel set between philosophy and poetry I know of nothing finer, as of nothing more pathetically hopeless, than Plato's return upon himself in his last dialogue 'The Laws.' There are who find that dialogue (left unrevised) insufferably dull, as no doubt it is without form and garrulous. But I think they will read it with a new tolerance, may-be even with a touch of feeling, if upon second thoughts they recognize in its twistings and turnings, its prolixities and repetitions, the scruples of an old man who, knowing that his time in this world is short, would not·go out of it pretending to know more than he does, and even in matters concerning which he was once very sure has come to divine that, after all, as Renan says, 'La verité consiste dans les nuances.' Certainly 'the soul's dark cottage battered and decayed' does in that last dialogue admit some wonderful flashes,

> From Heaven descended to the low-roofed house
> Of Socrates,

or rather to that noble 'banquet-hall deserted' which aforetime had entertained Socrates.

Suffer me, Mr. Vice-Chancellor and Gentlemen, before reaching my text, to remind ourselves of the characteristically beautiful setting. The place is Crete, and the three interlocutors — Cleinias a Cretan, Megillus a Lacedaemonian, and an Athenian stranger—have joined company on a pilgrimage to the cave and shrine of Zeus, from whom Minos, first lawgiver of the island, had reputedly derived not only his parentage but much parental instruction. Now the day being hot, even scorching, and the road from Cnossus to the Sacred Cave a long one, our three pilgrims, who have forgathered as elderly men, take it at their leisure, and propose to beguile it with talk upon Minos and his laws. 'Yes, and on the way,'

promises the Cretan, 'we shall come to cypress-groves exceedingly tall and fair, and to green meadows, where we may
repose ourselves and converse.' 'Good,' assents the Athenian.
'Ay, very good indeed, and better still when we arrive at them.
Let us push on.'

So they proceed. I have said that all three are elderly
men; that is, men who have had their opportunities, earned
their wages, and so nearly earned their discharge that now,
looking back on life, they can afford to see Man for what he
really is—at his best a noble plaything for the gods. Yet they
look forward, too, a little wistfully. They are of the world,
after all, and nowise so tired of it, albeit disillusioned, as to
have lost interest in the game or in the young who will carry
it on. So Minos and his laws soon get left behind, and the
talk (as so often befalls with Plato) is of the perfect citizen and
how to train him—of education, in short; and so, as ever with
Plato, we are back at length upon the old question which he
could never get out of his way—What to do with the poets?

It scarcely needs to be said that the Athenian has taken hold
of the conversation, and that the others are as wax in his hands.
'O Athenian stranger,' Cleinias addresses him—'inhabitant
of Attica I will not call you, for you seem to deserve rather
the name of Athene herself, because you go back to first
principles.' Thus complimented, the stranger lets himself go.
Yet somehow he would seem to have lost speculative nerve.

It was all very well in the 'Republic,' the ideal State, to be
bold and declare for banishing poetry altogether. But elderly
men have given up pursuing ideals; they have 'seen too many
leaders of revolts.' Our Athenian is driving now at practice
(as we say), at a well-governed State realizable on earth; and
after all it is hard to chase out the poets, especially if you yourself happen to be something of a poet at heart. Hear, then,
the terms on which, after allowing that comedies may be performed, but only by slaves and hirelings, he proceeds to allow
serious poetry.

And if any of the serious poets, as they are termed, who write
tragedy, come to us and say: 'O strangers, may we go to your city

and country, or may we not, and shall we bring with us our poetry? What is your will about these matters?'—how shall we answer the divine men? I think that our answer should be as follows:

'Best of strangers,' we will say to them, 'we also, according to our ability, are tragic poets, and our tragedy is the best and noblest: for our whole state is an imitation of the best and noblest life. . . . You are poets and we are poets, both makers of the same strains, rivals and antagonists in the noblest of dramas, which true law alone can perfect, as our hope is. Do not then suppose that we shall all in a moment allow you to erect your stage in the Agora, and introduce the fair voices of your actors, speaking above our own, and permit you to harangue our women and children and the common people in language other than our own, and very often the opposite of our own. For a State would be mad which gave you this license, until the magistrates had determined whether your poetry might be recited and was fit for publication or not. Wherefore, O ye sons and scions of the softer Muses! first of all show your songs to the Magistrates and let them compare them with our own, and if they are the same or better, we will give you a chorus; but if not, then, my friends, we cannot.'

Lame conclusion! Impotent compromise! How little applicable, at all events, to *our* Commonwealth! though, to be sure (you may say) we possess a relic of it in His Majesty's Licenser of Plays. As you know, there has been so much heated talk of late over the composition of the County Magistracy; yet I give you a countryman's word, Sir, that I have heard many names proposed for the Commission of the Peace, and on many grounds, but never one on the ground that its owner had a conservative taste in verse!

Nevertheless, as Plato saw, we must deal with these poets somehow. It is possible (though not, I think, likely) that in the ideal State there would be no Literature, as it is certain there would be no Professors of it; but since its invention men have never been able to rid themselves of it for any length of time. *Tamen usque recurret.* They may forbid Apollo, but still he comes leading his choir, the Nine:

> "Ἄκλητος μὲν ἔγωγε μένοιμί κεν· ἐς δὲ καλεύντων
> Θαρσήσας Μοίσαισι σὺν ἀμετέραισιν ἱκοίμαν.

And he may challenge us English boldly! For since Chaucer,

at any rate, he and his train have never been ἄκλητοι to us—least of all here in Cambridge.

Nay, we know that he should be welcome. Cardinal Newman, proposing the idea of a University to the Roman Catholics of Dublin, lamented that the English language had not, like the Greek, 'some definite words to express, simply and generally, intellectual proficiency or perfection, such as "health," as used with reference to the animal frame, and "virtue," with reference to our moral nature.' Well, it is a reproach to us that we do not possess the term: and perhaps again a reproach to us that our attempts at it—the word 'culture' for instance—have been apt to take on some soil of controversy, some connotative damage, from over-preaching on the one hand and impatience on the other. But we do earnestly desire the *thing*. We do prize that grace of intellect which sets So-and-so in our view as 'a scholar and a gentleman.' We do wish as many sons of this University as may be to carry forth that lifelong stamp from her precincts; and—this is my point—from our notion of such a man the touch of literary grace cannot be excluded. I put to you for a test Lucian's description of his friend Demonax:

His way was like other people's; he mounted no high horse; he was just a man and a citizen. He indulged in no Socratic irony. But his discourse was full of Attic grace; those who heard it went away neither disgusted by servility nor repelled by ill-tempered censure, but on the contrary lifted out of themselves by charity, and encouraged to more orderly, contented, hopeful lives.

I put it to you, that Lucian needs not to say another word, but we know that Demonax had loved letters, and partly by aid of them had arrived at being such a man. No; by consent of all, Literature is a nurse of noble natures, and right reading makes a full man in a sense even better than Bacon's; not replete, but complete rather, to the pattern for which Heaven designed him. In this conviction, in this hope, public spirited men endow Chairs in our Universities, sure that Literature is a good thing if only we can bring it to operate on young minds.

That he has in him some power to guide such operation a man must believe before accepting such a Chair as this. And now, Sir, the terrible moment is come when your ξένος must render some account—I will not say of himself, for that cannot be attempted—but of his business here. Well, first let me plead that while you have been infinitely kind to the stranger, feasting him and casting a gown over him, one thing not all your kindness has been able to do. With precedents, with traditions such as other Professors enjoy, you could not furnish him. The Chair is a new one, or almost new, and for the present would seem to float in the void, like Mahomet's coffin. Wherefore, being one who (in my Lord Chief Justice Crewe's phrase) would 'take hold of a twig or a twine-thread to uphold it'; being also prone (with Bacon) to believe that 'the counsels to which Time hath not been called, Time will not ratify'; I do assure you that, had any legacy of guidance been discovered among the papers left by my predecessor, it would have been eagerly welcomed and as piously honoured. O, trust me, Sir!—if any design for this Chair of English Literature had been left by Dr. Verrall, it is not I who would be setting up any new stage in your agora! But in his papers—most kindly searched for me by Mrs. Verrall—no such design can be found. He was, in truth, a stricken man when he came to the Chair, and of what he would have built we can only be sure that, had it been this or had it been that, it would infallibly have borne the impress of one of the most beautiful minds of our generation. The gods saw otherwise; and for me, following him, I came to a trench and stretched my hands to a shade.

For me, then, if you put questions concerning the work of this Chair, I must take example from the artist in *Don Quixote*, who being asked what he was painting answered modestly, 'That is as it may turn out.' The course is uncharted, and for sailing directions I have but these words of your Ordinance:

It shall be the duty of the Professor to deliver courses of lectures on English Literature from the age of Chaucer onwards, and otherwise to promote, so far as may be in his power, the study in the University of the subject of English Literature.

And I never even knew that English Literature had a 'subject';
or, rather, supposed it to have several! To resume:

The Professor shall treat this subject on literary and critical rather
than on philological and linguistic lines:

—a proviso which at any rate cuts off a cantle, large in itself,
if not comparatively, of the new Professor's ignorance. But
I ask you to note the phrase 'to promote, so far as may be in
his power, the study'—not, you will observe, 'to teach'; for
this absolves me from raising at the start a question of some
delicacy for me, as Green launched his *Prolegomena to Ethics*
upon the remark that 'an author who seeks to gain general
confidence scarcely goes the right way to work when he begins
with asking whether there really is such a subject as that of
which he proposes to treat.' In spite of—mark, pray, that I
say *in spite of*—the activity of many learned Professors, some
doubt does lurk in the public mind if, after all, English Literature can, in any ordinary sense, be taught, and if the attempts
to teach it do not, after all, justify (as Wisdom is so often
justified of her grandparents) the silent sapience of those old
benefactors who abstained from endowing any such Chairs.

But that the study of English Literature can be promoted in
young minds by an elder one, that their zeal may be encouraged,
their tastes directed, their vision cleared, quickened, enlarged—
this, I take it, no man of experience will deny. Nay, since
our two oldest Universities have a habit of marking one
another with interest—an interest, indeed, sometimes heightened
by nervousness—I may point out that all this has been done of
late years, and eminently done, by a Cambridge man you gave
to Oxford. This, then, Mr. Vice-Chancellor—this or something like this, Gentlemen—is to be my task if I have the good
fortune to win your confidence.

Let me, then, lay down two or three principles by which I
propose to be guided. (1) For the first principle of all I put
to you that in studying any work of genius we should begin by
taking it *absolutely*; that is to say, with minds intent on discovering just what the author's mind intended; this being at
once the obvious approach to its meaning (its τὸ τί ἦν εἶναι,

the 'thing it was to be'), and the merest duty of politeness we owe to the great man addressing us. We should lay our minds open to what he wishes to tell, and if what he has to tell be noble and high and beautiful, we should surrender and let soak our minds in it.

Let me premise that in claiming, even insisting upon, the first place for this *absolute* study of a great work I use no disrespect towards those learned scholars whose labours will help you, Gentlemen, to enjoy it afterwards in other ways and from other aspects; since I hold there is no surer sign of intellectual ill-breeding than to speak, even to feel, slightingly of any knowledge oneself does not happen to possess. Still less do I aim to persuade you that any one should be able to earn a Cambridge degree by the process (to borrow Macaulay's phrase) of reading our great authors 'with his feet on the hob,' a posture I have not even tried, to recommend it for a contemplative man's recreation. These editors not only set us the priceless example of learning for learning's sake: but even in practice they clear our texts for us, and afterwards—when we go more minutely into our author's acquaintance, wishing to learn all we can about him—by increasing our knowledge of detail they enhance our delight. Nay, with certain early writers—say Chaucer or Dunbar, as with certain highly allusive ones—Bacon, or Milton, or Sir Thomas Browne— some apparatus must be supplied from the start. But on the whole I think it a fair contention that such helps to studying an author are secondary and subsidiary; that, for example, with any author who by consent is less of his age than for all time, to study the relation he bore to his age may be important indeed, and even highly important, yet must in the nature of things be of secondary importance, not of the first.

But let us examine this principle a little more attentively— for it is the palmary one. As I conceive it, that understanding of literature which we desire in our Euphues, our gracefully-minded youth, will include knowledge in varying degree, yet is itself something distinct from knowledge. Let us illustrate this upon Poetry, which the most of us will allow to be the highest form of literary expression, if not of all artistic expression. Of all the testimony paid to Poetry, none commands better witness than this—that, as Johnson said of Gray's *Elegy*, it 'abounds with images which find a mirror in every mind, and with sentiments to which every bosom returns an echo.' When George Eliot said, 'I never before met with so many of my own feelings expressed just as I should like them,' she but repeated of Wordsworth (in homelier, more familiar fashion) what Johnson said of Gray; and the same testimony lies implicit in Emerson's fine remark that 'Universal history, the poets, the romancers'—all good writers, in short—'do not anywhere make us feel that we intrude, that this is for our betters. Rather it is true that, in their greatest strokes, there we feel most at home.' The mass of evidence, of which these are samples, may be summarized thus: As we dwell here between two mysteries, of a soul within and an ordered Universe without, so among us are granted to dwell certain men of more delicate intellectual fibre than their fellows—men whose minds have, as it were, filaments to intercept, apprehend, conduct, translate home to us stray messages between these two mysteries, as modern telegraphy has learnt to search out, snatch, gather home human messages astray over waste waters of the Ocean.

If, then, the ordinary man be done this service by the poet, that (as Dr. Johnson defines it) 'he feels what he remembers to have felt before, but he feels it *with a great increase of sensibility*'; or even if, though the message be unfamiliar, it suggest to us, in Wordsworth's phrase, to 'feel that we are greater than we know,' I submit that we respond to it less by anything that usually passes for knowledge, than by an improvement of sensibility, a tuning up of the mind to the poet's pitch; so that the man we are proud to send forth from our Schools will be remarkable less for something he can take out of his wallet and exhibit for knowledge, than for *being* something, and that 'something' a man of unmistakable intellectual breeding, whose trained judgment we can trust to choose the better and reject the worse.

But since this refining of the critical judgment happens to be less easy of practice than the memorizing of much that passes for knowledge—of what happened to Harriet or what Blake said to the soldier—and far less easy to examine on, the pedagogic mind (which I implore you not to suppose me confusing with the scholarly) for avoidance of trouble tends all the while to dodge or obfuscate what is essential, piling up accidents and irrelevancies before it until its very face is hidden. And we should be the more watchful not to confuse the pedagogic mind with the scholarly since it is from the scholar that the pedagogue pretends to derive his sanction; ransacking the great genuine commentators—be it a Skeat or a Masson or (may I add for old reverence' sake?) an Aldis Wright—fetching home bits of erudition, *non sua poma*, and announcing 'This *must* be the true Sion, for we found it in a wood.'

Hence a swarm of little school-books pullulates annually, all upside down and wrong from beginning to end; and hence a worse evil afflicts us, that the English schoolboy starts with a false perspective of any given masterpiece, his pedagogue urging, obtruding lesser things upon his vision until what is really important, the poem or the play itself, is seen in distorted glimpses, if not quite blocked out of view.

This same temptation—to remove a work of art from the category for which the author designed it into another where it can be more conveniently studied—reaches even above the schoolmaster to assail some very eminent critics. I cite an example from a book of which I shall hereafter have to speak with gratitude as I shall always name it with respect—*The History of English Poetry*, by Dr. Courthope, sometime Professor of Poetry at Oxford. In his fourth volume, and in his estimate of Fletcher as a dramatist, I find this passage:

But the critical test of a play's quality is only applied when it is read. So long as the illusion of the stage gives credit to the action, and the words and gestures of the actor impose themselves on the imagination of the spectator, the latter will pass over a thousand imperfections which reveal themselves to the reader, who, as he has to satisfy himself with the drama of silent images, will not be content if this in any way falls short of his conception of truth and nature,

—which seems equivalent to saying that the crucial test of the frieze of the Parthenon is its adaptability to an apartment in Bloomsbury. So long as the illusion of the Acropolis gave credit to Pheidias' design, and the sunlight of Attica imposed its delicate intended shadows edging the reliefs, the countrymen of Pericles might be tricked; but the visitor to the British Museum, as he has to satisfy himself with what happens indoors in the atmosphere of the West Central Postal Division of London, will not be content if Pheidias in any way fall short of *his* conception of truth and nature. Yet Fletcher (I take it) constructed his plays as plays; the illusion of the stage, the persuasiveness of the actor's voice, were conditions for which he wrought, and on which he had a right to rely; and, in short, any critic behaves uncritically who, distrusting his imagination to recreate the play as a play, elects to consider it in the category of something else.

In sum, if the great authors never oppress us with airs of condescension, but, like the great lords they are, put the meanest of us at our ease in their presence, I see no reason why we should pay to any commentator a servility not demanded by his master.

My next two principles may be more briefly stated.

(2) I propose next, then, that since our investigations will deal largely with style, that curiously personal thing; and since (as I have said) they cannot in their nature be readily brought to rule-of-thumb tests, and may therefore so easily be suspected of evading all tests, of being mere dilettantism; I propose (I say) that my pupils and I rebuke this suspicion by constantly aiming at the concrete, at the study of such definite beauties as we can see presented in print under our eyes; always seeking the author's intention, but eschewing, for the present at any rate, all general definitions and theories, through the sieve of which the particular achievement of genius is so apt to slip. And having excluded them at first in prudence, I make little doubt we shall go on to exclude them in pride. Definitions, formulae (some would add, creeds) have their use in any society in that they restrain the ordinary unintellectual man

from making himself a public nuisance with his private opinions.
But they go a very little way in helping the man who has a real
sense of prose or verse. In other words, they are good discipline for some thyrsus-bearers, but the initiated have little use
for them. As Thomas à Kempis 'would rather feel com-
punction than understand the definition thereof,' so the
initiated man will say of the 'Grand Style,' for example—'Why
define it for me?' When Viola says simply:

> I am all the daughters of my father's house,
> And all the brothers too,

or Macbeth demands of the Doctor:

> Canst thou not minister to a mind diseased,
> Pluck from the memory a rooted sorrow . . .?

or Hamlet greets Ophelia, reading her Book of Hours, with

> Nymph, in thy orisons
> Be all my sins remembered!

or when Milton tells of his dead friend how

> Together both, ere the high lawns appear'd
> Under the opening eyelids of the morn,
> We drove afield,

or describes the battalions of Heaven:

> On they move
> Indissolubly firm; nor obvious hill,
> Nor strait'ning vale, nor wood, nor stream divides
> Their perfect ranks,

or when Gray exalts the great commonplace;

> The boast of heraldry, the pomp of power,
> And all that beauty, all that wealth e'er gave,
> Awaits alike th' inevitable hour.
> The paths of glory lead but to the grave,

or when Keats casually drops us such a line as

> The journey homeward to habitual self,

or, to come down to our own times and to a living poet, when
I open on a page of William Watson and read:

> O ancient streams, O far descended woods,
> Full of the fluttering of melodious souls! . . .

'why then (will say the initiated one), why worry me with any
definition of the Grand Style in English, when here, and here,

and again here—in all these lines, simple or intense or exquisite or solemn—I recognize and feel the *thing*?'

Indeed, Sir, the long and the short of the argument lie just here. Literature is not an abstract Science, to which exact definitions can be applied. It is an Art rather, the success of which depends on personal persuasiveness, on the author's skill to give as on ours to receive.

(3) For our third principle I will ask you to go back with me to Plato's wayfarers, whom we have left so long under the cypresses; and loth as we must be to lay hands on our father Parmenides, I feel we must treat the gifted Athenian stranger to a little manhandling. For did you not observe—though Greek was a living language and to his metropolitan mind the only language—how envious he showed himself to seal up the well, or allow it to trickle only under permit of a public analyst: to treat all innovation as suspect, even as, a hundred odd years ago, the Lyrical Ballads were suspect?

But the very hope of this Chair, Sir (as I conceive it), relies on the courage of the young. As Literature is an Art and therefore not to be pondered only, but practised, so ours is a living language and therefore to be kept alive, supple, active in all honourable use. The orator can yet sway men, the poet ravish them, the dramatist fill their lungs with salutary laughter or purge their emotions by pity or terror. The historian 'superinduces upon events the charm of order.' The novelist —well, even the novelist has his uses; and I would warn you against despising any form of art which is alive and pliant in the hands of men. For my part, I believe, bearing in mind Mr. Barrie's *Peter Pan* and the old bottles he renovated to hold that joyous wine, that even Musical Comedy, in the hands of a master, might become a thing of beauty. Of the Novel, at any rate—whether we like it or not—we have to admit that it does hold a commanding position in the literature of our times, and to consider how far Mr. Lascelles Abercrombie was right the other day when he claimed, on the first page of his brilliant study of Thomas Hardy, that 'the right to such a position is not to be disputed; for here, as elsewhere, the right to a position is no more than the power to maintain it.' You may agree with that or you may not; you may or may not deplore the forms that literature is choosing nowadays; but there is no gainsaying that it is still very much alive. And I would say to you, Gentlemen, 'Believe, and be glad that Literature and the English tongue are both alive.' Carlyle, in his explosive way, once demanded of his countrymen, 'Shakespeare or India? If you had to surrender one to retain the other, which would you choose?' Well, our Indian Empire is yet in the making, while the works of Shakespeare are complete and purchasable in whole calf; so the alternatives are scarcely *in pari materia*; and moreover let us not be in a hurry to meet trouble half way. But in English Literature, which, like India, is still in the making, you have at once an Empire and an emprise. In that alone you have inherited something greater than Sparta. Let us strive, each in his little way, to adorn it.

But here at the close of my hour, the double argument, that Literature is an Art and English a living tongue, has led me right up to a fourth principle, the plunge into which (though I foresaw it from the first) all the coward in me rejoices at having to defer to another lecture. I conclude then, Gentlemen, by answering two suspicions, which very likely have been shaping themselves in your minds. In the first place, you will say, 'It is all very well for this man to talk about "cultivating an increased sensibility," and the like; but we know what *that* leads to—to quackery, to aesthetic chatter: "Isn't this pretty? Don't you admire that?"' Well, I am not greatly frightened. To begin with, when we come to particular criticism I shall endeavour to exchange it with you in plain terms; a manner which (to quote Mr. Robert Bridges' *Essay on Keats*) 'I prefer, because by obliging the lecturer to say definitely what he means, it makes his mistakes easy to point out, and in this way the true business of criticism is advanced.' But I have a second safeguard, more to be trusted: that here in Cambridge, with all her traditions of austere scholarship, any one who indulges in loose discinct talk will be quickly recalled to his tether. Though at the time Athene be not kind enough to descend from heaven and pluck him backward by the hair, yet the very *genius loci* will walk home with him from the lecture room, whispering monitions, cruel to be kind.

'But,' you will say alternatively, 'if we avoid loose talk on these matters we are embarking on a mighty difficult business.' Why, to be sure we are; and that, I hope, will be half the enjoyment. After all, we have a number of critics among whose methods we may search for help—from the Persian monarch who, having to adjudicate upon two poems, caused the one to be read to him, and at once, without ado, awarded the prize to the other, up to the great Frenchman whom I shall finally invoke to sustain my hope of building something; that is if you, Gentlemen, will be content to accept me less as a Professor than as an Elder Brother.

The Frenchman is Sainte-Beuve, and I pay a debt, perhaps appropriately here, by quoting him as translated by the friend of mine, now dead, who first invited me to Cambridge and taught me to admire her—one Arthur John Butler, sometime a Fellow of Trinity, and later a great pioneer among Englishmen in the study of Dante. Thus while you listen to the appeal of Sainte-Beuve, I can hear beneath it a more intimate voice, not for the first time encouraging me.

Sainte-Beuve then—*si magna licet componere parvis*—is delivering an Inaugural Lecture in the École Normale, the date being April 12th, 1858. 'Gentlemen,' he begins, 'I have written a good deal in the last thirty years; that is, I have scattered myself about a good deal; so that I need to gather myself together, in order that my words may come before you with all the more freedom and confidence.' That is his opening; and he ends:

As time goes on, you will make me believe that I can for my part be of some good to you: and with the generosity of your age you will repay me, in this feeling alone, far more than I shall be able to give you in intellectual direction, or in literary insight. If in one sense I bestow on you some of my experience, you will requite me, and in a more profitable manner, by the sight of your ardour for what is noble: you will accustom me to turn oftener and more willingly towards the future in your company. You will teach me again to hope.

ON THE LINEAGE OF ENGLISH LITERATURE

I

Because a great deal of what I have to say this morning, if not heretical, will yet run contrary to the vogue and practice of the Schools for these thirty years, I shall take the leap into my subject over a greater man's back and ask you to listen with particular attention to the following long passage from a writer whose opinion you may challenge, but whose authority to speak as a master of English prose no one in this room will deny—Cardinal Newman.

When [says he] we survey the stream of human affairs for the last three thousand years, we find it to run thus: At first sight there is so much fluctuation, agitation, ebbing and flowing, that we may despair to discern any law in its movements, taking the earth as its bed and mankind as its contents; but on looking more closely and attentively we shall discern, in spite of the heterogeneous materials and the various histories and fortunes which are found in the race of man during the long period I have mentioned, a certain formation amid the chaos—one and one only—and extending, though not over the whole earth, yet through a very considerable portion of it. . . .
Looking at the countries which surround the Mediterranean Sea as a whole, I see them to be from time immemorial the seat of an association of intellect and mind such as to deserve to be called the Intellect and the Mind of the Human Kind. Starting as it does, and advancing from certain centres, till their respective influences intersect and conflict, and then at length intermingle and combine, a common Thought has been generated, and a common Civilization defined and established. Egypt is one such starting point, Syria another, Greece a third, Italy a fourth, and North Africa a fifth—afterwards France and Spain. As time goes on, and as colonization and conquest work their changes, we see a great association of nations formed, of which the Roman Empire is the maturity and the most intelligible expression: an association, however, not political but mental, based on the same intellectual ideas and advancing by common intellectual methods. . . . In its earliest age it included far more of the Eastern world than it has since; in these later times it has taken into its compass a new hemisphere; in the Middle Ages it lost Africa, Egypt, and Syria, and extended itself to Germany, Scandinavia, and the British Isles. At one time its territory was

15

flooded by strange and barbarous races, but the existing civilization was vigorous enough to vivify what threatened to stifle it, and to assimilate to the old social forms what came to expel them: and thus the civilization of modern times remains what it was of old; not Chinese, or Hindoo, or Mexican, or Saracen . . . but the lineal descendant, or rather the continuation—*mutatis mutandis*—of the civilization which began in Palestine and Greece.

Other Civilizations—the Chinese, for instance, or the Hindoo—there have been, and are; but Newman is speaking of the civilization common to Europe, and not lightly to be abjured by any nation. To omit, then, all minor debts: such as what of arithmetic, what of astronomy, what of geography, we owe to the Saracen, from Palestine we derive the faith of Europe shared (in the language of the Bidding Prayer) by all Christian people dispersed throughout the world; as to Greece we owe the rudiments of our Western art, philosophy, letters; and not only the rudiments but the continuing inspiration, so that—though entirely superseded in worship, as even in the Athens of Pericles they were worshipped only by an easy, urbane, more than half humorous tolerance—Apollo and the Muses, Zeus and the great ones of Olympus, Hermes and Hephaestus, Athene in her armour, with her vanquisher the foam-born irresistible Aphrodite—these remain the authentic gods of our literature, beside whom the gods of northern Europe—Odin, Thor, Freya—are strangers, unhomely, uncanny as the shadows of unfamiliar furniture on the walls of a home. Sprung though great numbers of us are from the loins of Northmen, it is in these gracious deities of the South that we find the familiar and the real; as from the heroes of the sister-island, Cucullain and Concobar, we turn to Hercules, to Perseus, to Bellerophon, even to actual men of history, saying 'Give us Leonidas, give us Horatius, give us Regulus. These are the mighty ones we understand, and from whom, in a direct line of tradition, we understand Harry of Agincourt, Philip Sidney and our Nelson.'

Now since, of the Mediterranean peoples, the Hebrews discovered the Unseen God whom the body of Western civilization has learnt to worship; since the Greeks invented art philosophy, letters; since Rome found and developed the idea of imperial government, of imperial colonies as superseding merely fissiparous ones, of settling where she conquered (*ubi Romanus vicit ibi habitat*) and so extending with Government that system of law which Europe still obeys; we cannot be surprised that Israel, Greece, Rome—each in turn—set store on a pure ancestry.   Though Christ be the veritable Son of God, his ancestry must be traced back through his supposed father Joseph to the stem of Jesse, and so to Abraham, father of the race.   Again, as jealously as the Evangelist claimed Jesus for a Hebrew of the Hebrews, so, if you will turn to the *Menexenus* of Plato in the Oration of Aspasia over the dead who perished in battle, you hear her claim that 'No Pelopidae: scions of Pelops, or Cadmus, or Egyptus, or Danaus, nor the rest of the crowd of born foreigners dwell with us; but ours is the land of pure Hellenes, free from admixture.'   These proud Athenians, as you know, wore brooches in the shape of golden grass-hoppers, to signify that they were αὐτόχθονες, children of Attica, sprung direct from her soil.   And so, again, the true Roman, while enlarging Rome's citizenship over Asia, Africa, Gaul, to our remote Britain, insisted, even in days of the later Empire, on his pure descent from Aeneas and Romulus:

> Unde Ramnes et Quirites proque prole posterum
> Romuli matrem crearet et nepotem Caesarem.

Here is a boast that we English must be content to forgo. We may wear a rose on St. George's day, if we are clever enough to grow one.   The Welsh, I dare say, have less difficulty with the leek.   But April the 23rd is not a time of roses that we can pluck them as we pass, nor can we claim St. George as a com-patriot, *Cappadocius nostras.*   We have, to be sure, a few legendary heroes, of whom King Arthur and Robin Hood are (I suppose) the greatest; but, save in some Celtic corners of the land, we have few fairies, and these no great matter; while, as for tutelary gods, our springs, our wells, our groves, cliffs, mountain-sides, either never possessed them or possess them no longer.   Not of our landscape did it happen that

> The lonely mountains o'er,
> And the resounding shore,
> A voice of weeping heard, and loud lament;
> From haunted spring, and dale
> Edg'd with poplar pale,
> The parting Genius is with sighing sent

—for the sufficient reason that no tutelary gods of importance were ever here to be dispersed.

Let me press this home upon you by an illustration which I choose with the double purpose of enforcing my argument and sending you to make acquaintance (if you have not already made it) with a lovely poem.

In one of Pliny's letters you will find a very pleasant description of the source of the Clitumnus, a small Umbrian river which, springing from a rock in a grove of cypresses, descends into the Tinia, a tributary of the Tiber.

Have you ever [writes Pliny to his friend Romanus] seen the source of the Clitumnus? I suppose not, as I never heard you mention it. Let me advise you to go there at once. I have just visited it and am sorry that I put off my visit so long. At the foot of a little hill, covered with old and shady cypress trees, a spring gushes and bursts into a number of streamlets of various size. Breaking, so to speak, forth from its imprisonment, it expands into a broad basin, so clear and transparent that you may count the pebbles and little pieces of money which are thrown into it. From this point the force and weight of the water, rather than the slope of the ground, hurry it onward. What was a mere spring becomes a noble river, broad enough to allow vessels to pass each other as they sail with or against the stream. The current is so strong, though the ground is level, that barges of beam, as they go down, require no assistance of oars; while to go up is as much as can be done with oars and long poles. . . . The banks are clothed with abundant ash and poplar, so distinctly reflected in the transparent waters that they seem to be growing at the bottom of the river and can be counted with ease. The water is as cold as snow and as pure in colour. Hard by the spring stands an ancient and venerable temple with a statue of the river-god Clitumnus, clothed in the customary robe of state. The Oracles here delivered attest the presence of the deity. Close in the precinct stand several little chapels dedicated to particular gods, each of whom owns his distinctive name and special worship, and is the tutelary deity of a runlet. For beside the principal spring, which is, as it were, the parent of all the rest, there are several smaller ones which have their distinct sources but unite their waters with the Clitumnus, over which a bridge is thrown, separating the sacred part of the river from that which is open to general use. Above the bridge you may only go in a boat; below it, you may swim. The people of the town of Hispallum, to whom Augustus gave this place, furnish baths and lodgings at the public expense. There are several small dwelling-houses on the banks, in specially picturesque situations, and they stand quite close to the water-side. In short, everything in the neighbourhood will give you pleasure. You may also amuse yourself with numberless inscriptions on the pillars and walls, celebrating the praises of the stream and of its tutelary god. Many of these you will admire, and some will make you laugh. But no! You are too well cultivated to laugh at such things. Farewell.

Clitumnus still gushes from its rock among the cypresses, as in Pliny's day. The god has gone from his temple, on the frieze of which you may read this later inscription: 'Deus Angelorum, qui fecit Resurrectionem.' After many centuries and almost in our day, by the brain of Cavour and the sword of Garibaldi, he has made a resurrection for Italy. As part of that resurrection (for no nation can live and be great without its poet) was born a true poet, Carducci. He visited the bountiful, everlasting source, and of what did he sing? Possess yourselves, as for a shilling you may, of his Ode *Alle fonti del Clitumno*, and read: for few nobler poems have adorned our time. He sang of the weeping willow, the ilex, ivy, cypress, and the presence of the god still immanent among them. He sang of Umbria, of the ensigns of Rome, of Hannibal swooping down over the Alps; he sang of the nuptials of Janus and Camesena, progenitors of the Italian people; of nymphs, naiads, and the moonlight dances of Oreads; of flocks descending to the river at dusk, of the homestead, of the bare-footed mother, the clinging child, the father, clad in goat-skins, guiding the ox-waggon; and he ends on the very note of Virgil's famous apostrophe:

Sed neque Medorum silvae, ditissima terra . . .

with an invocation of Italy—Italy, mother of bullocks for agriculture, of wild colts for battle, mother of corn and of the

vine, Roman mother of enduring laws and mediaeval mother of
illustrious arts. The mountains, woods and waters of green
Umbria applaud the song, and across their applause is heard
the whistle of the railway train bearing promise of new industries
and a new national life.

> E tu, pia madre di giovenchi invitti
> a franger glebe e rintegrar maggesi
> e d' annitrenti in guerra aspri polledri,
> Italia madre,
>
> madre di biade e viti e leggi eterne
> ed incliti arti a raddolcir la vita
> salve! a te i canti de l' antica lode
> io rinovello.
>
> Plaudono i monti al carme e i boschi e l' acque
> de l' Umbria verde: in faccia a noi fumando
> ed anelando nuove industrie in corsa
> fischia il vapore.
>
> And thou, O pious mother of unvanquished
> Bullocks to break glebe, to restore the fallow,
> And of fierce colts for neighing in the battle:
> Italy, mother,
>
> Mother of corn and vines and of eternal
> Laws and illustrious arts the life to sweeten,
> Hail, hail, all hail! The song of ancient praises
> Renew I to thee!
>
> The mountains, woods and waters of green Umbria
> Applaud the song: and here before us fuming
> And longing for new industries, a-racing
> Whistles the white steam.[1]

I put it to you, Gentlemen, that, worthy as are the glories of
England to be sung, this note of Carducci's we cannot decently
or honestly strike. Great lives have been bled away into
Tweed and Avon: great spirits have been oared down the
Thames to Traitors' Gate and the Tower. Deeds done on the
Cam have found their way into history. But I once traced
the Avon to its source under Naseby battlefield, and found it

---

[1] I quote from a translation by Mr. E. J. Watson, published by Messrs.
J. W. Arrowsmith, of Bristol.

issuing from the fragments of a stucco swan.   No god mounts
guard over the head-water of the Thames; and the only
Englishman who boldly claims a divine descent is (I undertand)
an impostor who runs an Agapemone.   In short we are a
mixed race, and our literature is derivative.   Let us confine
our pride to those virtues, not few, which are honestly ours.
A Roman noble, even to-day, has some excuse for reckoning a
god in his ancestry, or at least a wolf among its wet-nurses: but
of us English even those who came over with William the Norman have the son of a tanner's daughter for escort.   I very
well remember that, the other day, writers who vindicated our
hereditary House of Lords against a certain Parliament Act
commonly did so on the ground that since the Reform Bill of
1832, by inclusion of all that was eminent in politics, war and
commerce, the Peerage had been so changed as to know itself
no longer for the same thing.   That is our practical way.

At all events, the men who made our literature had never a
doubt, as they were careless to dissimulate, that they were
conquering our tongue to bring it into the great European
comity, the civilization of Greece and Rome.   An Elizabethan
writer, for example, would begin almost as with a formula by
begging to be forgiven that he has sought to render the divine
accent of Plato, the sugared music of Ovid, into our uncouth
and barbarous tongue.   There may have been some mock-
modesty in this, but it rested on a base of belief.   Much of the
glory of English Literature was achieved by men who, with the
splendour of the Renaissance in their eyes, supposed themselves
to be working all the while upon pale and borrowed shadows.

Let us pass the enthusiasms of days when 'bliss was it in
that dawn to be alive' and come down to Alexander Pope and
the Age of Reason.   Pope at one time proposed to write a
History of English Poetry, and the draft scheme of that History
has been preserved.   How does it begin?   Why thus:

Era I

1. School of Provence	Chaucer's Visions, *Romaunt of the Rose.* *Piers Plowman.* Tales from Boccace. Gower.

2. School of Chaucer
- Lydgate.
- T. Occleve.
- Walt. de Mapes (a bad error, that!).
- Skelton.

3. School of Petrarch
- E. of Surrey.
- Sir Thomas Wyatt.
- Sir Philip Sidney.
- G. Gascoyn.

4. School of Dante
- Lord Buckhurst's *Induction.*   *Gorboduc.*
- Original of Good Tragedy.   Seneca his model.

—and so on. The scheme after Pope's death came into the hands of Gray, who for a time was fired with the notion of writing the History in collaboration with his friend Mason. Knowing Gray's congenital self-distrust, you will not be surprised that in the end he declined the task and handed it over to Warton. But, says Mant in his Life of Warton, 'their design'—that is, Gray's design with Mason—'was to introduce specimens of the Provençal poetry, and of the Scaldic, British and Saxon, as preliminary to what first deserved to be called English poetry, about the time of Chaucer, from whence their history properly so called was to commence.' A letter of Gray's on the whole subject, addressed to Warton, is extant, and you may read it in Dr. Courthope's *History of English Poetry.*

Few in this room are old enough to remember the shock of awed surmise which fell upon young minds presented, in the late 'seventies or early 'eighties of the last century, with Freeman's *Norman Conquest* or Green's *Short History of the English People*; in which, as through parting clouds of darkness, we beheld our ancestry, literary as well as political, radiantly legitimized; though not, to be sure, in the England that we knew—but far away in Sleswick, happy Sleswick! 'Its pleasant pastures, its black-timbered homesteads, its prim little townships looking down on inlets of purple water, were then but a wild waste of heather and sand, girt along the coast with sunless woodland, broken here and there with meadows which crept down to the marshes and to the sea.' But what of that? There—surely there, in Sleswick—had been discovered for us our august mother's marriage lines; and if the most of that bright assurance came out of an old political skit, the *Germania* of Tacitus, who recked at the time?   For along followed Mr. Stopford Brooke with an admirable little Primer published at one shilling, to instruct the meanest of us in our common father's actual name—Beowulf.

Beowulf is our old English Epic. . . . There is no mention of our England. . . . The whole poem, pagan as it is, is English to its very root.   It is sacred to us; our Genesis, the book of our origins.

Now I am not only incompetent to discuss with you the more recondite beauties of *Beowulf* but providentially forbidden the attempt by the conditions laid down for this Chair.   I gather —and my own perusal of the poem and of much writing about it confirms the belief—that it has been largely over-praised by some critics, who have thus naturally provoked others to under-rate it.   Such things happen.   I note, but without subscribing to it, the opinion of Vigfússon and York Powell, the learned editors of the *Corpus Poeticum Boreale*, that in the *Beowulf* we have 'an epic completely metamorphosed in form, blown out with long-winded empty repetitions and comments by a book poet, so that one must be careful not to take it as a type of the old poetry,' and I seem to hear as from the grave the very voice of my old friend the younger editor in that unfaltering pronouncement.   But on the whole I rather incline to accept the cautious surmise of Professor W. P. Ker that 'a reasonable view of the merit of *Beowulf* is not impossible, though rash enthusiasm may have made too much of it; while a correct and sober taste may have too contemptuously refused to attend to Grendel and the Firedrake'; and to leave it at that.   I speak very cautiously because the manner of the late Professor Freeman, in especial, had a knack of provoking in gentle breasts a resentment which the mind in its frailty too easily converted to a prejudice against his matter: while to men trained to admire Thucydides and Tacitus and acquainted with Lucian's 'Way to Write History' ($\Pi\hat{\omega}s$ $\delta\epsilon\hat{\iota}$ $\iota\sigma\tau o\rho\iota\alpha\nu$ $\sigma\upsilon\gamma\gamma\rho\alpha\phi\epsilon\iota\nu$) his loud insistence that the art was not an art but a science, and moreover recently invented by Bishop Stubbs, was a perpetual irritant.

But to return to *Beowulf*—You have just heard the opinions of scholars whose names you must respect. I, who construe Anglo-Saxon with difficulty, must admit the poem to contain many fine, even noble, passages. Take for example Hrothgar's lament for Æschere:

> Hróðgar maþelode, helm Scyldinga:
> 'Ne frin þú æfter sælum; sorh is geniwod
> Denigea leódum; deád is Æschere,
> Yrmenláfes yldra bróþor,
> Mín rún-wita, ond min ræd-bora;
> Eaxl-gestealla, ðonne we on orlege
> Hafelan wéredon, þonne hniton feþan,
> Eoferas cnysedan: swylc scolde eorl wesan
> *Æþeling* ær-gód, swylc Æschere wæs.'[1]

This is simple, manly, dignified. It avoids the besetting sin of the Anglo-Saxon gleeman—the pretentious trick of calling things 'out of their right names' for the sake of literary effect (as if e.g. the sea could be improved by being phrased into 'the seals' domain'). Its Anglo-Saxon *staccato*, so tiresome in sustained narrative, here happens to suit the broken utterance of mourning. In short, it exhibits the Anglo-Saxon Muse at her best, not at her customary. But set beside it a passage in which Homer tells of a fallen warrior—at haphazard, as it were, a single corpse chosen from the press of battle:

> πολλὰ δὲ χερμάδια μεγάλ' ἀσπίδας ἐστυφέλιξαν
> μαρναμένων ἀμφ' αὐτόν· ὁ δ' ἐν στροφάλιγγι κονίης
> κεῖτο μέγας μεγαλωστί, λελασμένος ἱπποσυνάων.

Can you—can any one—compare the two passages and miss to see that they belong to two different kingdoms of poetry? I lay no stress here on 'architectonics.' I waive that the *Iliad* is a well-knit epic and the story of *Beowulf* a shapeless

---

[1] 'Hrothgar spake, helm of the Scyldings: Ask not after good tidings. Sorrow is renewed among the Dane-folk. Dead is Æschere, Yrmenlaf's elder brother, who read me rune and bore me rede; comrade at shoulder when we fended our heads in war and the boar-helms rang. Even so should we each be an atheling passing good, as Æschere was.'

monstrosity. I ask you but to note the difference of note, of accent, of mere music. And I have quoted you but a passage of the habitual Homer. To assure yourselves that he can rise even from this habitual height to express the extreme of majesty and of human anguish, in poetry which betrays no false note, no strain upon the store of emotion man may own with self-respect and exhibit without derogation of dignity, turn to the last book of the *Iliad* and read of Priam raising to his lips the hand that has murdered his son. I say confidently that no one unable to distinguish this, as poetry, from the very best of *Beowulf* is fit to engage upon business as a literary critic.

In *Beowulf* then, as an imported poem, let us allow much barbarian merit. It came of dubious ancestry, and it had no progeny. The pretence that our glorious literature derives its lineage from *Beowulf* is in vulgar phrase 'a put up job'; a falsehood grafted upon our text - books by Teutonic and Teutonizing professors who can bring less evidence for it than will cover a threepenny-piece. Its run for something like that money, in small educational manuals, has been in its way a triumph of pedagogic *réclame*.

Our rude forefathers—the author of *The Rape of the Lock* and of the *Elegy written in a Country Churchyard*—knew nothing of the Exeter and Vercelli Books, nothing of the Ruthwell Cross. But they were poets, practitioners of our literature in the true line of descent, and they knew certain things which all such artists know by instinct. So, before our historians of thirty-odd years ago started to make Chaucer and *Beowulf* one, these rude forefathers made them two. 'Nor am I confident they erred.' Rather I am confident, and hope in succeeding lectures to convince you, that, venerable as Anglo-Saxon is, and worthy to be studied as the mother of our vernacular speech (as for a dozen other reasons which my friend Professor Chadwick will give you), its value is historical rather than literary, since from it our Literature is not descended. Let me repeat it in words that admit of no misunderstanding—*From Anglo-Saxon Prose, from Anglo-Saxon Poetry our living Prose and Poetry have save linguistically, no derivation.* I shall attempt to demonstrate that, whether or not Anglo-Saxon literature, such as it was, died of inherent weakness, die it did, and of its collapse the *Vision of Piers Plowman* may be regarded as the last dying spasm. I shall attempt to convince you that Chaucer did not inherit any secret from Caedmon or Cynewulf, but deserves his old title, 'Father of English Poetry,' because through Dante, through Boccaccio, through the lays and songs of Provence, he explored back to the Mediterranean, and opened for Englishmen a commerce in the true intellectual mart of Europe. I shall attempt to heap proof on you that whatever the agency — whether through Wyat or Spenser, Marlowe or Shakespeare, or Donne, or Milton, or Dryden, or Pope, or Johnson, or even Wordsworth—always our literature has obeyed, however unconsciously, the precept *Antiquam exquirite matrem*, 'Seek back to the ancient mother'; always it has recreated itself, has kept itself pure and strong, by harking back to bathe in those native—yes, *native*—Mediterranean springs.

Do not presume me to be right in this. Rather, if you will, presume me to be wrong until the evidence is laid out for your judgment. But at least understand to-day how profoundly a man, holding that view, must deplore the whole course of academical literary study during these thirty years or so, and how distrust what he holds to be its basic fallacies.

For, literature being written in language, yet being something quite distinct, and the development of our language having been fairly continuous, while the literature of our nation exhibits a false start—a break, silence, repentance, then a renewal on right glorious lines—our students of literature have been drilled to follow the specious continuance while ignoring the actual break, and so to commit the one most fatal error in any study; that of mistaking the inessential for the essential.

As I tried to persuade you in my Inaugural Lecture, our first duty to Literature is to study it absolutely, to understand, in Aristotelian phrase, its τὸ τί ἦν εἶναι; what it *is* and what it *means*. If that be our quest, and the height of it be realized, it is nothing to us—or almost nothing—to know of a certain alleged poet of the fifteenth century, that he helped us over a local or temporary disturbance in our vowel-endings. It is everything to have acquired and to possess such a norm of Poetry within us that we know whether or not what he wrote was POETRY.

Do not think this is easy. The study of right literary criticism is much more difficult than the false path usually trodden; so difficult, indeed, that you may easily count the men who have attempted to grasp the great rules and apply them to writing as an art to be practised. But the names include some very great ones—Aristotle, Horace, Quintilian, Corneille, Boileau, Dryden, Johnson, Lessing, Coleridge, Goethe, Sainte-Beuve, Arnold: and the study, though it may not find its pattern in our time, is not unworthy to be proposed for another attempt before a great University

II

Some of you whose avocations call them, from time to time, to Newmarket may have noted, at a little distance out from Cambridge, a by-road advertised as leading to Quy and Swaffham. It also leads to the site of an old Roman villa; but you need not interrupt your business to visit this, since the best thing discovered there—a piece of tessellated pavement —has been removed and deposited in the Geological Museum here in Cambridge, in Downing Street, where you may study it very conveniently. It is not at all a first-class specimen of its kind: not to be compared, for example, with the wonderful pavement at Dorchester, or with that (measuring 35 feet by 20) of the great villa unearthed, a hundred years ago, at Stonesfield in Oxfordshire: but I take it as the handiest, and am going to build a small conjecture upon it, or rather a small suggestion of a guess. Remember there is no harm in guessing so long as we do not pretend our guess-work to be something else.

I will ask you to consider first that in these pavements, laid

bare for us as 'the whistling rustic tends his plough,' we have
work dating somewhere between the first and fifth centuries,
work of unchallengeable beauty, work of a beauty certainly not
rivalled until we come to the Norman builders of five or six
hundred years later.   I want you to let your minds dwell on
these long stretches of time—four hundred years or so of
Roman occupation (counting, not from Caesar's raids, but
from the serious invasion of 43 A.D. under Aulus Plautius, say
to some while after the famous letter of Honorius, calling home
the legions).   You may safely put it at four hundred years,
and then count six hundred as the space before the Normans
arrive—a thousand years altogether, or but a fraction—one
short generation—less than the interval of time that separates
us from King Alfred.   In the great Cathedral of Winchester
(where sleep, by the way, two gentle writers specially beloved,
Izaak Walton and Jane Austen) above the choir-screen to the
south, you may see a line of painted chests, of which the
inscription on one tells you that it holds what was mortal of
King Canute.

> Here are sands, ignoble things,
> Dropp'd from the ruin'd sides of Kings.

But if you walk around to the north of the altar you will find
yourself treading on tiles not so very far short of twice that
antiquity.

I want you to-day to understand just what such a pavement
as that preserved for your inspection in Downing Street meant
to the man who saw it laid and owned it these fifteen hundred
years—more or less—ago.   *Ubi Romanus vicit, ibi habitat*—
'where the Roman has conquered, there he settles': but whether
he conquered or settled he carried these small tiles, these
tessellae, as religiously as ever Rachel stole her teraphin.
'Wherever his feet went there went the tessellated pavement
for them to stand on.   Even generals on foreign service carried
in panniers on muleback the little coloured cubes or *tessellae*
for laying down a pavement in each camping-place, to be taken
up again when they moved forward.   In England the same

sweet emblems of the younger gods of poetic legend, of love, youth, plenty, and all their happy naturalism, are found constantly repeated.'[1] I am quoting these sentences from a local historian, but you see how these relics have a knack of inspiring prose at once scholarly and imaginative, as (for a more famous instance) the urns disinterred at Walsingham once inspired Sir Thomas Browne's.   To continue and adapt the quotation:

Bacchus with his wild rout, Orpheus playing to a spellbound audience, Apollo singing to the lyre, Venus in Mars' embrace, Neptune with a host of seamen, scollops, and trumpets, Narcissus by the fountain, Jove and Ganymede, Leda and the swan, wood-nymphs and naiads, satyrs and fauns, masks, hautboys, cornucopiae, flowers and baskets of golden fruit—what touches of home they must have seemed to these old dwellers in the Cambridgeshire wilds!

Yes, touches of home!   For the owner of this villa (you may conceive) is the grandson or even great-great-grandson of the colonist who first built it, following in the wake of the legionaries.   The family has prospered and our man is now a considerable landowner.   He was born in Britain: his children have been born here: and here he lives a comfortable, well-to-do, out-of-door life, in its essentials I daresay not so very unlike the life of an English country squire to-day.   Instead of chasing foxes or hares he hunts the wolf and the wild boar; but the sport is good and he returns with an appetite.   He has added a summer parlour to the house, with a northern aspect and no heating-flues: for the old parlour he has enlarged the praefurnium, and through the long winter evenings sits far better warmed than many a master of a modern country-house.   A belt of trees on the brow of the rise protects him from the worst winds, and to the south his daughters have planted violet-beds which will breathe odorously in the spring. He has rebuilt and enlarged the slave-quarters and outhouses, replaced the stucco pillars around the atrium with a colonnade of polished stone, and, where stucco remains, has repainted it

[1] From *A History of Oxfordshire* by Mr. J. Meade Falkner, author of Murray's excellent Handbook of Oxfordshire.

in fresh colours. He knows that there are no gaps or weak spots in his stockade fence—wood is always cheap. In a word he has improved the estate; is modestly proud of it; and will be content, like the old Athenian, to leave his patrimony not worse but something better than he found it.

Sensible men—and the Romans were eminently that—as a rule contrive to live decently, or, at least, tolerably. What struck Arthur Young more than anything else in his travels through France on the very eve of the Revolution seems to have been the general good-tempered happiness of the French gentry on their estates. We may moralize of the Roman colonists as of the French proprietors that 'unconscious of their doom the little victims played'; but we have no right to throw back on them the shadow of what was to come or to cloud the picture of a useful, peaceable, maybe more than moderately happy life, with our later knowledge of disaster mercifully hidden from it.

Although our colonist and his family have all been born in Britain, are happy enough here on the whole, and talk without more than half meaning it, and to amuse themselves with speculations half-wistful, of daring the tremendous journey and setting eyes on Rome some day, their pride is to belong to her, to Rome, the imperial City, the city afar: their windows open back towards her as Daniel's did towards Jerusalem—*Urbs quam dicunt Romam*—*the* City. Along the great road, hard by, her imperial writ runs. They have never subscribed to the vow of Ruth, 'Thy people shall be my people and thy God my God.' They dwell under the Pax Romana, not merely protected by it but as *citizens*. Theirs are the ancestral deities portrayed on that unfading pavement in the very centre of the villa—Apollo and Daphne, Bacchus and Ariadne:

> For ever warm and still to be enjoyed,
> For ever panting, and for ever young.

Parcels come to them, forwarded from the near military station; come by those trade-routes, mysterious to us, concerning which a most illuminating book waits to be written by somebody. There are parcels of seeds—useful vegetables and potherbs, helichryse (marigolds as we call them now) for the flower garden, for the colonnade even roses with real Italian earth damp about their roots. There are parcels of books, too—rolls rather, or tablets—wherein the family reads about Rome; of its wealth, the uproar of its traffic, the innumerable chimneys smoking, *fumum et opes strepitumque*. For they are always reading of Rome; feeling themselves, as they read, to belong to it, to be neither savage nor even rustic, but by birthright *of the city*, urbane; and what these exiles read is of how Horace met a bore on the Sacred Road (which would correspond, more or less, with our Piccadilly):

> Along the Sacred Road I strolled one day
> Deep in some bagatelle (you know my way)
> When up comes one whose face I scarcely knew—
> 'The dearest of dear fellows! how d' ye do?'
> —He grasped my hand. 'Well, thanks! The same to you?'

—or of how Horace apologizes for protracting a summer jaunt to his country seat:

> Five days I told you at my farm I 'd stay,
> And lo! the whole of August I 'm away.
> Well but, Maecenas, you would have me live,
> And, were I sick, my absence you 'd forgive.
> So let me crave indulgence for the fear
> Of falling ill at this bad time of year.
> When, thanks to early figs and sultry heat,
> The undertaker figures with his suite;
> When fathers all and fond mammas grow pale
> At what may happen to their young heirs male,
> And courts and levees, town-bred mortals' ills,
> Bring fevers on, and break the seals of wills.[1]

Consider those lines; then consider how long it took the inhabitants of this island—the cultured ones who count as readers or writers—to recapture just that note of urbanity. Other things our forefathers—Britons, Saxons, Normans, Dutch or French refugees—discovered by the way; worthier things if you will; but not until the eighteenth century do you find just that note recaptured; the note of easy confidence that

[1] Conington's translation.

our London had become what Rome had been, the Capital
city. You begin to meet it in Dryden; with Addison it is
fairly established. Pass a few years, and with Samuel Johnson
it is taken for granted. His *London* is Juvenal's Rome, and
the same satire applies to one as applied to the other. But
against the urbane lines written by one Horace some while
before Juvenal let us set a passage from another Horace—
Horace Walpole, seventeen hundred years later and some little
while ahead of Johnson. He, like our Roman colonist, is a
settler in a new country, Twickenham; and like Flaccus he
loves to escape from town life.

TWICKENHAM, *June 8th*, 1747.

To the Hon. H. S. CONWAY.

You perceive by my date that I am got into a new camp, and have
left my tub at Windsor. It is a little plaything-house that I got out
of Mrs. Chevenix's shop, and the prettiest bauble you ever saw. It
is set in enamelled meadows with filagree hedges:

> A small Euphrates through the place is roll'd,
> And little finches wave their wings of gold.

Two delightful roads, that *you* would call dusty, supply me continually with coaches and chaises: barges as solemn as Barons of the
Exchequer move under my window; Richmond Hill and Ham Walks
bound my prospect; but, thank God! the Thames is between me
and the Duchess of Queensberry. Dowagers as plenty as flounders
inhabit all around, and Pope's ghost is just now skimming under my
window by the most poetical moonlight. . . . The Chevenixes had
tricked it out for themselves; up two pairs of stairs is what they call
Mr. Chevenix's library, furnished with three maps, one shelf, a bust
of Sir Isaac Newton and a lame telescope without any glasses. Lord
John Sackville *predeceased* me here and instituted certain games
called *cricketalia*, which have been celebrated this very evening in
honour of him in a neighbouring meadow.

You will think I have removed my philosophy from Windsor with
my tea-things hither; for I am writing to you in all tranquility while a
Parliament is bursting about my ears. You know it is going to be
dissolved. . . . They say the Prince has taken up two hundred
thousand pounds, to carry elections which he won't carry—he had
much better have saved to it buy the Parliament after it is chosen.

There you have Horace Walpole, the man-about-town, almost
precisely echoing Horatius Flaccus, the man-about-town; and

this (if you will bring your minds to it) is just the sort of passage a Roman colonist in Britain would open upon, out of his parcel of new books, and read, *and understand*, some eighteen hundred years ago.

What became of it all?—of that easy colonial life, of the men and women who trod those tessellated pavements? 'Wiped out,' say the historians, knowing nothing, merely guessing: for you may with small trouble assure yourselves that the fifth and sixth centuries in the story of this island are a blind spot, concerning which one man's guess may be as good as another's. 'Wiped out,' they will commonly agree; for while, as I warned you in another lecture, the pedantic mind, faced with a difficulty, tends to remove it conveniently into a category to which it does not belong, still more prone is the pedantic mind to remove it out of existence altogether. So 'wiped out' is the theory; and upon it a sympathetic imagination can invent what sorrowful pictures it will of departing legions, the last little cloud of dust down the highway, the lovers by the gate watching it, not comprehending; the peaceful homestead in the background, ripe for doom—and what-not.

Or, stay! There is another theory to which the late Professor Freeman inclined (if so sturdy a figure could be said to incline), laying stress on a passage in Gildas, that the Romans in Britain, faced by the Saxon invader, got together their money, and bolted away into Gaul. 'The Romans that were in Britain gathered together their gold-hoard, hid part in the ground and carried the rest over to Gaul,' writes Gildas. 'The hiding in the ground,' says Freeman, 'if of course a guess to explain the frequent finding of Roman coins'—which indeed it *does* explain better than the guess that they were carried away, and perhaps better than the schoolboy's suggestion that during their occupation of Britain the Romans spent most of their time in dropping money about. Likely enough, large numbers of the colonists *did* gather up what they could and flee before the approaching storm; but by no means all, I think. For (since, where all is uncertain, we must reason from what is probable of human nature) in the first place men with large estates do not behave in that way before a danger which creeps upon them little by little, as this Saxon danger did. These colonists could not dig up their fields and carry *them* over to Gaul. They did not keep banking accounts; and in the course of four hundred years their main wealth had certainly been sunk in the land. They could not carry away their villas. We know that many of them did not carry away the *tessellae* for which (as we have seen) they had so peculiar a veneration; for these remain. Secondly, if the colonists left Britain in a mass, when in the middle of the sixth century we find Belisarius offering the Goths to trade Britain for Sicily, as being 'much larger and this long time subservient to Roman rule,'[1] we must suppose either (as Freeman appears to suppose) that Belisarius did not know what he was offering, or that he was attempting a gigantic 'bluff,' or lastly that he really was offering an exchange not flatly derisory; of which three possible suppositions I prefer the last as the likeliest. Nor am I the less inclined to choose it, because these very English historians go on to clear the ground in a like convenient way of the Celtic inhabitants, exterminating them as they exterminated the Romans, with a wave of the hand, quite in the fashion of Mr. Podsnap. 'This is un-English: therefore for me it merely ceases to exist.'

'*Probable extirpation of the Celtic inhabitants*' jots down Freeman in his margin, and proceeds to write:

In short, though the literal extirpation of a nation is an impossibility, there is every reason to believe that the Celtic inhabitants of those parts of Britain which had become English at the end of the sixth century had been as nearly extinguished as a nation could be. The women doubtless would be largely spared, but as far as the male sex is concerned we may feel sure that death, emigration, or personal slavery were the only alternatives which the vanquished found at the hands of our fathers.

Upon this passage, if brought to me in an undergraduate essay, I should have much to say. The style, with its abstract nouns ('the literal extirpation of a nation is an impossibility'), its

---

[1] *Bell. Goth.* ii, ᴏ.

padding and periphrasis ('there is every reason to believe' . . . 'as far as the male sex is concerned we may feel sure') betrays the loose thought.   It begins with 'in short' and proceeds to be long-winded.   It commits what even schoolboys know to be a solecism by inviting us to consider three 'alternatives'; and what can I say of 'the women doubtless would be largely spared,' save that besides scanning in iambics it says what Freeman never meant and what no-one outside of an Aristophanic comedy could ever suggest?   'The women doubtless would be largely spared'!   It reminds me of the young lady in Cornwall who, asked by her vicar if she had been confirmed, admitted blushingly that 'she had reason to believe, partially so.'

'The women doubtless would be largely spared'!—But I thank the Professor for teaching me that phrase, because it tries to convey just what I am driving at.   The Jutes, Angles, Saxons, did not extirpate the Britons, whatever you may hold concerning the Romans.   For, once again, men do not behave in that way, and certainly will not when a live slave is worth money.   Secondly, the very horror with which men spoke, centuries after, of Anderida quite plainly indicates that such a wholesale massacre was exceptional, monstrous.   If not exceptional, monstrous, why should this particular slaughter have lingered so ineffaceably in their memories?   Finally— and to be as curt as the question deserves—the Celtic Briton in the island was not exterminated and never came near to being exterminated: but on the contrary, remains equipollent with the Saxon in our blood, and perhaps equipollent with that mysterious race we call Iberian, which came before either and endures in this island to-day, as any one travelling it with eyes in his head can see.   Pict, Dane, Norman, Frisian, Huguenot French—these and others come in.   If mixture of blood be a shame, we have purchased at the price of that shame the glory of catholicism; and I know of nothing more false in science or more actively poisonous in politics or in the arts than the assumption that we belong as a race to the Teutonic family.

Dane, Norman, Frisian, French Huguenot—they all come

in. And will you refuse a hearing when I claim that the Roman
came in too? Bethink you how deeply Rome engraved itself
on this island and its features. Bethink you that, as human
nature is, no conquering race ever lived or could live—even in
garrison—among a tributary one without begetting children
on it. Bethink you yet further of Freeman's admission that
in the wholesale (and quite hypothetical) general massacre 'the
women doubtless would be largely spared'; and you advance
nearer to my point. I see a people which for four hundred
years was permeated by Rome. If you insist on its being a
Teutonic people (which I flatly deny) then you have one which
alone of Teutonic peoples has inherited the Roman gift of con-
solidating conquest, of colonizing in the wake of its armies;
of driving the road, bridging the ford, bringing the lawless
under its sense of law. I see that this nation of ours concurrently, when it seeks back to what alone can inspire and
glorify these activities, seeks back, not to any supposed native
North, but south to the Middle Sea of our civilization and
steadily to Italy, which we understand far more easily than
France—though France has helped us times and again. Putting these things together, I retort upon the ethnologists—for
I come from the West of England, where we suffer incredible
things from them—'*Semper ego auditor tantum?*' I hazard
that the most important thing in our blood is that purple drop
of the imperial murex we derive from Rome.

You must, of course, take this for nothing more than it
pretends to be—a conjecture, a suggestion. I will follow it
up with two statements of fact, neither doubtful nor disputable.

The first is, that when English poetry awoke, long after the
Conquest (or, as I should prefer to put it, after the Crusades)
it awoke a new thing; in its vocabulary as much like Anglo-
Saxon poetry as ever you will, but in metre, rhythm, lilt—and
more, in style, feeling, imaginative play—and yet more again,
in knowledge of what it aimed to be, in the essentials, in the
qualities that make Poetry Poetry—as different from Anglo-
Saxon poetry as cheese is from chalk, and as much more
nutritious. Listen to this:

> Bytuene Mershe ant Averil
>> When spray biginnith to spring,
> The lutel foul hath hire wyl
>> On hire lud to synge:
> Ich libbe in love-longinge
> For semlokest of alle thynge,
> He may me blisse bringe,
> Icham in hire bandoun.
> An hendy hap ichabbe y-hent,
> Ichot from hevene it is me sent,
> From alle wymmen my love is lent,
>> And lvht on Alisoun.

Here you have alliteration in plenty; you even have what some hold to be the pattern of Anglo-Saxon alliterative verse (though in practice disregarded, may be, as often as not), the chosen initial used twice in the first line and once at least in the second:

> From alle wymmen my *l*ove is *l*ent,
> And *l*yht on A*l*isoun.

But if a man cannot see a difference infinitely deeper than any similarity between this son of Alison and the old Anglo-Saxon verse—*a difference of nature*—I must despair of his literary sense.

What has happened? Well, in Normandy, too, and in another tongue, men are singing much the same thing in the same way:

> A la fontenelle
> Qui sort seur l'araine,
> Trouvai pastorella
> Qui n'iert pas vilaine . . .
>> Merci, merci, douce Marote,
>> N'oçiez pas vostre ami doux,

and this Norman and the Englishman were singing to a new tune, which was yet an old tune re-set to Europe by the Provence, the Roman Province; by the troubadours—Pons de Capdeuil, Bernard de Ventadour, Bertrand de Born, Pierre Vidal, and the rest, with William of Poitou, William of Poitiers.

Read and compare; you will perceive that the note then set persists and has never perished. Take Giraud de Borneil:

> Bel companhos, si dormetz o velhatz
> Non dortmatz plus, qu'el jorn es apropchatz—

and set it beside a lyric of our day, written without a thought of Giraud de Borneil:

Heigh! brother mine, art a-waking or a-sleeping:
Mind'st thou the merry moon a many summers fled?
Mind'st thou the green and the dancing and the leaping?
Mind'st thou the haycocks and the moon above them creeping? . . .

Or take Bernard de Ventadour's:

> Quand erba vertz, e fuelha par
> E'l flor brotonon per verjan,
> E'l rossinhols autet e clar
> Leva sa votz e mov son chan,
> Joy ai de luy, e joy ai de la flor,
> Joy ai de me, e de me dons maior.

Why, it runs straight off into English verse:

> When grass is green and leaves appear
>   With flowers in bud the meads among,
> And nightingale aloft and clear
>   Lifts up his voice and pricks his song,
> Joy, joy have I in song and flower,
> Joy in myself, and in my lady more.

And that may be doggerel; yet what is it but

> It was a lover and his lass,
> With a hey and a ho and a hey nonino,
> That o'er the green cornfield did pass
>   In the spring-time, the only pretty ring-time—

or

> When daffodils begin to peer,
>   With heigh! the doxy over the dale,
> Why then comes in the sweet o' the year;
>   For the red blood reigns in the winter's pale.

Nay, flatter the Anglo-Saxon tradition by picking its very best—and I suppose it hard to find better than the much-admired opening of *Piers Plowman*, in which that tradition shot up like the flame of a dying candle:

> Bote in a Mayes morwnynge—on Malverne hulles
> Me bi-fel a ferly—a feyrie me thouhte;
> I was weori of wandringe—and wente me to reste
> Under a brod banke—bi a bourne syde,
> And as I lay and leonede—and lokede on the watres,
> I slumberde in a slepynge—hit sownede so murie.

This is good, solid stuff, no doubt: but tame, inert, if not actually lifeless. As M. Jusserand says of Anglo-Saxon poetry in general, it is like the river Saône—one doubts which way it flows. How tame in comparison with this, for example!

> In somer, when the shawes be sheyne,
>   And leves be large and long,
> Hit is full mery in feyre foreste
>   To here the foulys song:
>
> To se the dere draw to the dale
>   And leve the hilles hee,
> And shadow hem in the leves grene
>   Under the grene-wode tre.
>
> Hit befel on Whitsontide,
>   Erly in a May mornyng,
> The Son up feyre can shyne,
>   And the briddis mery can syng.
>
> 'This is a mery mornyng,' said litell John,
>   'Be Hym that dyed on tre;
> A more mery man than I am one
>   Lyves not in Cristianté.
>
> 'Pluk up thi hert, my dere mayster,'
>   Litull John can sey,
> 'And thynk hit is a full fayre tyme
>   In a mornyng of May.'

There is no doubting which way *that* flows! And this vivacity, this new beat of the heart of poetry, is common to Chaucer and the humblest ballad-maker; it pulses through any book of lyrics printed yesterday, and it came straight to us out of Provence, the Roman Province. It was the Provençal Troubadour who, like the Prince in the fairy tale, broke through the hedge of briers and kissed Beauty awake again.

You will urge that he wakened Poetry not in England alone

but all over Europe, in Dante before our Chaucer, in the trouvères and minnesingers as well as in our ballad-writers. To that I might easily retort, 'So much the better for Europe, and the more of it the merrier, to win their way into the great comity.' But here I put in my second assertion, that we English have had above all nations lying wide of the Mediterranean, the instinct to refresh and renew ourselves at Mediterranean wells; that again and again our writers—our poets especially—have sought them as the hart panteth after the water-brooks. If you accept this assertion, and if you believe as well that our literature, surpassing Rome's, may vie with that of Athens—if you believe that a literature which includes Chaucer, Spenser, Shakespeare, Pope, Wordsworth, Shelley— the Authorized Verson of Holy Writ, with Browne, Bunyan, Swift, Addison, Johnson, Arnold, Newman—has entered the circle to take its seat with the first—why then, heartily believing this with you, I leave you to find some better explanation than mine if you can.

But what I content myself with asserting here you can scarcely deny. Chaucer's initial and enormous debt to Dante and Boccaccio stands in as little dispute as Dunbar's to Chaucer. On that favourite poet of mine, Sir Thomas Wyat, I descanted in a former lecture. He is one of your glories here, having entered St. John's College at the age of twelve (which must have been precocious even for those days). Anthony Wood asserts that after finishing his course here, he proceeded to Cardinal Wolsey's new College at Oxford; but, as Christ Church was not founded until 1524, and Wyat, still precocious, had married a wife two years before that, the statement (to quote Dr. Courthope) 'seems no better founded than many others advanced by that patriotic but not very scrupulous author.' It is more to the point that he went travelling, and brought home from France, Italy, afterwards Spain—always from Latin altars—the flame of lyrical poetry to England; the flame of the Petrarchists, caught from the Troubadours, clarified (so to speak) by the salt of humane letters. On what our Elizabethan literature owes to the Classical revival uncounted volumes have been written and hundreds more will be written; I will but remind you of what Spenser talked about with Gabriel Harvey, what Daniel disputed with Campion; that Marlowe tried to re-incarnate Machiavelli, that Jonson was a sworn Latinist and the 'tribe of Ben' a classical tribe; while, as for Shakespeare, go and reckon the proportion of Italian and Roman names in his *dramatis personae*. Of Donne's debt to France, Italy, Rome, Greece, you may read much in Professor Grierson's great edition, and I daresay Professor Grierson would be the first to allow that all has not yet been computed. You know how Milton prepared himself to be a poet. Have you realized that, in those somewhat strangely constructed sonnets of his, Milton was deliberately modelling upon the Horatian Ode, as his *confrère*, Andrew Marvell, was avowedly attempting the like in his famous *Horatian Ode* on Cromwell's Return from Ireland—so that if Cromwell had returned (like Mr. Quilp), walked in and caught his pair of Latin Secretaries scribbling verse, one at either end of the office table, both might colourably have pleaded that they were, after all, writing Latin. Put together Dryden's various Prefaces and you will find them one solid monument to his classical faith. Of Pope, Gray, Collins, you will not ask me to speak. What is salt in Cowper you can taste only when you have detected that by a stroke of madness he missed, or barely missed, being our true English Horace, that almost more nearly than the rest he hit what the rest had been seeking. Then, of the 'romantic revival'—enemy of false classicism, not of classicism—bethink you what, in his few great years, Wordsworth owed directly to France of the early Revolution; what Keats drew forth out of Lemprière: and again how Tennyson wrought upon Theocritus, Virgil, Catullus; upon what Arnold constantly shaped his verse; how Browning returned ever upon Italy to inspire his best and correct or redeem his worse.

Of Anglo-Saxon prose I know little indeed, but enough of the world to feel reasonably sure that if it contained any single masterpiece—or anything that could be paraded as a master piece—we should have heard enough about it long before now. It was invented by King Alfred for excellent political reasons; but, like other ready-made political inventions in this country, it refused to thrive. I think it can be demonstrated, that the true line of intellectual descent in prose lies through Bede (who wrote in Latin, the 'universal language'), and not through the Blickling Homilies, or Ælfric, or the Saxon Chronicle. And I am sure that Freeman is perversely wrong when he laments as a 'great mistake' that the first Christian missionaries from Rome did not teach their converts to pray and give praise in the vernacular. The vernacular being what it was, these men did better to teach the religion of the civilized world—*orbis terrarum*—in the language of the civilized world. I am not thinking of its efficiency for spreading the faith; but neither is Freeman; and, for that, we must allow these old missionaries to have known their own business. I am thinking only of how this 'great mistake' affected our literature; and if you will read Professor Saintsbury's *History of English Prose Rhythm* (pioneer work, which yet wonderfully succeeds in illustrating what our prose-writers from time to time were trying to do); if you will study the Psalms in the Prayer Book Version; if you will consider what Milton, Clarendon, Sir Thomas Browne, were aiming at; what Addison, Gibbon, Johnson; what Landor, Thackeray, Newman, Arnold, Pater; I doubt not your rising from the perusal convinced that our nation, in this storehouse of Latin to refresh and replenish its most sacred thoughts, has enjoyed a continuous blessing: that the Latin of the Vulgate and the Offices has been a background giving depth and, as the painters say, 'value' to nine-tenths of our serious writing.

And now, since this and a previous lecture run something counter to a great deal of that teaching in English Literature which nowadays passes most acceptably, let me avoid offence, so far as may be, by defining one or two things I am *not* trying to do.

I am not persuading you to despise your linguistic descent. English is English—our language; and all its history to be venerated by us.

I am not persuading you to despise linguistic study. *All* learning is venerable.

I am not persuading you to behave like Ascham, and turn English prose into pedantic Latin; nor would I have you doubt that in the set quarrel between Campion, who wished to divert English verse into strict classical channels, and Daniel, who vindicated our free English way (derived from Latin through the Provençal), Daniel was on the whole, right, Campion on the whole, wrong: though I believe that both ways yet lie open, and we may learn, if we study them intelligently, a hundred things from the old classical metres.

I do not ask you to forget what there is of the Northmen in your blood. If I desired this, I could not worship William Morris as I do, among the later poets.

I do not ask you to doubt that the barbarian invaders from the north, with their myths and legends, brought new and most necessary blood of imagination into the literary material —for the time almost exhausted—of Greece and Rome.

Nevertheless, I do contend that when Britain (or, if you prefer it, Sleswick),

> When Sleswick first at Heaven's command
> Arose from out the azure main,

she differed from Aphrodite, that other foam-born, in sundry important features of ear, of lip, of eye.

Lastly, if vehement assertions on the one side have driven me into too vehement dissent on the other, I crave pardon; not for the dissent but for the vehemence, as sinning against the very principle I would hold up to your admiration—the old Greek principle of avoiding excess.

But I *do* commend the patient study of Greek and Latin authors—in the original or in translation—to all of you who would write English; and for three reasons.

(1) In the first place they will correct your insularity of mind; or, rather, will teach you to forget it. The Anglo-Saxon, it has been noted, ever left an empty space around his

houses; and that, no doubt, is good for a house. It is not so good for the mind.

(2) Secondly, we have a tribal habit, confirmed by Protestant meditation upon a Hebraic religion, of confining our literary enjoyment to the written word and frowning down the drama, the song, the dance. A fairly attentive study of modern lyrical verse has persuaded me that this exclusiveness may be carried too far, and threatens to be deadening. 'I will sing and give praise,' says the Scripture, 'with the best member that I have' —meaning the tongue. But the old Greek was an 'all round man' as we say. He sought to praise and give thanks with all his members, and to tune each to perfection. I think his way worth your considering.

(3) Lastly, and chiefly, I commend these classical authors to you because they, in the European civilization which we all inherit, conserve the norm of literature; the steady grip on the essential; the clean outline at which in verse or in prose —in epic, drama, history, or philosophical treatise—a writer should aim.

THE ART OF READING

I

In the third book of the *Ethics*, and in the second chapter, Aristotle, dealing with certain actions which, though bad in themselves, admit of pity and forgiveness because they were committed involuntarily, through ignorance, instances 'the man who did not know a subject was forbidden, like Aeschylus with the Mysteries,' and 'the man who only meant to show how it worked, like the fellow who let off the catapult' (ἡ δεῖξαι βουλόμενος ἀφεῖναι, ὡς ὁ τὸν καταπέλτην).

I feel comfortably sure, Gentlemen, that in a previous course of lectures *On the Art of Writing*, unlike Aeschylus I divulged no mysteries: but I am troubled with speculations over that man and the catapult, because I really was trying to tell you how the thing worked; and Aristotle, with a reticence which (as Horace afterwards noted) may lend itself to obscurity, tells us neither what happened to that exponent of ballistics, nor to the engine itself, nor to the other person.

My discharge, such as it was, at any rate provoked another Professor (*emeritus*, learned, sagacious, venerable) to retort that the true business of a Chair such as this is to instruct young men how to *read* rather than how to write. Well, be it so. I accept the challenge.

I propose in this and some ensuing lectures to talk of the Art and Practice of Reading, particularly as applied to English Literature: to discuss on what ground and through what faculties an Author and his Reader meet: to enquire if, or to what extent, reading of the best Literature can be taught; and supposing it to be taught, if or to what extent it can be examined upon; with maybe an interlude or two, to beguile the way.

II

The first thing, then, to be noted about the reading of English (with which alone I am concerned) is that for Englishmen it has been made, by Act of Parliament, compulsory.

The next thing to be noted is that in our schools and Colleges and Universities it has been made, by Statute or in practice, all but impossible.

The third step is obvious—to reconcile what we cannot do with what we must: and to that aim I shall, under your patience, direct this lecture. I shall be relieved at all events, and from the outset, of the doubt by which many a Professor, here and elsewhere, has been haunted: I mean the doubt whether there really *is* such a subject as that of which he proposes to treat. Anything that requires so much human ingenuity as reading English in an English University *must* be an art.

III

But I shall be met, of course, by the question 'How is the reading of English made impossible at Cambridge?' and I pause here, on the edge of my subject, to clear away that doubt.

It is no fault of the University.

The late Philip Gilbert Hamerton, whom some remember as an etcher, wrote a book which he entitled (as I think, too magniloquently) *The Intellectual Life.* He cast it in the form of letters—'To an Author who kept very Irregular Hours,' 'To a Young Etonian who thought of becoming a Cotton-spinner,' 'To a Young Gentleman who had firmly resolved never to wear anything but a Grey Coat' (but Mr. Hamerton couldn't quite have meant that), 'To a Lady of High Culture who found it difficult to associate with persons of her Own Sex,' 'To a Young Gentleman of Intellectual Tastes, who, without having as yet any Particular Lady in View, had expressed, in a General Way, his Determination to get Married.' The volume is well worth reading. In the first letter of all, addressed 'To a Young Man of Letters who worked Excessively,' Mr. Hamerton fishes up from his memory, for admonishment, this salutary instance:

A tradesman, whose business affords an excellent outlet for energetic bodily activity, told me that having attempted, in addition to his ordinary work, to acquire a foreign language which seemed likely to be useful to him, he had been obliged to abandon it on account of alarming cerebral symptoms. This man has immense vigour and energy, but the digestive functions, in this instance, are sluggish. However, when he abandoned study, the cerebral inconveniences disappeared, and have never returned since.

IV

Now we all know, and understand, and like that man: for the simple reason that he is every one of us.

You or I (say) have to take the Modern Languages Tripos, Section A (English), in 1917.[1] First of all (and rightly) it is demanded of us that we show an acquaintance, and something more than a bowing acquaintance, with Shakespeare. Very well; but next we have to write a paper and answer questions on the outlines of English Literature from 1350 to 1832—almost 500 years—, and next to write a paper and show particular knowledge of English Literature between 1700 and 1785— eighty-five years. Next comes a paper on passages from selected English verse and prose writings—the Statute discreetly avoids calling them literature—between 1200 and 1500, exclusive of Chaucer; with questions on language, metre, literary history and literary criticism: then a paper on Chaucer with questions on language, metre, literary history and literary criticism: lastly a paper on writing in the Wessex dialect of Old English, with questions on language, metre and literary history.

Now if you were to qualify yourself for all this as a scholar should, and in two years, you would certainly deserve to be addressed by Mr. Hamerton as 'A Young Man of Letters who worked Excessively'; and to work excessively is not good for any one. Yet, on the other hand, you are precluded from using, for your 'cerebral inconveniences,' the heroic remedy exhibited by Mr. Hamerton's enterprising tradesman, since on

[1] This lecture was given in 1916. At that time I was engaged against a system of English teaching which I believed to be thoroughly bad. That system has since given place in Cambridge to another, which I am prepared to defend as a better.

that method you would not attain to the main object of your
laudable ambition, a Cambridge degree.

But the matter is very much worse than your Statute makes
it out. Take one of the papers in which some actual acquaintance with Literature is required—the Special Period
from 1700 to 1785; then turn to your *Cambridge History of
English Literature*, and you will find that the mere bibliography of those eighty-five years occupies something like five
or six hundred pages—five or six hundred pages of titles and
authors in simple enumeration! The brain reels; it already
suffers 'cerebral inconveniences.' But stretch the list back to
Chaucer, back through Chaucer to those alleged prose writings
in the Wessex dialect, then forward from 1785 to Wordsworth,
to Byron, to Dickens, Carlyle, Tennyson, Browning, Meredith,
even to this year in which literature still lives and engenders;
and the brain, if not too giddy indeed, stands as Satan stood
on the brink of Chaos—

> Pondering his voyage; for no narrow frith
> He had to cross—

and sees itself, with him, now plumbing a vast vacuity, and
anon nigh-foundered, 'treading the crude consistence.'

The whole business of reading English Literature in two
years, to *know* it in any reputable sense of the word—let alone
your learning to write English—is, in short, impossible. And
the framers of the Statute, recognizing this, have craftily
compromised by setting you to work on such things as 'the
Outlines of English Literature'; which are not Literature at all
but are only what some fellow has to say about it, hastily summarizing his estimates of many works, of which on a generous
computation he has probably read one-third; and by examining
you on (what was it all?) 'language, metre, literary history and
literary criticism,' which again are not Literature, or at least
(as a Greek would say in his idiom) escape their own notice
being Literature. For English Literature, as I take it, is *that
which sundry men and women have written memorably in English
about Life*. And so I come to the art of reading *that*, which
is Literature.

V

I shall again take leave to leap into my subject over another man's back, or, rather over two men's backs. No doubt it has happened to many of you to pick up in a happy moment some book or pamphlet or copy of verse which just says the word you have unconsciously been listening for, almost craving to speak for yourself, and so sends you off hot-foot on the trail. And if you have had that experience, it may also have happened to you that, after ranging, you returned on the track 'like faithful hound returning,' in gratitude, or to refresh the scent; and that, picking up the book again, you found it no such wonderful book after all, or that some of the magic had faded by process of the change in yourself which itself had originated. But the word was spoken.

Such a book—pamphlet I may call it, so small it was—fell into my hands some ten years ago; *The Aims of Literary Study* —no very attractive title—by Dr. Corson, a distinguished American Professor (and let me say that, for something more than ten—say for twenty—years much of the most thoughtful as well as the most thorough work upon English comes to us from America). I find, as I handle again the small duodecimo volume, that my own thoughts have taken me a little wide, perhaps a little astray, from its suggestions. But for loyalty's sake I shall start just where Dr. Corson started, with a passage from Browning's *A Death in the Desert*, supposed (you will remember)—

Supposed of Pamphylax the Antiochene

narrating the death of St. John the Evangelist, John of Patmos; the narrative interrupted by this gloss:

[This is the doctrine he was wont to teach,
How divers persons witness in each man,
Three souls which make up one soul: *first*, to wit,
A soul of each and all the bodily parts,
Seated therein, which works, and is *What Does*,
And has the use of earth, and ends the man
Downward: but, tending upward for advice,
Grows into, and again is grown into

> By the next soul, which, seated in the brain,
> Useth the first with its collected use,
> And feeleth, thinketh, willeth,—is *What Knows*:
> Which, duly tending upward in its turn,
> Grows into, and again is grown into
> By the last soul, that uses both the first,
> Subsisting whether they assist or no,
> And, constituting man's self, is *What Is*—
> And leans upon the former

(Mark the word, Gentlemen;—'*leans* upon the former'— leaning back, as it were felt by him, on this very man who had leaned on Christ's bosom, being loved)

> And leans upon the former, makes it play,
> As that played off the first: and, tending up,
> Holds, is upheld by, God, and ends the man
> Upward in that dread point of intercourse,
> Nor needs a place, for it returns to Him.
> *What Does, What Knows, What Is;* three souls, one man.
> I give the glossa of Theotypas.]

What Does, What Knows, What Is—there is no mistaking what Browning means, nor in what degrees of hierarchy he places this, that, and the other. . . . Does it not strike you how curiously men to-day, with their minds perverted by hate, are inverting that order?—all the highest value set on *What Does* —*What Knows* suddenly seen to be of importance, but only as important in feeding the guns, perfecting explosives, collaring trade—all in the service of *What Does*, of 'Efficiency'; no one stopping to think that 'Efficiency' is—must be—a relative term! Efficient for what?—for *What Does, What Knows* or perchance, after all, for *What Is*? No! banish the humanities and throw everybody into practical science: not into that study of natural science, which can never conflict with the 'humanities' since it seeks discovery for the pure sake of truth, or charitably to alleviate man's lot—

> Sweetly, rather, to ease, loose and bind,
> As need requires, this frail fallen humankind . . .

—but to invent what will be commercially serviceable in besting your neighbour, or in gassing him, or in slaughtering him neatly and wholesale. But still the whisper (not ridiculous in its day) will assert itself, that *What Is* comes first, holding and upheld by God; still through the market clamour for a 'Business Government' will persist the voice of Plato murmuring that, after all, the best form of government is government by good men: and the voice of some small man faintly protesting 'But I don't want to be governed by business men; because I know them and, without asking much of life, I have a hankering to die with a shirt on my back.'

VI

But let us postpone *What Is* for a moment, and deal with *What Does* and *What Knows*. They too, of course, have had their oppositions, and the very meaning of a University such as Cambridge—its *fons*, its *origo*, the reason of its being—was to assert *What Knows* against *What Does* in a mediaeval world pranced over by men-at-arms, Normans, English, Burgundians, Scots. Ancillary to Theology, which then had a meaning vastly different from its meaning to-day, the University tended as portress of the gate of knowledge—of such knowledge as the Church required, encouraged, or permitted—and kept the flag of intellectual life, as I may put it, flying above that gate and over the passing throngs of 'doers' and mailed-fisters. The University was a *Seat of Learning*: the Colleges, as they sprang up, were *Houses of Learning*.

But note this, which in their origin and still in the frame of their constitution differentiates Oxford and Cambridge from all their ancient sisters and rivals. These two (and no third, I believe, in Europe) were corporations of Teachers, existing for Teachers, governed by Teachers. In a Scottish University the students by vote choose their Rector: but here or at Oxford no undergraduate, no Bachelor, counts at all in the government, both remaining alike *in statu pupillari* until qualified as Masters—*Magistri*. Mark the word, and mark also the title of one who obtained what in those days would be the highest of degrees (but yet gave him no voting strength above a Master). He was a Professor—'Sanctae Theologiae Professor.' To this day every country clergyman who comes up to Cambridge to record his vote does so by virtue of his capacity to teach what he learned here—in theory, that is. Scholars were included in College foundations on a sort of pupil-teacher-supply system: living in rooms with the lordly masters, and valeting them for the privilege of 'reading with' them. We keep to this day the pleasant old form of words. Now for various reasons—one of which, because it is closely germane to my subject, I shall particularly examine—Oxford and Cambridge, while conserving almost intact their mediaeval frame of government, with a hundred other survivals which Time but makes, through endurance, more endearing, have, insensibly as it were, and across (it must be confessed) intervals of sloth and gross dereliction of duty, added a new function to the cultivation of learning—that of furnishing out of youth a succession of men capable of fulfilling high offices in Church and State.

Some may regret this. I think many of us must regret that a deeper tincture of learning is not required of the average pass-man, or injected into him. But speaking roughly about fact, I should say that, while we elders up here are required —nay, presumed—to *know* certain things, we aim that our young men shall *be* of a certain kind; and I see no cause to disown a sentence in the very first lecture I had the honour of reading before you—'The man we are proud to send forth from our Schools will be remarkable less for something he can take out of his wallet and exhibit for knowledge, than for *being* something, and that "something" recognizable for a man of unmistakable intellectual breeding, whose trained judgment we can trust to choose the better and reject the worse.'

The reasons which have led our older Universities to deflect their functions (whether for good or ill) so far from their first purpose are complicated if not many. Once admit young men in large numbers, and youth (I call any Dean or Tutor to witness) must be compromised with; will construe the laws of its seniors in its own way, now and then breaking them; and will inevitably end by getting something of its own way. The growth of gymnastic, the insensible gravitation of the elderly towards Fenner's—there to snatch a fearful joy and explain that the walk was good for them; the Union and other debating societies; College rivalries; the festivities of May Week; the invasion of women students: all these may have helped. But I must dwell discreetly on one compelling and obvious cause —the increased and increasing unwieldiness of Knowledge. And that is the main trouble, as I guess.

VII

Let us look it fair in the face: because it is the main practical difficulty with which I propose that we grapple. Against Knowledge I have, as the light cynic observed of a certain lady's past, only one serious objection—that there is so much of it. There is indeed so much of it that if with the best will in the world you devoted yourself to it as a mere scholar, you could not possibly digest its accumulated and still accumulating stores. As Sir Thomas Elyot wrote in the sixteenth century (using, you will observe, the very word of Mr. Hamerton's energetic but fed-up tradesman), 'Inconveniences always doe happen by ingurgitation and excessive feedings.' An old schoolmaster and a poet—Mr. James Rhoades, late of Sherborne—comments in words which I will quote, being unable to better them:

This is no less true of the mind than of the body. I do not know that a well-informed man, as such, is more worthy of regard than a well-fed one. The brain, indeed, is a nobler organ than the stomach, but on that very account is the less to be excused for indulging in repletion. The temptation, I confess, is greater, because for the brain the banquet stands ever spread before our eyes, and is, unhappily, as indestructible as the widow's meal and oil.

Only think what would become of us if the physical food, by which our bodies subsist, instead of being consumed by the eater, was passed on intact by every generation to the next, with the superadded hoards of all the ages, the earth's productive power meanwhile increasing year by year beneath the unflagging hand of Science, till, as Comus says, she

> would be quite surcharged with her own weight
> And strangled with her waste fertility.

Should we rather not pull down our barns, and build smaller, and make bonfires of what they would not hold? And yet, with regard to Knowledge, the very opposite of this is what we do. We store the whole religiously, and that though not twice alone, as with the bees in Virgil, but scores of times in every year, is the teeming produce gathered in. And then we put a fearful pressure on ourselves and others to gorge of it as much as ever we can hold.

My author puts it somewhat dithyrambically: but there you have it, Gentlemen.

If you crave for Knowledge, the banquet of Knowledge grows and groans on the board until the finer appetite sickens. If, still putting all your trust in Knowledge, you try to dodge the difficulty by specializing, you produce a brain bulging out inordinately on one side, on the other cut flat down and mostly paralytic at that: and in short so long as I hold that the Creator has an idea of a man, so long shall I be sure that no uneven specialist realizes it. The real tragedy of the Library at Alexandria was not that the incendiaries burned immensely, but that they had neither the leisure nor the taste to discriminate.

VIII

The old schoolmaster whom I quoted just now goes on:

I believe, if the truth were known, men would be astonished at the small amount of learning with which a high degree of culture is compatible. In a moment of enthusiasm I ventured once to tell my 'English set' that if they could really master the ninth book of *Paradise Lost*, so as to rise to the height of its great argument and incorporate all its beauties in themselves, they would at one blow, by virtue of that alone, become highly cultivated men. . . . More and more various learning might raise them to the same height by different paths, but could hardly raise them higher.

Here let me interpose and quote the last three lines of that Book—three lines only; simple, unornamented, but for every man and every woman who have dwelt together since our first parents, in mere statement how wise!

> Thus they in mutual accusation spent
> The fruitless hours, *but neither self-condemning*;
> And of their vain contest appear'd no end.

A parent afterwards told me (my schoolmaster adds) that his son went home and so buried himself in the book that food and sleep that day had no attraction for him. Next morning, I need hardly say, the difference in his appearance was remarkable: he had outgrown all his intellectual clothes.

The end of this story strikes me, I confess, as rapid, and may be compared with that of the growth of Delian Apollo in the Homeric hymn; but we may agree that, in reading, it is not quantity so much that tells, as quality and thoroughness of digestion.

IX

What Does—What Knows—What Is. . . .

I am not likely to depreciate to you the value of *What Does*, after spending my first twelve lectures up here, on the art and practice of Writing, encouraging you to *do* this thing which I daily delight in trying to do: as God forbid that any one should hint a slightening word of what our sons and brothers are doing just now, and doing for us! But Peace being the normal condition of man's activity, I look around me for a vindication of what is noblest in *What Does* and am content with a passage from George Eliot's poem *Stradivarius*, the gist of which is that God himself might conceivably make better fiddles than Stradivari's, but by no means certainly; since, as a fact, God orders his best fiddles of Stradivari. Says the great workman:

> 'God be praised,
> Antonio Stradivari has an eye
> That winces at false work and loves the true,
> With hand and arm that play upon the tool
> As willingly as any singing bird
> Sets him to sing his morning roundelay,
> Because he likes to sing and likes the song.'
> Then Naldo: ''Tis a pretty kind of fame
> At best, that comes of making violins;
> And saves no masses, either. Thou wilt go
> To purgatory none the less.'
> But he:
> ''Twere purgatory here to make them ill;
> And for my fame—when any master holds

'Twixt chin and hand a violin of mine,
He will be glad that Stradivari lived,
Made violins, and made them of the best.
The masters only know whose work is good:
They will choose mine, and while God gives them skill
I give them instruments to play upon,
God choosing me to help Him.'
                              'What!   Were God
At fault for violins, thou absent?'
                                   'Yes;
He were at fault for Stradivari's work.'
'Why, many hold Giuseppe's violins
As good as thine.'
                  'May be: they are different.
His quality declines: he spoils his hand
With over-drinking.   But were his the best,
He could not work for two.   My work is mine,
And heresy or not, if my hand slacked
I should rob God—since He is fullest good—
Leaving a blank instead of violins.
I say, not God Himself can make man's best
Without best men to help him. . . .
                              'Tis God gives skill,
But not without men's hands: He could not make
Antonio Stradivari's violins
Without Antonio.   Get thee to thy easel.'

So much then for *What Does*: I do not depreciate it.

X

Neither do I depreciate—in Cambridge, save the mark!—
What Knows.   All knowledge is venerable; and I suppose you
will find the last vindication of the scholar's life at its baldest
in Browning's *A Grammarian's Funeral*:

Others mistrust and say, 'But time escapes:
      Live now or never!'
He said, 'What 's time?   Leave Now for dog and apes!
      Man has Forever.'
Back to his book then; deeper drooped his head:
      Calculus racked him:
Leaden before, his eyes grew dross of lead:
      Tussis attacked him. . . .

So, with the throttling hands of death at strife,
  Ground he at grammar;
Still, thro' the rattle, parts of speech were rife:
  While he could stammer
He settled *Hoti's* business—let it be!—
  Properly based *Oun*—
Gave us the doctrine of the enclitic *De,*
  Dead from the waist down.
Well, here 's the platform, here 's the proper place:
  Hail to your purlieus,
All ye highfliers of the feathered race,
  Swallows and curlews!
Here 's the top-peak; the multitude below
  Live, for they can, there:
This man decided not to Live but Know—
  Bury this man there.

Nevertheless Knowledge is not, cannot be, everything; and indeed, as a matter of experience, cannot even be counted upon to educate. Some of us have known men of extreme learning who yet are, some of them, uncouth in conduct, others violent and overbearing in converse, others unfair in controversy, others even unscrupulous in action—men of whom the sophist Thrasymachus in Plato's *Republic* may stand for the general type. Nay, some of us will subscribe with the old schoolmaster whom I will quote again, when he writes:

To myself personally, as an exception to the rule that opposites attract, a very well-informed person is an object of terror. His mind seems to be so full of facts that you cannot, as it were, see the wood for the trees; there is no room for perspective, no lawns and glades for pleasure and repose, no vistas through which to view some towering hill or elevated temple; everything in that crowded space seems of the same value: he speaks with no more awe of *King Lear* than of the last Cobden prize essay; he has swallowed them both with the same ease, and got the facts safe in his pouch; but he has no time to ruminate because he must still be swallowing; nor does he seem to know what even Macbeth, with Banquo's murderers then at work, found leisure to remember—that good digestion must wait on appetite, if health is to follow both.

Now that may be put a trifle too vivaciously, but the moral is true. Bacon tells us that reading maketh a full man. Yes, and too much of it makes him too full. The two words of the

Greek upon knowledge remain true, that the last triumph of Knowledge is *Know Thyself*. So Don Quixote repeats it to Sancho Panza, counselling him how to govern his Island:

First, O son, thou hast to fear God, for in fearing Him is wisdom, and being wise thou canst not err.

But secondly thou hast to set thine eyes on what thou art, endeavouring to *know thyself—which is the most difficult knowledge that can be conceived.*

But to know oneself is to know that which alone can know *What Is*. So the hierarchy runs up.

XI

What Does, What Knows, What Is. . . .

I have happily left myself no time to-day to speak of *What Is*: happily, because I would not have you even approach it towards the end of an hour when your attention must be languishing. But I leave you with two promises, and with two sayings from which as this lecture took its start its successors will proceed.

The first promise is, that *What Is*, being the spiritual element in man, is the highest object of his study.

The second promise is that, nine-tenths of what is worthy to be called Literature being concerned with this spiritual element, for that it should be studied, from first up to *n*thly, before anything else.

And my two quotations are for you to ponder:

(1) This, first:

That all spirit is mutually attractive, as all matter is mutually attractive, is an ultimate fact beyond which we cannot go. . . . Spirit to spirit—as in water face answereth to face, so the heart of man to man.

(2) And this other, from the writings of an obscure Welsh clergyman of the seventeenth century:

You will never enjoy the world aright till the sea itself floweth in your veins, till you are clothed with the heavens and crowned with the stars.

ON READING THE BIBLE

I

The Education Act of 1870, often in these days too sweepingly denounced, did a vast deal of good along with no small amount of definite harm. At the head (I think) of the harmful effects must be set its discouragement of Bible reading; and this chiefly through its encouraging parents to believe that they could henceforth hand over the training of their children to the State, lock, stock and barrel. You all remember the picture in Burns of *The Cotter's Saturday Night*:

> The cheerfu' supper done, wi' serious face,
>> They, round the ingle, form a circle wide;
> The sire turns o'er, wi' patriarchal grace,
>> The big ha'-Bible, ance his father's pride.
> His bonnet rev'rently is laid aside,
> His lyart haffets wearing thin and bare;
>> Those strains that once did sweet in Zion glide,
> He wales a portion with judicious care,
> And 'Let us worship God!' he says, with solemn air.

But you know that the sire bred on the tradition of 1870, and now growing grey, does nothing of that sort on a Saturday night: that, Saturday being tub-night, he inclines rather to order the children into the back-kitchen to get washed; that on Sunday morning, having seen them off to a place of worship, he inclines to sit down and read, in place of the Bible, his Sunday newspaper: that in the afternoon he again shunts them off to Sunday-school. Now—to speak first of the children—it is good for them to be tubbed on Saturday night; good for them also, I daresay, to attend Sunday-school on the following afternoon; but not good in so far as they miss to hear the Bible read by their parents and

> Pure religion breathing household laws.

'Pure religion'?—Well perhaps that begs the question: and I dare say Burns' cotter when he waled 'a portion with judicious care,' waled it as often as not to contradict and confute a neighbouring religionist; that often he contradicted and confuted very crudely. But we may call it simple religion anyhow, sincere religion, parental religion, household religion: and for a certainty no 'lessons' in day-school or Sunday-school have, for tingeing a child's mind, an effect comparable with that of a religion pervading the child's home, present at bedside and board:

> Here a little child I stand,
> Heaving up my either hand;
> Cold as paddocks tho' they be,
> Here I lift them up to Thee;
> For a benison to fall
> On our meat and on us all.   Amen.

—permeating the house, subtly instilled by the very accent of his father's and his mother's speech. For the grown man—well, I happen to come from a part of England where men, in all my days, have been curiously concerned with religion and are yet so concerned; so much that you can scarce take up a local paper and turn to the correspondence column but you will find some heated controversy raging over Free Will and Predestination, the Validity of Holy Orders, Original Sin, Redemption of the many or the few:

> Go it Justice, go it Mercy!
> Go it Douglas, go it Percy!

But the contestants do not write in the language their fathers used. They seem to have lost the vocabulary, and to have picked up, in place of it, the jargon of the Yellow Press, which does not tend to clear definition on points of theology. The mass of all this controversial stuff is no more absurd, no more frantic, than it used to be: but in language it has lost its dignity with its homeliness. It has lost the colouring of the Scriptures, the intonation of the Scriptures, the Scriptural *habit*.

If I turn from it to a passage in Bunyan, I am conversing with a man who, though he has read few other books, has imbibed and soaked the Authorized Version into his fibres so that he cannot speak but Biblically. Listen to this:

As to the situation of this town, it lieth just between the two worlds, and the first founder, and builder of it, so far as by the best, and most authentic records I can gather, was one Shaddai; and he built it for his own delight. He made it the mirror, and glory of all that he made, even the Top-piece beyond anything else that he did in that country: yea, so goodly a town was Mansoul, when first built, that it is said by some, the Gods at the setting up thereof, came down to see it, and sang for joy. . . .

The wall of the town was well built, yea so fast and firm was it knit and compact together, that had it not been for the townsmen themselves, they could not have been shaken, or broken for ever.

Or take this:

Now as they were going along and talking, they espied a Boy feeding his Father's Sheep. The Boy was in very mean Cloaths, but of a very fresh and well-favoured Countenance, and as he sate by himself he Sung. . . . Then said their Guide, Do you hear him? I will dare to say, that this Boy lives a merrier Life, and wears more of that Herb called Heart's-ease in his Bosom, than he that is clad in Silk and Velvet.

I choose ordinary passages, not solemn ones in which Bunyan is consciously scriptural. But you cannot miss the accent.

That is Bunyan, of course; and I am far from saying that the labouring men among whom I grew up, at the fishery or in the hayfield, talked with Bunyan's magic. But I do assert that they had something of the accent; enough to be *like*, in a child's mind, the fishermen and labourers among whom Christ found his first disciples. They had the large simplicity of speech, the cadence, the accent. But let me turn to Ireland, where, though not directly derived from our English Bible, a similar scriptural accent survives among the peasantry and is, I hope, ineradicable. I choose two sentences from a book of 'Memories' recently written by the survivor of the two ladies who together wrote the incomparable 'Irish R.M.' The first was uttered by a small cultivator who was asked why his potato-crop had failed:

'I couldn't hardly say' was the answer. 'Whatever it was, God spurned them in a boggy place.'

Is that not the accent of Isaiah?

He will surely violently turn and toss thee like a ball into a large country.

The other is the benediction bestowed upon the late Miss Violet Martin by a beggar-woman in Skibbereen:

Sure ye 're always laughing!   That ye may laugh in the sight of the Glory of Heaven!

II

But one now sees, or seems to see, that we children did, in our time, read the Bible a great deal, if perforce we were taught to read it in sundry bad ways: of which perhaps the worst was that our elders hammered in all the books, all the parts of it, as equally inspired and therefore equivalent.   Of course this meant among other things that they hammered it all in literally: but let us not sentimentalize over that.   It really did no child any harm to believe that the universe was created in a working week of six days, and that God sat down and looked at it on Sunday, and behold it was very good.   A week is quite a long while to a child, yet a definite division rounding off a square job.   The bath-taps at home usually, for some unexplained reason, went wrong during the week-end: the plumber came in on Monday and carried out his tools on Saturday at mid-day.   These little analogies really do (I believe) help the infant mind, and not at all to its later detriment.   Nor shall I ask you to sentimentalize overmuch upon the harm done to a child by teaching him that the bloodthirsty jealous Jehovah of the Book of Joshua is as venerable (being one and the same un-alterably, 'with whom is no variableness, neither shadow of turning') as the Father, 'the same Lord, whose property is always to have mercy,' revealed to us in the Gospel, invoked for us at the Eucharist.   I do most seriously hold it to be fatal if we grow up and are fossilized in any such belief.   But over this business of teaching the Book of Joshua to children I am in some doubt.   A few years ago an Education Committee, of which I happened to be Chairman, sent ministers of religion about, two by two, to test the religious instruction given in Elementary Schools.   Of the two who worked around my immediate neighbourhood, one was a young priest of the

Church of England, a mediaevalist with an ardent passion for ritual; the other a gentle Congregational minister, a mere holy and humble man of heart. They became great friends in the course of these expeditions, and they brought back this report —'It is positively wicked to let these children grow up being taught that there is no difference in value between Joshua and St. Matthew: that the God of the Lord's Prayer is the same who commanded the massacre of Ai.' Well, perhaps it is. Seeing how bloodthirsty old men can be in these days, one is tempted to think that they can hardly be caught too young and taught decency, if not mansuetude. But I do not remember, as a child, feeling any horror about it, or any difficulty in reconciling the two concepts. Children *are* a bit bloodthirsty, and I observe that two volumes of the late Captain Mayne Reid—*The Rifle Rangers*, and *The Scalp Hunters*—have just found their way into *The World's Classics* and are advertised alongside of Ruskin's *Sesame and Lilies* and the *De Imitatione Christi*. I leave you to think this out; adding but this for a suggestion: that as the Hebrew outgrew his primitive tribal beliefs, so the bettering mind of man casts off the old clouts of primitive doctrine, he being in fact better than his religion. You have all heard preachers trying to show that Jacob was somehow a better fellow than Esau. You have all, I hope, rejected every such explanation. Esau was a decent fellow: Jacob was not. The instinct of a young man meets that wall, and there is no passing it. Later, the mind of the youth perceives that the writer of Jacob's history has a tribal mind, and supposes throughout that for the advancement of his tribe many things are permissible and even admirable which a later and urbaner mind rejects as detestably sharp practice. And the story of Jacob becomes the more valuable to us historically as we realize what a hero he is to the bland chronicler.

But of another thing, Gentlemen, I am certain: that we were badly taught in that these books, while preached to us as equivalent, were kept in separate compartments. We were taught the Books of Kings and Chronicles as history. The prophets were the Prophets, inspired men predicting the future —which they only did by chance, as every inspired man does. Isaiah was never put into relation with his time at all; which means everything to our understanding of Isaiah, whether of Jerusalem or of Babylon. We ploughed through Kings and Chronicles, and made out lists of rulers, with dates and capital events. Isaiah was all fine writing about nothing at all, and historically we were concerned with him only to verify some far-fetched reference to the Messiah in this or that Evangelist. But there is not, never has been, really fine literature—like Isaiah—composed about nothing at all. If we had only been taught to read Isaiah concurrently with the Books of the Kings, what a fire it would have kindled among the dry bones of our studies!

Then said the Lord unto Isaiah, Go forth now to meet Ahaz, thou, and Shear-jashub thy son, at the end of the conduit of the upper pool in the highway of the fuller's field.

Scholars, of course, know the political significance of that meeting. But if we had only known it; if we had only been taught what Assyria was — with its successive monarchs Tiglath-pileser, Shalmaneser, Sargon, Sennacherib; and why Syria and Israel and Egypt were trying to cajole or force Judah into alliance; what a difference this passage would have meant to us!

I daresay, after all, that the best way is not to bother a boy too early and overmuch with history; that the best way is to let him ramp at first through the Scriptures even as he might through *The Arabian Nights*: to let him take the books as they come, merely indicating, for instance, that Job is a great poem, the Psalms great lyrics, the story of Ruth a lovely idyll, the Song of Songs the perfection of an Eastern love-poem. Well and what then? He will certainly get less of *The Cotter's Saturday Night* into it, and certainly more of the truth of the East. There he will feel the whole splendid barbaric story for himself: the flocks of Abraham and Laban: the trek of Jacob's sons to Egypt for corn: the figures of Rebekah at the well, Ruth at the gleaning, and Rizpah beneath the gibbet: Sisera bowing in weariness: Saul—great Saul—by the tent-prop with the jewels in his turban:

All its lordly male-sapphires, and rubies courageous at heart.

Or consider—to choose one or two pictures out of the tremendous procession—consider Michal, Saul's royal daughter: how first she is given in marriage to David to be a snare for him; how, loving him, she saves his life, letting him down from the window and dressing up an image on the bed in his place: how, later, she is handed over to another husband, Phaltiel, how David demands her back, and she goes:

And her husband (Phaltiel) went with her along weeping behind her to Bahurim. Then said Abner unto him, Go, return. And he returned.

Or, still later, how the revulsion takes her, Saul's daughter, as she sees David capering home before the ark, and how her affection had done with this emotional man of the ruddy countenance, so prone to weep in his bed:

And as the ark of the Lord came into the city of David, Michal Saul's daughter—

Mark the three words—

Michal Saul's daughter looked through a window, and saw King David leaping and dancing before the Lord; and she despised him in her heart.

The whole story goes into about ten lines. Your psychological novelist nowadays, given the wit to invent it, would make it cover five hundred pages at least.

Or take the end of David in the first two chapters of the First Book of Kings, with its tale of Oriental intrigues, plots, treacheries, murderings in the depths of the horrible palace wherein the old man is dying. Or read of Solomon and his ships and his builders, and see his Temple growing (as Heber put it) like a tall palm, with no sound of hammers. Or read again the end of Queen Athaliah:

And when Athaliah heard the noise of the guard and of the people, she came to the people into the temple of the Lord.—And when she looked, behold, the king stood by a pillar, as the manner was, and

* C 974

the princes and the trumpeters by the king, and all the people of the land rejoiced, and blew with trumpets: And Athaliah rent her clothes, and cried Treason, Treason.—But Jehoiada the priest commanded the captains of the hundreds, the officers of the host, and said unto them, Have her forth without the ranges. . . .

—And they laid hands on her; and she went by the way by the which the horses came into the king's house: and there was she slain.

Let a youngster read this, I say, just as it is written; and how the true East—sound, scent, form, colour—pours into the narrative!—cymbals and trumpets, leagues of sand, caravans trailing through the heat, priest and soldiery and kings going up between them to the altar; blood at the foot of the steps, blood everywhere, smell of blood mingled with spices, sandalwood, dung of camels!

Yes, but how—if you will permit the word—how the *enjoyment* of it as magnificent literature might be enhanced by a scholar who would condescend to whisper, of his knowledge, the magical word here or there, to the child as he reads! For an instance.—

No child—no grown man with any sense of poetry—can deny his ear to the Forty-fifth Psalm; the one that begins 'My heart is inditing a good matter,' and plunges into a hymn of royal nuptials. First (you remember) the singing-men, the sons of Korah, lift their chant to the bridegroom, the King:

Gird thy sword upon thy thigh, O most mighty. . . . And in thy majesty ride prosperously.

Or as we hear it in the Book of Common Prayer:

Good luck have thou with thine honour . . .
because of the word of truth, of meekness, and righteousness·
and thy right hand shall teach thee terrible things. . . .
All thy garments smell of myrrh, aloes, and cassia: out of the ivory palaces, whereby they have made thee glad.

Anon they turn to the Bride:

Hearken, O daughter, and consider, and incline thine ear; forget also thine own people, and thy father's house. . . .
The King's daughter is all glorious within: her clothing is of wrought gold.
She shall be brought unto the king in raiment of needlework: the virgins that be her fellows shall bear her company. And the daughter

of Tyre shall be there with a gift. Instead of thy fathers shall be thy children, whom thou mayest make princes in all the earth.

For whom (wonders the young reader, spell-bound by this), for what happy bride and bridegroom was this glorious chant raised? Now suppose that, just here, he has a scholar ready to tell him what is likeliest true—that the bridegroom was Ahab—that the bride, the daughter of Sidon, was no other than Jezebel, and became what Jezebel now is—with what an awe of surmise would two other passages of the history toll on his ear?

And one washed the chariot in the pool of Samaria; and the dogs licked up his blood. . . .

And when he (Jehu) was come in, he did eat and drink, and said, Go, see now this cursed woman, and bury her: for she is a king's daughter.

And they went to bury her: but they found no more of her than the skull, and the feet, and the palms of her hands.

Wherefore they came again, and told him. And he said, This is the word of the Lord, which he spake by his servant Elijah the Tishbite, saying, In the portion of Jezreel shall dogs eat the flesh of Jezebel . . . so that men shall not say, This is Jezebel.

III

I shall ask you, first, to assent with me, that the Authorized Version of the Holy Bible is, as a literary achievement, one of the greatest in our language; nay, with the possible exception of the complete works of Shakespeare, the very greatest. You will hardly deny this.

As little, or less, will you deny that more deeply than any other book—more deeply even than all the writings of Shakespeare—far more deeply—it has influenced our literature. Here let me repeat a short passage from a former lecture of mine (May 15, 1913, five years ago). I had quoted some few glorious sentences such as:

Thine eyes shall see the king in his beauty: they shall behold the land that is very far off.

And a man shall be as an hiding-place from the wind, and a covert from the tempest; as rivers of water in a dry place, as the shadow of a great rock in a weary land. . . .

So when this corruptible shall have put on incorruption, and this mortal shall have put on immortality . . .

and having quoted these I went on:

When a nation has achieved this manner of diction, these rhythms for its dearest beliefs, a literature is surely established. . . . Wycliff, Tyndale (above all), Coverdale and others before the Forty-seven had wrought. The Authorized Version, setting a seal on all, set a seal on our national style. . . . It has cadences homely and sublime, yet so harmonizes them that the voice is always one. Simple men—holy and humble men of heart like Izaak Walton and Bunyan —have their lips touched and speak to the homelier tune. Proud men, scholars—Milton, Sir Thomas Browne—practise the rolling Latin sentence; but upon the rhythms of our Bible they, too, fall back—'The great mutations of the world are acted, or time may be too short for our designs.' 'Acquaint thyself with the Choragium of the stars.' 'There is nothing immortal but immortality.' The precise man Addison cannot excel one parable in brevity or in heavenly clarity: the two parts of Johnson's antithesis come to no more than this: 'Our Lord has gone up to the sound of a trump; with the sound of a trump our Lord has gone up.' The Bible controls its enemy Gibbon as surely as it haunts the curious music of a light sentence of Thackeray's. It is in everything we see, hear, feel, because it is in us, in our blood.

If that be true, or less than gravely overstated: if the English Bible hold this unique place in our literature; if it be at once a monument, an example and (best of all) a well of English undefiled, no stagnant water, but quick, running, curative, refreshing, vivifying; may we not agree, Gentlemen, to require the weightiest reason why our instructors should continue to hedge in the temple and pipe the fountain off in professional conduits, forbidding it to irrigate freely our ground of study?

It is done so complacently that I do not remember to have met one single argument put up in defence of it; and so I am reduced to guess-work. What *can* be the justifying reason for an embargo on the face of it so arbitrary, if not senseless?

Does it reside perchance in some primitive instinct of *taboo*; of a superstition of fetish-worship fencing off sacred things as unmentionable, and reinforced by the bad Puritan notion that holy things are by no means to be enjoyed?

Or are we forbidden on the ground that our Bible is directly inspired? Well, inspiration is a dangerous term. It is dangerous mainly because it is a relative term, a term of degrees. You may say definitely of some things that the writer was inspired, as you may certify a certain man to be mad—that is, so thoroughly and convincingly mad that you can order him under restraint. But quite a number of us are (as they say in my part of the world) 'not exactly,' and one or two of us here and there at moments may have a touch even of inspiration. So of the Bible itself: I suppose that few nowadays would contend it to be all inspired *equally*. 'No,' you may say, 'not all equally: but all of it *directly*, as no other book is.'

To that I might answer, 'How do you *know* that direct inspiration ceased with the Revelation of St. John the Divine, and closed the book? It may be: but how do you know, and what authority have you to say that Wordsworth's *Tintern Abbey*, for example, or Browning's great Invocation of Love was not directly inspired? Certainly the men who wrote them were rapt above themselves: and, if not directly, Why indirectly, and how?'

But I pause on the edge of a morass, and spring back to firmer ground. Our Bible, as we have it, is a translation, made by forty-seven men and published in the year 1611. The original—and I am still on firm ground because I am quoting now from *The Cambridge History of English Literature*—'either proceeds from divine inspiration, as some will have it or, according to others, is the fruit of the religious genius of the Hebrew race. From either point of view the authors are highly gifted individuals' (*sic*)—

highly gifted individuals, who, notwithstanding their diversities, and the progressiveness observable in their representations of the nature of God, are wonderfully consistent in the main tenor of their writings, and serve, in general, for mutual confirmation and illustration. In some cases, this may be due to the revision of earlier productions by later writers, which has thus brought more primitive conceptions into a degree of conformity with maturer and profounder views; but, even in such cases, the earlier conception often lends itself, without wrenching, to the deeper interpretation and the completer exposition. The Bible is not distinctively an intellectual achievement.

In all earnest I protest that to write about the Bible in such a fashion is to demonstrate inferentially that it has never quickened you with its glow; that, whatever your learning, you have missed what the unlearned Bunyan, for example, so admirably caught—the true *wit* of the book. The writer, to be sure, is dealing with the originals. Let us more humbly sit at the feet of the translators. 'Highly gifted individuals,' or no, the sort of thing the translators wrote was 'And God said, Let there be light,' 'A sower went forth to sow,' 'The Kingdom of Heaven is like unto leaven, which a woman took,' 'The wages of sin is death,' 'The trumpet shall sound,' 'Jesus wept,' 'Death is swallowed up in victory.'

Let me quote you for better encouragement, as well as for relief, a passage from Matthew Arnold on the Authorized Version:

> The effect of Hebrew poetry can be preserved and transferred in a foreign language as the effect of other great poetry cannot. The effect of Homer, the effect of Dante, is and must be in great measure lost in a translation, because their poetry is a poetry of metre, or of rhyme, or both; and the effect of these is not really transferable. A man may make a good English poem with the matter and thoughts of Homer and Dante, may even try to reproduce their metre, or rhyme: but the metre and rhyme will be in truth his own, and the effect will be his, not the effect of Homer or Dante. Isaiah's, on the other hand, is a poetry, as is well known, of parallelism; it depends not on metre and rhyme, but on a balance of thought, conveyed by a corresponding balance of sentence; and the effect of this *can* be transferred to another language. . . . Hebrew poetry has in addition the effect of assonance and other effects which cannot perhaps be transferred; but its main effect, its effect of parallelism of thought and sentence, can.

I take this from the preface to his little volume in which Arnold confesses that his 'paramount object is to get Isaiah enjoyed.'

IV

Sundry men of letters besides Matthew Arnold have pleaded for a literary study of the Bible, and specially of our English Version, that we may thereby enhance our enjoyment of the work itself and, through this, enjoyment and understanding of the rest of English Literature, from 1611 down. Specially among these pleaders let me mention Mr. F. B. Money-Coutts (later Lord Latymer) and a Cambridge man, Dr. R. G. Moulton, Professor of Literary Theory and Interpretation in the University of Chicago. Of both these writers I shall have something to say. But first and generally, if you ask me why all their pleas have not yet prevailed, I will give you my own answer — the fault as usual lies in ourselves, in our own tameness and incuriosity.

There is no real trouble with the *taboo* set up by professionals and puritans, if we have the courage to walk past it as Christian walked between the lions; no real tyranny we could not overthrow, if it were worth while, with a push; no need at all for us to 'wreathe our sword in myrtle boughs.' What tyranny exists has grown up through the quite well-meaning labours of quite well-meaning men: and I have never heard any serious reason given why we should not include portions of the English Bible in our English Tripos, if we choose.

> Nos te,
> Nos facimus, Scriptura, deam.

Then why don't we choose?

To answer this, we must (I suggest) seek somewhat further back. The Bible—that is to say the body of the old Hebrew Literature clothed for us in English—comes to us in our childhood. But how does it come?

Let me, amplifying a hint from Dr. Moulton, ask you to imagine a volume including the great books of our own literature all bound together in some such order as this: *Paradise Lost*, Darwin's *Descent of Man*, *The Anglo-Saxon Chronicle*, Walter Map, Mill *On Liberty*, Hooker's *Ecclesiastical Polity*, *The Annual Register*, Froissart, Adam Smith's *Wealth of Nations*, *Domesday Book*, *Le Morte d'Arthur*, Campbell's *Lives of the Lord Chancellors*, Boswell's *Johnson*, Barbour's *The Bruce*, Hakluyt's *Voyages*, Clarendon, Macaulay, the plays of Shakespeare, Shelley's *Prometheus Unbound*, *The*

Faerie Queene, Palgrave's *Golden Treasury*, Bacon's *Essays*, Swinburne's *Poems and Ballads*, FitzGerald's *Omar Khayyàm*, Wordsworth, Browning, *Sartor Resartus*, Burton's *Anatomy of Melancholy*, Burke's *Letters on a Regicide Peace*, *Ossian*, *Piers Plowman*, Burke's *Thoughts on the Present Discontents*, Quarles, Newman's *Apologia*, Donne's *Sermons*, Ruskin, Blake, *The Deserted Village*, *Manfred*, Blair's *Grave*, *The Complaint of Deor*, Bailey's *Festus*, Thompson's *Hound of Heaven*.

Will you next imagine that in this volume most of the authors' names are lost; that, of the few that survive, a number have found their way into wrong places; that Ruskin for example is credited with *Sartor Resartus*; that *Laus Veneris* and *Dolores* are ascribed to Queen Elizabeth, *The Anatomy of Melancholy* to Charles II; and that, as for the titles, these were never invented by the authors, but by a Committee?

Will you still go on to imagine that all the poetry is printed as prose; while all the long paragraphs of prose are broken up into short verses, so that they resemble the little passages set out for parsing or analysis in an examination paper?

This device, as you know, was first invented by the exiled translators who published the Geneva Bible (as it is called) in 1557; and for pulpit use, for handiness of reference, for 'waling a portion,' it has its obvious advantages: but it is, after all and at the best, a very primitive device: and, for my part, I consider it the deadliest invention of all for robbing the book of outward resemblance to literature and converting it to the aspect of a gazetteer—a *biblion a-biblion*, as Charles Lamb puts it.

Have we done? By no means. Having effected all this, let us pepper the result over with italics and numerals, print it in double columns, with a marginal gutter on either side, each gutter pouring down an inky flow of references and cross references. Then, and not till then, is the outward disguise complete—so far as you are concerned. It remains only then to appoint it to be read in Churches, and oblige the child to get selected portions of it by heart on Sundays. But you are yet to imagine that the authors themselves have taken a hand in the game: that the later ones suppose all the earlier ones to have been predicting all the time in a nebulous fashion what they themselves have to tell, and indeed to have written mainly with that object: so that Macaulay and Adam Smith, for example, constantly interrupt the thread of their discourse to affirm that what they tell us must be right because Walter Map or the author of *Piers Plowman* foretold it ages before.

Now a grown man—that is to say, a comparatively un-impressionable man—that is again to say, a man past the age when to enjoy the Bible is priceless—has probably found out somehow that the word prophet does not (in spite of vulgar usage) mean 'a man who predicts.' He has experienced too many prophets of that kind—especially since 1914—and he respects Isaiah too much to rank Isaiah among them. He has been in love, belike; he has read the Song of Solomon: he very much doubts if, on the evidence, Solomon was the kind of lover to have written that Song, and he is quite certain that when the lover sings to his beloved:

Thy two breasts are like two young roes that are twins. Thy neck is as a tower of ivory; thine eyes like the fishpools in Heshbon, by the gate of Bath-rabbim.

—he knows, I say, that this is not a description of the Church and her graces, as the chapter-heading audaciously asserts. But he is lazy; too lazy even to commend the Revised Version for striking Solomon out of the Bible, calling the poem The Song of Songs, omitting the absurd chapter-headings, and printing the poetry as poetry ought to be printed. The old-fashioned arrangement was good enough for him. Or he goes to church on Christmas Day and listens to a first lesson, of which the old translators made nonsense, and, in two passages at least, stark nonsense. But, again, the old nonsense is good enough for him; soothing in fact. He is not even quite sure that the Bible, looking like any other book, ought to be put in the hands of the young.

In all this I think he is wrong. I am sure he is wrong if our contention be right, that the English Bible should be studied by us all for its poetry and its wonderful language as well as for

its religion—the religion and the poetry being in fact emotion-
ally inseparable.   For thus, in Euripides' phrase, we clothe the
Bible in a dress through which its beauty will best shine.

V

If you ask me How? I answer—first begging you to bear in
mind that we are planning the form of the book for our purpose,
and that other forms will be used for other purposes—that we
should start with the simplest alterations, such as these:

(1) The books should be re-arranged in their right order, so
far as this can be ascertained (and much of it has been ascertained).   I am told, and I can well believe, that this would at
a stroke clear away a mass of confusion in strictly Biblical
criticism.   But that is not my business.   I know that it would
immensely help our *literary* study.

(2) I should print the prose continuously, as prose is ordinarily and properly printed: and the poetry in verse lines, as
poetry is ordinarily and properly printed.   And I should print
each on a page of one column, with none but the necessary
notes and references, and these so arranged that they did not
tease and distract the eye.

(3) With the verse we should, I hold, go farther even than
the Revisers.   As you know, much of the poetry in the Bible,
especially of such as was meant for music, is composed in
stanzaic form, or in strophe and anti-strophe, with prelude
and conclusion, sometimes with a choral refrain.   We should
print these, I contend, in their proper form, just as we should
print an English poem in its proper form.

I shall conclude to-day with a striking instance of this, with
four strophes from the 107th Psalm, taking leave to use at
will the Authorised, the Revised and the Coverdale Versions.
Each strophe, you will note, has a double refrain.   As Dr.
Moulton points out, the one puts up a cry for help, the other
an ejaculation of praise after the help has come.   Each refrain
has a sequel verse, which appropriately changes the motive
and sets that of the next stanza:

(i)

They wandered in the wilderness in a solitary way;
They found no city to dwell in.
Hungry and thirsty,
Their soul fainted in them.
> *Then they cried unto the Lord in their trouble,*
> *And he delivered them out of their distresses.*

He led them forth by a straight way,
That they might go to a city of habitation.
> *Oh that men would praise the Lord for his goodness,*
> *And for his wonderful works to the children of men!*

For he satisfieth the longing soul,
And filleth the hungry soul with goodness.

(ii)

Such as sit in darkness, and in the shadow of death,
Being bound in affliction and iron;
Because they rebelled against the words of God,
And contemned the counsel of the most High:
Therefore he brought down their heart with labour;
They fell down, and there was none to help.
> *Then they cried unto the Lord in their trouble,*
> *And he saved them out of their distresses.*

He brought them out of darkness and the shadow of death,
And brake their bands in sunder.
> *Oh that men would praise the Lord for his goodness,*
> *And for his wonderful works to the children of men!*

For he hath broken the gates of brass,
And cut the bars of iron in sunder.

(iii)

Fools because of their transgression,
And because of their iniquities, are afflicted,
Their soul abhorreth all manner of meat;
And they draw near unto death's door.
> *Then they cry unto the Lord in their trouble,*
> *And he saveth them out of their distresses.*

He sendeth his word and healeth them,
And delivereth them from their destructions.
> *Oh that men would praise the Lord for his goodness,*
> *And for his wonderful works to the children of men!*

And let them offer the sacrifices of thanksgiving,
And declare his works with singing!

(iv)

They that go down to the sea in ships,
That do business in great waters;
These see the works of the Lord,
And his wonders in the deep.
For he commandeth, and raiseth the stormy wind,
Which lifteth up the waves thereof.
They mount up to the heaven,
They go down again to the depths;
Their soul melteth away because of trouble.
They reel to and fro,
And stagger like a drunken man,
And are at their wits' end.
    Then they cry unto the Lord in their trouble,
    And he bringeth them out of their distresses.
He maketh the storm a calm,
So that the waves thereof are still.
Then are they glad because they be quiet;
So he bringeth them unto the haven where they would be.
    Oh that men would praise the Lord for his goodness,
    And for his wonderful works to the children of men!
Let them exalt him also in the assembly of the people,
And praise him in the seat of the elders!

VI

My task from this point is mainly practical: to choose a particular book of Scripture and show (if I can) not only that it deserves to be enjoyed, in its English rendering, as a literary masterpiece, an indisputable classic for us, as surely as if it had first been composed in English; but that it can, for purposes of study, serve the purpose of any true literary school of English as readily, and as usefully, as the Prologue to *The Canterbury Tales* or *Hamlet* or *Paradise Lost*. I shall choose the Book of Job for several reasons, presently to be given; but beg you to understand that, while taking it for a striking illustration, I use it but to illustrate; that what may be done with Job may, in degree, be done with Ruth, with Esther, with the Psalms, the Song of Songs, Ecclesiastes; with Isaiah of Jerusalem, Ezekiel, sundry of the prophets; even with St. Luke's Gospel or St. Paul's letters to the Churches.

My first reason, then, for choosing Job has already been given. It is the most striking illustration to be found. Many of the Psalms touch perfection as lyrical strains: of the ecstasy of passion in love I suppose the Song of Songs to express the very last word. There are chapters of Isaiah that snatch the very soul and ravish it aloft. In no literature known to me are short stories told with such sweet austerity of art as in the Gospel parables—I can even imagine a high and learned artist in words, after rejecting them as divine on many grounds, surrendering in the end to their divine artistry. But for high seriousness combined with architectonic treatment on a great scale; for sublimity of conception, working malleably within a structure which is simple, severe, complete, having a beginning, a middle and an end; for diction never less than adequate, constantly right and therefore not seldom superb as theme, thought and utterance soar up together and make one miracle, I can name no single book of the Bible to compare with Job.

My second reason is that the poem, being brief, compendious and quite simple in structure, can be handily expounded; Job is what Milton precisely called it, 'a brief model.' And my third reason (which I must not hide) is that two writers whom I mentioned a while back—Lord Latymer and Professor R. G. Moulton—have already done this for me. A man who drives at practice must use the tools other men have made, so he use them with due acknowledgment; and this acknowledgment I pay by referring you to Book II of Lord Latymer's *The Poet's Charter*, and to the analysis of Job with which Professor Moulton introduces his *Literary Study of the Bible*.

VII

When Milton (determined to write a grand epic) was casting about for his subject, he had a mind for some while to attempt the story of Job. You may find evidence for this in a MS. preserved here in Trinity College Library. You will find printed evidence in a passage of his *Reason of Church Government*:

Time serves not now [he writes], and perhaps I might seem too profuse to give any certain account of what the mind at home, in the spacious circuits of her musing, hath liberty to propose to herself, though of highest hope and hardest attempting; whether that epic form whereof the two poems of Homer, and those other two of Virgil and Tasso, are a diffuse, and the book of Job a brief model . . .

Again, we know Job to have been one of the three stories meditated by Shelley as themes for great lyrical dramas, the other two being the madness of Tasso and *Prometheus Unbound*. Shelley never abandoned this idea of a lyrical drama on Job; and if Milton abandoned the idea of an epic, there are passages in *Paradise Lost* as there are passages in *Prometheus Unbound* that might well have been written from this other story. Take the lines

> Why am I mock'd with death, and lengthen'd out
> To deathless pain? How gladly would I meet
> Mortality my sentence, and be earth
> Insensible! how glad would lay me down
> As in my mother's lap! There I should rest
> And sleep secure; . . .

What is this, as Lord Latymer asks, but an echo of Job's words?—

> For now should I have lien down and been quiet;
> I should have slept; then had I been at rest:
> With kings and counsellers of the earth,
> Which built desolate places for themselves . . .
> There the wicked cease from troubling;
> And there the weary be at rest.

There is no need for me to point out how exactly, though from two nearly opposite angles, the story of Job would hit the philosophy of Milton and the philosophy of Shelley to the very heart. What is the story of the afflicted patriarch but a direct challenge to a protestant like Milton (I use the word in its strict sense) to justify the ways of God to man? It is the very purpose of the Book of Job, as it is the declared purpose of *Paradise Lost*: and since both poems can only work out the justification by long argumentative speeches, both poems lamentably fail as real solutions of the difficulty. To this I shall recur, and here merely observe that *qui s'excuse s'accuse*:

a God who can only explain himself by the help of long-winded scolding, or of long-winded advocacy, though he employ an archangel for advocate, has given away the half of his case by the implicit admission that there are two sides to the question. And when we have put aside the poetical ineptitude of a Creator driven to apology, it remains that to Shelley the Jehovah who, for a sort of wager, allowed Satan to torture Job merely for the game of testing him, would be no better than any other tyrant; would be a miscreant Creator, abominable as the Zeus of the *Prometheus Unbound.*

You may urge that Milton and Shelley dropped Job for hero because both felt him to be a merely static figure; and that the one chose Satan, the rebel angel, the other chose Prometheus the rebel Titan, because both are active rebels; and as epic and drama require action, each of these heroes makes the thing move; that Satan and Prometheus are not passive sufferers like Job but souls as quick and fiery as Byron's Lucifer:

> Souls who dare use their immortality—
> Souls who dare look the Omnipotent tyrant in
> His everlasting face, and tell him that
> His evil is not good.

Very well, urge this: urge it with all your might. All the while you will be doing just what I desire you to do, using Job alongside *Prometheus Unbound* and *Paradise Lost* as a comparative work of literature.

But, if you ask me for my own opinion why Milton and Shelley dropped their intention to make poems on the Book of Job, it is that they no sooner tackled it than they found it to be a magnificent poem already, and a poem on which, with all their genius, they found themselves unable to improve.

I want you to realize a thing most simple, demonstrable by five minutes of practice, yet so confused by conventional notions of what poetry is that I dare say it to be equally demonstrable that Milton and Shelley discovered it only by experiment. Does this appear to you a bold thing to say of so tremendous an artist as Milton? Well, of course it would be

cruel to quote in proof his paraphrases of Psalms cxiv and
cxxxvi: to set against the Authorized Version's

> When Israel went out of Egypt,
> The house of Jacob from a people of strange language

such pomposity as

>> When the blest seed of Terah's faithful son
>> After long toil their liberty had won—

or against

> O give thanks . . .
> To him that stretched out the earth above the waters:
>> for his mercy endureth for ever.
> To him that made great lights:
>> for his mercy endureth for ever

such stuff as

>>> Who did the solid earth ordain
>>> To rise above the watery plain;
>>>> *For his mercies aye endure,*
>>>> *Ever faithful, ever sure.*
>>> Who, by his all-commanding might,
>>> Did fill the new-made world with light;
>>>> *For his mercies aye endure,*
>>>> *Ever faithful, ever sure*

—verses yet further weakened by the late Sir William Baker for
Hymns Ancient and Modern.

It were cruel, I say, to condemn these attempts as little above
those of Sternhold and Hopkins, or even of those of Tate and
Brady: for Milton made them at fifteen years old, and he who
afterwards consecrated his youth to poetry soon learned to
know better. And yet, bearing in mind the passages in *Paradise
Lost* and *Paradise Regained* which paraphrase the Scriptural
narrative, I cannot forbear the suspicion that, though as an
artist he had the instinct to feel it, he never quite won to
knowing the simple fact that the thing had already been done
and surpassingly well done: he, who did so much to liberate
poetry from rhyme—he—even he who in the grand choruses of
Samson Agonistes did so much to liberate it from strict metre
—never quite realized, being hag-ridden by the fetish that rides
between two panniers, the sacred and the profane, that this

translation of Job already belongs to the category of poetry, *is* poetry, already above metre, and in its English rhythm far on its way to the insurpassable. If rhyme be allowed to that greatest of arts, if metre, is not rhythm above both for her service? Hear in a sentence how this poem uplifts the rhythm of the Vulgate:

> *Ecce, Deus magnus vincens scientiam nostram: numerus annorum ejus inestimabilis!*

But hear, in a longer passage, how our English rhythm swings and sways to the Hebrew parallels:

> Surely there is a mine for silver,
> And a place for gold which they refine.
> Iron is taken out of the earth,
> And brass is molten out of the stone.
> Man setteth an end to darkness,
> And searcheth out to the furthest bound
> The stones of thick darkness and of the shadow of death.
> He breaketh open a shaft away from where men sojourn;
> They are forgotten of the foot that passeth by;
> They hang afar from men, they swing to and fro.
> As for the earth, out of it cometh bread:
> And underneath it is turned up as it were by fire.
> The stones thereof are the place of sapphires,
> And it hath dust of gold.
> That path no bird of prey knoweth,
> Neither hath the falcon's eye seen it:
> The proud beasts have not trodden it,
> Nor hath the fierce lion passed thereby.
> He putteth forth his hand upon the flinty rock;
> He overturneth the mountains by the roots.
> He cutteth out channels among the rocks;
> And his eye seeth every precious thing.
> He bindeth the streams that they trickle not;
> And the thing that is hid bringeth he forth to light.
> But where shall wisdom be found?
> And where is the place of understanding?
> Man knoweth not the price thereof;
> Neither is it found in the land of the living.
> The deep saith, It is not in me:
> And the sea saith, It is not with me.
> It cannot be gotten for gold,
> Neither shall silver be weighed for the price thereof.

It cannot be valued with the gold of Ophir,
With the precious onyx, or the sapphire.
Gold and glass cannot equal it:
Neither shall the exchange thereof be jewels of fine gold.
No mention shall be made of coral or of crystal:
Yea, the price of wisdom is above rubies.
The topaz of Ethiopia shall not equal it,
Neither shall it be valued with pure gold.
Whence then cometh wisdom?
And where is the place of understanding?
Seeing it is hid from the eyes of all living,
And kept close from the fowls of the air.
Destruction and Death say,
We have heard a rumour thereof with our ears.
God understandeth the way thereof,
And he knoweth the place thereof.
For he looketh to the ends of the earth,
And seeth under the whole heaven;
To make a weight for the wind;
Yea, he meteth out the waters by measure.
When he made a decree for the rain, ʼ
And a way for the lightning of the thunder:
Then did he see it, and declare it;
He established it, yea, and searched it out.
And unto man he said,
Behold, the fear of the Lord, *that* is wisdom;
And to depart from evil is understanding.

Is that poetry? Surely it is poetry. Can you improve it
with the embellishments of rhyme and strict scansion?   Well,
sundry bold men have tried, and I will choose for your judgment the rendering of a part of the above passage by one who
is by no means the worst of them—a hardy anonymous Scots-
man.   His version was published at Falkirk in 1869:

His hand on the rock the adventurer puts,
And mountains entire overturns by the roots;
New rivers in rocks are enchased by his might,
And everything precious revealed to his sight;
The floods from o'er-flowing he bindeth at will,
And the thing that is hid bringeth forth by his skill.

But where real wisdom is found can he shew?
Or the place understanding inhabiteth?   No!
Men know not the value, the price of this gem;

'Tis not found in the land of the living with them.
It is not in me, saith the depth; and the sea
With the voice of an echo, repeats, Not in me.
Whence then cometh wisdom? And where is the place
Understanding hath chosen, since this is the case? . . .

Enough! This not only shows how that other rendering can be spoilt even to the point of burlesque by an attempt, on preconceived notions, to embellish it with metre and rhyme, but it also hints that parallel verse will actually resent and abhor such embellishment even by the most skilled hand. Yet, I repeat, our version of Job is poetry undeniable. What follows?

Why, it follows that in the course of studying it as literature we have found experimentally settled for us—and on the side of freedom—a dispute in which scores of eminent critics have taken sides: a dispute revived but yesterday (if we omit the blank and devastated days of this War) by the writers and apostles of *vers libres*. 'Can there be poetry without metre?' 'Is free verse a true poetic form?' Why, our Book of Job being poetry, unmistakable poetry, of course there can, to be sure it is. These apostles are butting at an open door. Nothing remains for them but to go and write *vers libres* as fine as those of Job in our English translation. Or suppose even that they write as well as M. Paul Fort, they will yet be writing ancestrally, not as innovators but as renewers. Nothing is done in literature by arguing whether or not this or that be possible or permissible. The only way to prove it possible or permissible is to go and do it: and then you are lucky indeed if some ancient writers have not forestalled you.

VIII

For another question (much argued, you will remember, a few years ago) 'Is there—can there be—such a thing as a Static Theatre, a Static Drama?'

Most of you (I daresay) remember M. Maeterlinck's definition of this and his demand for it. To summarize him roughly, he contends that the old drama—the traditional, the conventional drama—lives by action; that, in Aristotle's phrase, it represents men doing, πράττοντες, and resolves itself into a struggle of human wills—whether against the gods, as in ancient tragedy, or against one another, as in modern. M. Maeterlinck tells us:

There is a tragic element in the life of every day that is far more real, far more penetrating, far more akin to the true self that is in us, than is the tragedy that lies in great adventure. . . . It goes beyond the determined struggle of man against man, and desire against desire; it goes beyond the eternal conflict of duty and passion. Its province is rather to reveal to us how truly wonderful is the mere act of living, and to throw light upon the existence of the soul, self-contained in the midst of ever-restless immensities; to hush the discourse of reason and sentiment, so that above the tumult may be heard the solemn uninterrupted whisperings of man and his destiny.

To the tragic author [he goes on, later], as to the mediocre painter who still lingers over historical pictures, it is only the violence of the anecdote that appeals, and in his representation thereof does the entire interest of his work consist. . . . Indeed when I go to a theatre, I feel as though I were spending a few hours with my ancestors, who conceived life as though it were something that was primitive, arid and brutal. . . . I am shown a deceived husband killing his wife, a woman poisoning her lover, a son avenging his father, a father slaughtering his children, murdered kings, ravished virgins, imprisoned citizens—in a word all the sublimity of tradition, but alas how superficial and material! Blood, surface-tears and death! What can I learn from creatures who have but one fixed idea, who have no time to live, for that there is a rival, a mistress, whom it behoves them to put to death?

M. Maeterlinck does not (he says) know if the Static Drama of his craving be impossible. He inclines to think—instancing some Greek tragedies such as *Prometheus* and *Choephori*—that it already exists. But may we not, out of the East—the slow, the stationary East—fetch an instance more convincing?

IX

The Drama of Job opens with a *Prologue* in the mouth of a Narrator.

There was a man in the land of Uz, named Job; upright, God-fearing, of great substance in sheep, cattle and oxen; blest

also with seven sons and three daughters.   After telling of their
family life, how wholesome it is, and pious, and happy—

The Prologue passes to a Council held in Heaven.   The
Lord sits there, and the sons of God present themselves, each
from his province.   Enters Satan (whom we had better call
the Adversary) from his sphere of inspection, the Earth, and
reports.   The Lord specially questions him concerning Job,
pattern of men.   The Adversary demurs.   'Doth Job fear
God for nought?   Hast thou not set a hedge about his prosperity?   But put forth thy hand and touch all that he hath,
and he will renounce thee to thy face.'   The Lord gives leave for
this trial to be made (you will recall the opening of *Everyman*):

So, in the midst of his wealth, a messenger came to Job
and says:

> The oxen were plowing,
> and the asses feeding beside them:
> and the Sabeans fell upon them,
> and took them away;
> yea, they have slain the servants with the edge of the sword;
> and I only am escaped alone to tell thee.

While he was yet speaking, there came also another, and said,
> The fire of God is fallen from heaven,
> and hath burned up the sheep, and the servants,
> and consumed them;
> and I only am escaped alone to tell thee.

While he was yet speaking, there came also another, and said,
> The Chaldeans made three bands,
> and fell upon the camels,
> and have taken them away,
> yea, and slain the servants with the edge of the sword;
> and I only am escaped alone to tell thee.

While he was yet speaking, there came also another, and said,
> Thy sons and thy daughters
> were eating and drinking wine in their eldest brother's house:
> and, behold,
> there came a great wind from the wilderness,
> and smote the four corners of the house,
> and it fell upon the young men,
> and they are dead;
> and I only am escaped alone to tell thee.

Then Job arose, and rent his mantle, and shaved his head, and fell down upon the ground, and worshipped; and he said.

> Naked came I out of my mother's womb,
>   and naked shall I return thither:
> the Lord gave, and the Lord hath taken away;
>   blessed be the name of the Lord.

So the Adversary is foiled, and Job has not renounced God.

A second Council is held in Heaven; and the Adversary, being questioned, has to admit Job's integrity, but proposes a severer test:

Skin for skin, yea, all that a man hath will he give for his life. But put forth thine hand now, and touch his bone and his flesh, and he will renounce thee to thy face.

Again leave is given: and the Adversary smites Job with the most hideous and loathsome form of leprosy. His kinsfolk (as we learn later) have already begun to desert and hold aloof from him as a man marked out by God's displeasure. But now he passes out from their midst, as one unclean from head to foot, and seats himself on the ash-mound—that is, upon the Mezbele or heap of refuse which accumulates outside Arab villages.

The dung [says Professor Moulton] which is heaped upon the Mezbele of the Hauran villages is not mixed with straw, which in that warm and dry land is not needed for litter, and it comes mostly from solid-hoofed animals, as the flocks and oxen are left over-night in the grazing places. It is carried in baskets in a dry state to this place . . . and usually burnt once a month. . . . The ashes remain. . . . If the village has been inhabited for centuries the Mezbele reaches a height far overtopping it. The winter rains reduce it into a compact mass, and it becomes by and by a solid hill of earth. . . . The Mezbele serves the inhabitants for a watchtower, and in the sultry evenings for a place of concourse, because there is a current of air on the height. There all day long the children play about it; and there the outcast, who has been stricken with some loathsome malady, and is not allowed to enter the dwellings of men, lays himself down, begging an alms of the passers-by by day, and by night sheltering himself among the ashes which the heat of the sun has warmed.

Here, then, sits in his misery 'the forsaken grandee'; and here yet another temptation comes to him—this time not ex pressly allowed by the Lord. Much foolish condemnation (and, I may add, some foolish facetiousness) has been heaped on Job's wife. As a matter of fact she is *not* a wicked woman. She has borne her part in the pious and happy family life, now taken away: she has uttered no word of complaint though all the substance be swallowed up and her children with it. But now the sight of her innocent husband thus helpless, thus incurably smitten, wrings, through love and anguish and indignation, this cry from her:

Dost thou still hold fast thine integrity? renounce God, and die.

But Job answered, soothing her:

Thou speakest as one of the foolish women speaketh. What? shall we receive good at the hand of God, and shall we not receive evil?

So the second trial ends, and Job has not sinned with his lips.

But now comes the third trial, which needs no Council in Heaven to decree it. Travellers by the mound saw this figure seated there, patient, uncomplaining, an object of awe even to the children who at first mocked him; they asked this man's history; and hearing of it, smote on their breasts, and made a token of it and carried the news into far countries: until it reached the ears of Job's three friends, all great tribesmen like himself—Eliphaz the Temanite, Bildad the Shuhite, and Zophar the Naamathite. These three made an appointment together to travel and visit Job. 'And when they lifted up their eyes afar off, and knew him not, they lifted up their voice, and wept.' Then they went up and sat down facing him on the ground. But the majesty of suffering is silent:

Here I and sorrows sit;
Here is my throne, bid kings come bow to it. . . .

No, not a word. . . . And, with the grave courtesy of Eastern men, they too are silent:

So they sat down with him upon the ground seven days and seven nights, and none spake a word unto him: for they saw that his grief was very great.

The Prologue ends. The scene is set. After seven days of silence the real drama opens.

Of the drama itself I shall attempt no analysis, referring you for this to the two books from which I have already quoted. My purpose being merely to persuade you that this surpassing poem can be studied, and ought to be studied, as literature, I shall content myself with turning it (so to speak) once or twice in my hand and glancing one or two facets at you.

To begin with, then, you will not have failed to notice, in the setting out of the drama, a curious resemblance between Job and the *Prometheus* of Aeschylus. The curtain in each play lifts on a figure solitary, tortured (for no reason that seems good to us) by a higher will which, we are told, is God's. The chorus of Sea-nymphs in the opening of the Greek play bears no small resemblance in attitude of mind to Job's three friends. When Job at length breaks the intolerable silence with

> Let the day perish wherein I was born,
> And the night which said, There is a man child conceived,

he uses just such an outburst as Prometheus: and, as he is answered by his friends, so the Nymphs at once exclaim to Prometheus

> Seest thou not that thou hast sinned?

But at once, for any one with a sense of comparative literature, is set up a comparison between the persistent West and the persistent East; between the fiery energizing rebel and the patient victim. Of these two, both good, one will dare everything to release mankind from thrall; the other will submit, and justify himself—mankind too, if it may hap—by submission.

At once this difference is seen to give a difference of form to the drama. Our poem is purely static. Some critics can detect little individuality in Job's three friends, to distinguish them. For my part I find Eliphaz more of a personage than the other two; grander in the volume of his mind, securer in wisdom; as I find Zophar rather noticeably a mean-minded greybeard, and Bildad a man of the stand-no-nonsense kind. But, to tell the truth, I prefer not to search for individuality in these men: I prefer to see them as three figures with eyes of stone, almost expressionless. For in truth they are the conventions, all through—the orthodox men—addressing Job, the reality; and their words come to this:

> Thou sufferest, therefore must have sinned.
> All suffering is, must be, a judgment upon sin.
> Else God is not righteous.

They are statuesque, as the drama is static. The speeches follow one another, rising and falling, in rise and fall magnificently and deliberately eloquent. Not a limb is seen to move, unless it be when Job half rises from the dust in sudden scorn of their conventions:

> No doubt but *ye* are the people,
> And wisdom shall die with you!

or again:

> Will *ye* speak unrighteously for God,
>   And talk deceitfully for him?
> Will *ye* respect *his* person?
>   Will *ye* contend for God?

Yet so great is this man, who has not renounced and will not renounce God, that still and ever he clamours for more knowledge of Him. Still getting no answer, he lifts up his hands and calls the great Oath of Clearance; in effect 'If I have loved gold overmuch, hated mine enemy, refused the stranger my tent, truckled to public opinion':

> If my land cry out against me,
>   And the furrows thereof weep together;
> If I have eaten the fruits thereof without money,
> Or have caused the owners thereof to lose their life:
>   Let thistles grow instead of wheat,
>   And cockle instead of barley.

With a slow gesture he covers his face:

> The words of Job are ended.

X

They are ended: even though at this point (when the debate seems to be closed) a young Aramaean Arab, Elihu, who has been loitering around and listening to the controversy, bursts in and delivers his young red-hot opinions. They are violent, and at the same time quite raw and priggish. Job troubles not to answer: the others keep a chilling silence. But while this young man rants, pointing skyward now and again, we see, we feel—it is most wonderfully conveyed—as clearly as if indicated by successive stage-directions, a terrific thunder-storm gathering; a thunder - storm with a whirlwind. It gathers; it is upon them; it darkens them with dread until even the words of Elihu dry on his lips:

> If a man speak, surely he shall be swallowed up.

It breaks and blasts and confounds them; and out of it the Lord speaks.

Now of that famous and marvellous speech, put by the poet into the mouth of God, we may say what may be said of all speeches put by man into the mouth of God. We may say, as of the speeches of the Archangel in *Paradise Lost*, that it is argument, and argument, by its very nature, admits of being answered. But, if to make God talk at all be anthropomorphism, here is anthropomorphism at its very best in its effort to reach to God.

There is a hush. The storm clears away; and in this hush the voice of the Narrator is heard again, pronouncing the Epilogue. Job has looked in the face of God and reproached him as a friend reproaches a friend. Therefore his captivity was turned, and his wealth returned to him, and he begat sons and daughters, and saw his sons' sons unto the fourth generation. So Job died, being old and full of years.

XI

Structurally a great poem; historically a great poem; philosophically a great poem; so rendered for us in noble English diction as to be worthy in any comparison of diction, structure, ancestry, thought! I conclude with these words of Lord Latymer:

There is nothing comparable with it except the *Prometheus Bound* of Aeschylus. It is eternal, illimitable . . . its scope is the relation between God and Man. It is a vast liberation, a great gaol-delivery of the spirit of Man; nay, rather a great Acquittal.

ON JARGON

I ASK leave this morning to interpose some words upon a kind of writing which, from a superficial likeness, commonly passes for prose in these days, and by lazy folk is commonly written for prose, yet actually is not prose at all; my excuse being the simple practical one that, by first clearing this sham prose out of the way, we shall the better deal with honest prose when we come to it. The proper difficulties of prose will remain: but we shall be agreed in understanding what it is, or at any rate what it is not, that we talk about. I remember to have heard somewhere of a religious body in the United States of America which had reason to suspect one of its churches of accepting spiritual consolation from a coloured preacher—an offence against the laws of the Synod—and despatched a Disciplinary Committee with power to act; and of the Committee's returning to report itself unable to take any action under its terms of reference, for that while a person undoubtedly coloured had undoubtedly occupied the pulpit and had audibly spoken from it in the Committee's presence, the performance could be brought within no definition of preaching known or discoverable. So it is with that infirmity of speech—that flux, that determination of words to the mouth, or to the pen—which, though it be familiar to you in parliamentary debates, in newspapers, and as the staple language of Blue Books, Committees, Official Reports, I take leave to introduce to you as prose which is not prose and under its real name of Jargon.

You must not confuse this Jargon with what is called Journalese. The two overlap, indeed, and have a knack of assimilating each other's vices. But Jargon finds, maybe, the most of its votaries among good douce people who have never written to or for a newspaper in their life, who would never talk of 'adverse climatic conditions' when they mean 'bad weather'; who have never trifled with verbs such as 'obsess,' 'recrudesce,' 'envisage,' 'adumbrate,' or with phrases such as 'the psychological moment,' 'the true inwardness,'

91

'it gives furiously to think.' Jargon dallies with Latinity—'sub silentio,' 'de die in diem,' 'cui bono?' (always in the sense, unsuspected by Cicero, of 'What is the profit?')—but not for the sake of style. Your journalist at the worst is an artist in his way: he daubs paint of this kind upon the lily with a professional zeal; the more flagrant (or, to use his own word, arresting) the pigment, the happier is his soul. Like the Babu he is trying all the while to embellish our poor language, to make it more floriferous, more poetical—like the Babu for example who, reporting his mother's death, wrote, 'Regret to inform you, the hand that rocked the cradle has kicked the bucket.'

There is metaphor: *there* is ornament: *there* is a sense of poetry, though as yet groping in a world unrealized. No such gusto marks—no such zeal, artistic or professional, animates —the practitioners of Jargon, who are, most of them (I repeat), douce respectable persons. Caution is its father: the instinct to save everything and especially trouble: its mother, Indolence. It looks precise, but is not. It is, in these times, *safe*: a thousand men have said it before and not one to your knowledge had been prosecuted for it. And so, like respectability in Chicago, Jargon stalks unchecked in our midst. It is becoming the language of Parliament: it has become the medium through which Boards of Government, County Councils, Syndicates, Committees, Commercial Firms, express the processes as well as the conclusions of their thought and so voice the reason of their being.

Has a Minister to say 'No' in the House of Commons? Some men are constitutionally incapable of saying 'no': but the Minister conveys it thus—'The answer to the question is in the negative.' That means 'no.' Can you discover it to mean anything else, or anything more except that the speaker is a pompous person?—which was no part of the information demanded.

That is Jargon, and it happens to be accurate. But as a rule Jargon is by no means accurate, its method being to walk circumspectly around its target; and its faith, that having done so it has either hit the bull's-eye or at least achieved something equivalent, and safer.

Thus the Clerk of a Board of Guardians will minute that

In the case of John Jenkins deceased, the coffin provided was of the usual character.

Now this is not accurate. 'In the case of John Jenkins deceased,' for whom a coffin was supplied, it is wholly superfluous to tell us that he is deceased. But actually John Jenkins never had more than one case, and that was the coffin. The Clerk says he had two—a coffin in a case: but I suspect the Clerk to be mistaken, and I am sure he errs in telling us that the coffin was of the usual character: for coffins have no character, usual or unusual.

For another example (I shall not tell you whence derived):

In the case of every candidate who is placed in the first class [So you see the lucky fellow gets a case as well as a first class. He might be a stuffed animal: perhaps he is] the class-list will show by some convenient mark (1) the Section or Sections for proficiency in which he is placed in the first class and (2) the Section or Sections (if any) in which he has passed with special distinction.

'The Section or Sections (if any)'—But, how, if they are not any, could they be indicated by a mark however convenient?

The Examiners will have regard to the style and method of the candidate's answers, and will give credit for excellence *in these respects.*

Have you begun to detect the two main vices of Jargon? The first is that it uses circumlocution rather than short straight speech. It says 'In the case of John Jenkins deceased, the coffin' when it means 'John Jenkins's coffin': and its yea is not yea, neither is its nay nay: but its answer is in the affirmative or in the negative, as the foolish and superfluous 'case' may be. The second vice is that it habitually chooses vague woolly abstract nouns rather than concrete ones. I shall have something to say by-and-by about the concrete noun, and how you should ever be struggling for it whether in prose or in verse. For the moment I content myself with advising you, if you

would write masculine English, never to forget the old tag of
your Latin Grammar:

> Masculine will only be
> Things that you can touch and see.

But since these lectures are meant to be a course in First
Aid to writing, I will content myself with one or two extremely
rough rules: yet I shall be disappointed if you do not find them
serviceable.

The first is: Whenever in your reading you come across
one of these words, *case, instance, character, nature, condition,
persuasion, degree*—whenever in writing your pen betrays you
to one or another of them—pull yourself up and take thought.
If it be 'case' (I choose it as Jargon's dearest child—'in Heaven
yclept Metonymy') turn to the dictionary, if you will, and seek
out what meaning can be derived from *casus*, its Latin ancestor:
then try how, with a little trouble, you can extricate yourself
from that case.

Here are some specimens to try your hand on:

(1) All those tears which inundated Lord Hugh Cecil's head were
dry in the case of Mr. Harold Cox.

Poor Mr. Cox! left gasping in his aquarium!

(2) [From a cigar-merchant] In any case, let us send you a case on
approval.

(3) It is contended that Consols have fallen in consequence: but
such is by no means the case.

'*Such*,' by the way, is another spoilt child of Jargon, especially
in Committee's Rules—'Co-opted members may be eligible
as such; such members to continue to serve for such time as'
—and so on.

(4) Even in the purely Celtic areas, only in two or three cases do
the Bishops bear Celtic names.

For 'cases' read 'dioceses.'

Instance. In most instances the players were below their form.

But what were they playing at?   Instances?

Character—Nature. There can be no doubt that the accident was
caused through the dangerous nature of the spot, the hidden character
of the by-road, and the utter absence of any warning or danger signal.

Mark the foggy wording of it all! And yet the man hit something and broke his neck! Contrast that explanation with the verdict of a coroner's jury in the West of England on a drowned postman—'We find that deceased met his death by an act of God, caused by sudden overflowing of the river Walkham and helped out by the scandalous neglect of the way-wardens.'

The Aintree course is notoriously of a trying nature.

On account of its light character, purity and age, Usher's whiskey is a whiskey that will agree with you.

Order. The mésalliance was of a pronounced order.

Condition. He was conveyed to his place of residence in an intoxicated condition.

'He was carried home drunk.'

Quality and *Section.* Mr. ——, exhibiting no less than five works, all of a superior quality, figures prominently in the oil section.

This was written of an exhibition of pictures.

Degree. A singular degree of rarity prevails in the earlier editions of this romance.

That is Jargon. In prose it runs simply 'The earlier editions of this romance are rare'—or 'are very rare'—or even (if you believe what I take leave to doubt) 'are singularly rare'; which should mean that they are rarer than the editions of any other work in the world.

Now what I ask you to consider about these quotations is that in each the writer was using Jargon to shirk prose, palming off periphrases upon us when with a little trouble he could have gone straight to the point. 'A singular degree of rarity prevails,' 'the accident was caused through the dangerous nature of the spot,' 'but such is by no means the case.' We may not be capable of much; but we can all write better than that, if we take a little trouble. In place of, 'the Aintree course is of a trying nature' we can surely say 'Aintree is a trying course' or 'the Aintree course is a trying one'—just that and nothing more.

Next, having trained yourself to keep a look-out for these worst offenders (and you will be surprised to find how quickly you get into the way of it), proceed to push your suspicions out among the whole cloudy host of abstract terms. 'How excellent a thing is sleep,' sighed Sancho Panza; 'it wraps a man round like a cloak'—an excellent example, by the way, of how to say a thing concretely: a Jargoneer would have said that 'among the beneficent qualities of sleep its capacity for withdrawing the human consciousness from the contemplation of immediate circumstances may perhaps be accounted not the least remarkable.' How vile a thing—shall we say?—is the abstract noun! It wraps a man's thoughts round like cotton wool.

Here is a pretty little nest of specimens, found in *The Times* newspaper by Messrs. H. W. and F. G. Fowler, authors of that capital little book *The King's English*:

> One of the most important reforms mentioned in the rescript is the unification of the organization of judicial institutions and the guarantee for all the tribunals of the independence necessary for securing to all classes of the community equality before the law.

I do not dwell on the cacophony; but, to convey a straight-forward piece of news, might not the Editor of *The Times* as well employ a man to write:

> One of the most important reforms is that of the Courts, which need a uniform system and to be made independent. In this way only can men be assured that all are equal before the law.

I think he might.

A day or two ago the musical critic of the *Standard* wrote this:

MR. LAMOND IN BEETHOVEN

> Mr. Frederick Lamond, the Scottish pianist, as an interpreter of Beethoven has few rivals. At his second recital of the composer's works at Bechstein Hall on Saturday afternoon he again displayed a complete sympathy and understanding of his material that extracted the very essence of aesthetic and musical value from each selection he undertook. The delightful intimacy of his playing and his unusual force of individual expression are invaluable assets, which, allied to his technical brilliancy, enable him to achieve an artistic triumph. The two lengthy Variations in E flat major (Op. 35) and in D major, the latter on the Turkish March from 'The Ruins of Athens,' when included in the same programme, require a

master hand to provide continuity of interest. *To say that Mr. Lamond successfully avoided moments that might at times, in these works, have inclined to comparative disinterestedness, would be but a moderate way of expressing the remarkable fascination with which his versatile playing endowed them,* but *at the same time* two of the sonatas given included a similar form of composition, and no matter how intellectually brilliant may be the interpretation, the extravagant use of a certain mode is bound in time to become somewhat ineffective. In the Three Sonatas, the E major (Op. 109), the A major (Op. 2, No. 2), and the C major (Op. 111), Mr. Lamond signalized his perfect insight into the composer's varying moods.

Will you not agree with me that here is no writing, here is no prose, here is not even English, but merely a flux of words to the pen?

Here again is a string, a concatenation—say, rather, a tiara —of gems of purest ray serene from the dark unfathomed caves of a Scottish newspaper:

The Chinese viewpoint, as indicated in this letter, may not be without interest to your readers, because it evidently is suggestive of more than an academic attempt to explain an unpleasant aspect of things which, if allowed to materialize, might suddenly culminate in disaster resembling the Chang-Sha riots. It also ventures to illustrate incidents having their inception in recent premature endeavours to accelerate the development of Protestant missions in China; but we would hope for the sake of the interests involved that what my correspondent describes as 'the irresponsible ruffian element' may be known by their various religious designations only within very restricted areas.

Well, the Chinese have given it up, poor fellows! and are asking the Christians—as to-day's newspapers inform us—to pray for them. Do you wonder? But that is, or was, the Chinese 'viewpoint'—and what a willow-pattern viewpoint! Observe its delicacy. It does not venture to interest or be interesting; merely to be 'not without interest.' But it does 'venture to illustrate incidents'—which, for a viewpoint, is brave enough: and this illustration 'is suggestive of more than an academic attempt to explain an unpleasant aspect of things which, if allowed to materialize, might suddenly culminate.' *What* materializes? The unpleasant aspect? or the things? Grammar says the 'things,' 'things which if allowed to materialize.'

* D 974

But things are materialized already, and as a condition of their
being things. It must˙be the aspect then, that materializes.
But, if so, it is also the aspect that culminates, and an aspect,
however unpleasant, can hardly do that, or at worst cannot
culminate in anything resembling the Chang-Sha riots. . . .
I give it up.

Let us turn to another trick of Jargon: the trick of Elegant
Variation, so rampant in the Sporting Press that there, without
needing to attend these lectures, the Undergraduate detects it
for laughter:

> Hayward and C. B. Fry now faced the bowling, which apparently
> had no terrors for the Surrey crack. The old Oxonian, however,
> took some time in settling to work. . . .

Yes, you all recognize it and laugh at it. But why do you
practise it in your Essays? An undergraduate brings me an
essay on Byron. In an essay on Byron I expect, nay exact, that
Byron shall be mentioned again and again. But my undergraduate has a blushing sense that to call Byron Byron twice on
one page is indelicate. So Byron, after starting bravely as
Byron, in the second sentence turns into 'that great but unequal
poet' and thenceforward I have as much trouble with Byron as
ever Telemachus with Proteus to hold and pin him back to his
proper self. Half-way down the page he becomes 'the gloomy
master of Newstead': overleaf he is reincarnated into 'the
meteoric darling of society': and so proceeds through successive avatars—'this arch-rebel,' 'the author of *Childe
Harold*,' 'the apostle of scorn,' 'the ex-Harrovian, proud, but
abnormally sensitive of his club-foot,' 'the martyr of Misso-
longhi,' 'the pageant-monger of a bleeding heart.' Now this
again is Jargon. It does not, as most Jargon does, come of
laziness; but it comes of timidity, which is worse. In literature
as in life he makes himself felt who not only calls a spade a
spade but has the pluck to double spades and re-double.

For another rule—just as rough and ready, but just as useful:
Train your suspicions to bristle up whenever you come upon
'as regards,' 'with regard to,' 'in respect of,' 'in connection
with,' 'according as to whether,' and the like. They are all

dodges of Jargon, circumlocutions for evading this or that simple statement: and I say that it is not enough to avoid them nine times out of ten, or nine-and-ninety times out of a hundred. You should *never* use them. Though I cannot admire his style, I admire the man who wrote to me, 'Re Tennyson—your remarks anent his *In Memoriam* make me sick': for though *re* is not a preposition of the first water, and 'anent' has enjoyed its day, the finish crowned the work. But here are a few specimens far, very far, worse:

The special difficulty in Professor Minocelsi's case [our old friend 'case' again] arose in *connexion with* the view he holds *relative to* the historical value of the opening pages of Genesis.

That is Jargon. In prose, even taking the miserable sentence as it stands constructed, we should write 'the difficulty arose over the view he holds about the historical value,' etc.

From a popular novelist:

I was entirely indifferent *as to* the results of the game, caring nothing at all *as to* whether *I had losses or gains*—

Cut out the first 'as' in 'as to,' and the second 'as to' altogether, and the sentence begins to be prose—'I was entirely indifferent to the results of the game, caring nothing at all whether I had losses or gains.'

But why, like Dogberry, have 'had losses'? Why not simply 'lose.' Let us try again. 'I was entirely indifferent to the results of the game, caring nothing at all whether I won or lost.'

Still the sentence remains absurd: for the second clause but repeats the first without adding one jot. For if you care not at all whether you win or lose, you must be entirely indifferent to the results of the game. So why not say 'I was careless if I won or lost,' and have done with it?

A man of simple and charming character, he was fitly *associated with* the distinction of the Order of Merit.

I take this gem with some others from a collection made three years ago, by the *Oxford Magazine*; and I hope you admire it as one beyond price. 'He was associated with the distinction of the Order of Merit' means 'he was given the Order of Merit.'

If the members of that Order make a society then he was associated with them; but you cannot associate a man with a distinction. The inventor of such fine writing would doubtless have answered Canning's Needy Knife-grinder with:

I associate thee with sixpence! I will see thee in another association first!

But let us close our *florilegium* and attempt to illustrate Jargon by the converse method of taking a famous piece of English (say Hamlet's soliloquy) and remoulding a few lines of it in this fashion:

To be, or the contrary? Whether the former or the latter be preferable would seem to admit of some difference of opinion; the answer in the present case being of an affirmative or of a negative character according as to whether one elects on the one hand to mentally suffer the disfavour of fortune, albeit in an extreme degree, or on the other to boldly envisage adverse conditions in the prospect of eventually bringing them to a conclusion. The condition of sleep is similar to, if not indistinguishable from, that of death; and with the addition of finality the former might be considered identical with the latter: so that in this connection it might be argued with regard to sleep that, could the addition be effected, a termination would be put to the endurance of a multiplicity of inconveniences, not to mention a number of downright evils incidental to our fallen humanity, and thus a consummation achieved of a most gratifying nature.

That is Jargon: and to write Jargon is to be perpetually shuffling around in the fog and cotton-wool of abstract terms; to be for ever hearkening, like Ibsen's Peer Gynt, to the voice of the Boyg exhorting you to circumvent the difficulty, to beat the air because it is easier than to flesh your sword in the thing. The first virtue, the touchstone of a masculine style, is its use of the active verb and the concrete noun. When you write in the active voice, 'They gave him a silver teapot,' you write as a man. When you write 'He was made the recipient of a silver teapot,' you write Jargon. But at the beginning set even higher store on the concrete noun. Somebody—I think it was FitzGerald—once posited the question 'What would have become of Christianity if Jeremy Bentham had had the writing of the Parables?' Without pursuing that dreadful enquiry I ask you to note how carefully the Parables—those exquisite short stories—speak only of 'things which you can touch and see'—'A sower went forth to sow,' 'The kingdom of heaven is like unto leaven, which a woman took'—and not the Parables only, but the Sermon on the Mount and almost every verse of the Gospel. The Gospel does not, like my young essayist, fear to repeat a word, if the word be good. The Gospel says, 'Render unto Caesar the things that are Caesar's'—not 'Render unto Caesar the things that appertain to that potentate.' The Gospel does not say 'Consider the growth of the lilies,' or even 'Consider how the lilies grow.' It says, 'Consider the lilies, how they grow.'

Or take Shakespeare. I wager you that no writer of English so constantly chooses the concrete word, in phrase after phrase forcing you to touch and see. No writer so insistently teaches the general through the particular. He does it even in *Venus and Adonis* (as Professor Wendell, of Harvard, pointed out in a brilliant little monograph on Shakespeare, published some few years ago). Read any page of *Venus and Adonis* side by side with any page of Marlowe's *Hero and Leander*, and you cannot but mark the contrast: in Shakespeare the definite, particular, visualized image, in Marlowe the beautiful generalisation, the abstract term, the thing seen at a literary remove. Take the two openings, both of which start out with the sunrise. Marlowe begins:

> Now had the Morn espied her lover's steeds:
> Whereat she starts, puts on her purple weeds,
> And, red for anger that he stay'd so long,
> All headlong throws herself the clouds among.

Shakespeare wastes no words on Aurora and her feelings, but gets to his hero and to business without ado:

> Even as the sun with purple-colour'd face—

(You have the sun visualized at once),

> Even as the sun with purple-colour'd face
> Had ta'en his last leave of the weeping morn,
> Rose-cheek'd Adonis hied him to the chase;
> Hunting he loved, but love he laugh'd to scorn.

When Shakespeare has to describe a horse, mark how definite
he is:

> Round-hoof'd, short-jointed, fetlocks shag and long,
> Broad breast, full eye, small head and nostril wide,
> High crest, short ears, straight legs and passing strong;
> Thin mane, thick tail, broad buttock, tender hide.

Or again, in a casual simile, how definite:

> Upon this promise did he raise his chin,
> Like a dive-dipper peering through a wave,
> Which, being look'd on, ducks as quickly in.

Or take, if you will, Marlowe's description of Hero's first
meeting with Leander:

> It lies not in our power to love or hate,
> For will in us is over-ruled by fate . . .,

and set against it Shakespeare's description of Venus' last
meeting with Adonis, as she came on him lying in his blood:

> Or as the snail whose tender horns being hit
> Shrinks backward in his shelly cave with pain,
> And there all smother'd up in shade doth sit,
> Long after fearing to creep forth again,
> So, at his bloody view—

I do not deny Marlowe's lines (if you will study the whole
passage) to be lovely. You may even judge Shakespeare's to
be crude by comparison. But you cannot help noting that
whereas Marlowe steadily deals in abstract, nebulous terms,
Shakespeare constantly uses concrete ones, which later on he
learned to pack into such verse as:

> Sleep that knits up the ravell'd sleeve of care.

Is it unfair to instance Marlowe, who died young? Then
let us take Webster for the comparison; Webster, a man of
genius or of something very like it, and commonly praised by
the critics for his mastery over definite, detailed, and what I
may call *solidified sensation.* Let us take this admired passage
from his *Duchess of Malfi*:

Ferdinand. How doth our sister Duchess bear herself
             In her imprisonment?
Bosola.   Nobly: I 'll describe her.
             She 's sad as one long used to 't, and she seems
             Rather to welcome the end of misery

> Than shun it: a behaviour so noble
> As gives a majesty to adversity.[1]
> You may discern the shape of loveliness
> More perfect in her tears than in her smiles;
> She will muse for hours together; [2] and her silence
> Methinks expresseth more than if she spake.

Now set against this the well-known passage from *Twelfth Night* where the Duke asks and Viola answers a question about someone unknown to him and invented by her—a mere phantasm, in short: yet note how much more definite is the language:

> *Viola.* My father had a daughter lov'd a man;
> As it might be, perhaps, were I a woman,
> *I* should your lordship.
>
> *Duke.*   And what 's her history?
> *Viola.* A blank, my lord.   She never told her love,
> But let concealment, like a worm i' the bud,
> Feed on her damask cheek; she pined in thought,
> And with a green and yellow melancholy
> She sat like Patience on a monument
> Smiling at grief.   Was not this love indeed?

Observe (apart from the dramatic skill of it) how, when Shakespeare *has* to use the abstract noun 'concealment,' on an instant it turns into a visible worm 'feeding' on the visible rose; how, having to use a second abstract word 'patience,' at once he solidifies it in tangible stone.

Turning to prose, you may easily assure yourselves that men who have written learnedly on the art agree in treating our maxim—to prefer the concrete term to the abstract, the particular to the general, the definite to the vague—as a canon of rhetoric.   Whately has much to say on it.   The late Mr. E. J. Payne, in one of his admirable prefaces to Burke (prefaces too little known and valued, as too often happens to scholarship hidden away in a schoolbook), illustrated the maxim by setting a passage from Burke's speech *On Conciliation with America* alongside a passage of like purport from Lord Brougham's *Inquiry into the Policy of the European Powers*.   Here is the deadly parallel:

---

[1] Note the abstract terms.
[2] Here we first come on the concrete: and beautiful it is.

BURKE

BROUGHAM

In large bodies the circulation of power must be less vigorous at the extremities. Nature has said it. The Turk cannot govern Ægypt and Arabia and Curdistan as he governs Thrace; nor has he the same dominion in Crimea and Algiers which he has at Brusa and Smyrna. Despotism itself is obliged to truck and huckster. The Sultan gets such obedience as he can. He governs with a loose rein, that he may govern at all; and the whole of the force and vigour of his authority in his centre is derived from a prudent relaxation in all his borders.

In all the despotisms of the East, it has been observed that the further any part of the empire is removed from the capital, the more do its inhabitants enjoy some sort of rights and privileges: the more inefficacious is the power of the monarch; and the more feeble and easily decayed is the organization of the government.

You perceive that Brougham has transferred Burke's thought to his own page: but will you not also perceive how pitiably, by dissolving Burke's vivid particulars into smooth generalities, he has enervated its hold on the mind?

'This particularizing style,' comments Mr. Payne, 'is the essence of Poetry; and in Prose it is impossible not to be struck with the energy it produces. Brougham's passage is excellent in its way: but it pales before the flashing lights of Burke's sentences.' The best instances of this energy of style, he adds, are to be found in the classical writers of the seventeenth century. 'When South says, "An Aristotle was but the rubbish of an Adam, and Athens but the rudiments of Paradise," he communicates more effectually the notion of the difference between the intellect of fallen and of unfallen humanity than in all the philosophy of his sermons put together.'

You may agree with me, or you may not, that South in this passage is expounding a fallacy; but you will agree with Mr. Payne and me that he utters it vividly.

Let me quote to you, as a final example of this vivid style of writing, a passage from Dr. John Donne far beyond and above anything that ever lay within South's compass:

The ashes of an Oak in the Chimney are no epitaph of that Oak, to tell me how high or how large that was; it tells me not what flocks it sheltered while it stood, nor what men it hurt when it fell. The dust of great persons' graves is speechless, too; it says nothing, it distinguishes nothing. As soon the dust of a wretch whom thou wouldest not, as of a prince whom thou couldest not look upon will trouble thine eyes if the wind blow it thither; and when a whirlewind hath blown the dust of the Churchyard into the Church, and the man sweeps out the dust of the Church into the Churchyard, who will undertake to sift those dusts again and to pronounce, This is the Patrician, this is the noble flowre [flour], and this the yeomanly, this the Plebeian bran? So is the death of *Iesabel* (*Iesabel* was a Queen) expressed. They shall not say *This is Iesabel*; not only not wonder that it is, nor pity that it should be; but they shall not say, they shall not know, *This is Iesabel*.

Carlyle noted of Goethe 'his emblematic intellect, his never-failing tendency to transform into *shape*, into *life*, the feeling that may dwell in him. Everything has form, has visual excellence: the poet's imagination bodies forth the forms of things unseen, and his pen turns them into shape.'

Consider this, Gentlemen, and maybe you will not hereafter set it down to my reproach that I wasted an hour of a May morning in a denunciation of Jargon, and in exhorting you upon a technical matter at first sight so trivial as the choice between abstract and definite words.

A lesson about writing your language may go deeper than language; for language (as in a former lecture I tried to preach to you) is your reason, your λόγος. So long as you prefer abstract words, which express other men's summarized concepts of things, to concrete ones which lie as near as can be reached to things themselves and are the first-hand material for your thoughts, you will remain, at the best, writers at secondhand. If your language be Jargon, your intellect, if not your whole character, will almost certainly correspond. Where your mind should go straight, it will dodge: the difficulties it should approach with a fair front and grip with a firm hand it will be seeking to evade or circumvent. For the Style is the Man, and where a man's treasure is there his heart, and his brain, and his writing, will be also.

THE COMMERCE OF THOUGHT

I

AMONG the fascinating books that have never been written (and they are still the most fascinating of all) I think my favourite is Professor So-and-So's *History of Trade-Routes from the Earliest Times*, a magnificent treatise, incomplete in three volumes. The title may not allure you, but I shall try to persuade you that you are mistaken about this book.

For a few examples—Who, hearing that British oysters, from Richborough, were served at Roman dinner-parties under the Empire, does not want to know how that long journey was contrived for them and how they were kept alive on the road? Or take the secret of the famous purple that was used to dye the Emperor's robe. As Browning asked, 'Who fished the murex up?' How did it reach the dyeing-vat? What was the process? Was the trade a monopoly? Again, you remember that navy of Tarshish, which came once in three years bringing Solomon gold and silver, ivory and apes and peacocks. Who would not wish to read one of its bills of lading, to construct a picture of the quays as the vessels freighted or discharged their cargo? As who would not eagerly read a description of that lumberers' camp on Lebanon to which Solomon sent ten thousand men a month by courses: 'a month they were in Lebanon and two months at home, and Adoniram was over the levy'? The conditions, you see, must have been hard, as the *corvée* was enormous. What truth, if any, underlies the legend that when Solomon died they embalmed and robed him and stood the corpse high on the unfinished wall that, under their great taskmaster's eye, the workmen should work and not 'slack' (as we say)? What a clerk-of-the-works!

Yet again—Where lay the famous tin-islands, the Cassiterides? How were the great ingots of Cornish tin delivered down to the coast and shipped on to Marseilles, Carthage, Tyre? We know that they were shaped pannier-wise, and carried by ponies. But where was the island of Ictis, where the ships received them? Our latest theorists will not allow it to have been St. Michael's Mount—the nearest of all, and the most obviously correspondent with the historian's description. They tell us hardily it was the Isle of Wight—or the Isle of Thanet. Ah, if these professors did not suffer from sea-sickness, how much simpler their hypotheses would be! Image the old Cornish merchant taking whole trains of ponies, laden with valuable ore, along the entire south of England, through dense forests and marauding tribes, to ship his ware at Thanet, when he had half a dozen better ports at his door!   Imagine a skipper from Marseilles— But the absurdities are endless, and I will not here pursue them.

For what other hidden port of trade was that Phoenician skipper bound who, held in chase off the Land's End by a Roman galley and, desperate of cheating her, deliberately (tradition tells) drove his ship ashore to save his merchants' secret? Through what phases, before this, had run and shifted the commercial struggle between young Greece and ancient Phoenicia imaged for us in Matthew Arnold's famous simile:

> As some grave Tyrian trader, from the sea,
>   Descried at sunrise an emerging prow
> Lifting the cool-hair'd creepers stealthily,
>   The fringes of a southward-facing brow
>   Among the Aegean isles:
> And saw the merry Grecian coaster come,
>   Freighted with amber grapes, and Chian wine,
>   Green bursting figs, and tunnies steep'd in brine;
> And knew the intruders on his ancient home,
>
> The young light-hearted masters of the waves;
>   And snatch'd his rudder, and shook out more sail,
>   And day and night held on indignantly
> O'er the blue Midland waters with the gale,
>   Betwixt the Syrtes and soft Sicily,
>   To where the Atlantic raves
> Outside the Western Straits, and unbent sails
>   There, where down cloudy cliffs, through sheets of foam,
>   Shy traffickers, the dark Iberians come;
> And on the beach undid his corded bales.

What commerce followed the cutting of Rome's great military roads?—that tremendous one, for instance, hewn along the cliffs close over the rapids that swirl through the Iron Gates of Danube. By what caravan tracks, through what depots, did the great slave traffic wind up out of Africa and reach the mart at Constantinople? What sort of men worked goods down the Rhône valley; and, if by water, by what contrivances? To come a little later, how did the Crusaders handle transport and commissariat? Through and along what line of *entrepôts* did Venice, Genoa, Seville ply their immense ventures? Who planted the vineyards of Bordeaux, Madeira, the Rhine-land, and from what stocks? Who, and what sort of man opened an aloe market in Socotra? Why, and on what instance, and how, did England and Flanders come to supply Europe, the one with wool, the other with fine linen and naperies?

Now of these and like questions—for of course I might multiply them by the hundred—I wish, first of all, to impress on you that they are of first importance if you would understand history; by which I mean, if you would take hold, in imagination, of the human motives which make history. Roughly (but, of course, very roughly) you may say of man that his wars and main migrations on this planet are ruled by the two great appetites which rule the strifes and migrations of the lower animals—love, and hunger. If under love we include the parental instinct in man to do his best for his mate and children (which includes feeding them, and later includes patrimonies and marriage portions) you get love and hunger combined, and doubled in driving power. Man, unlike the brutes, will also war for religion (I do not forget the Moslem invasion or the Crusades) and emigrate for religion (I do not forget the Pilgrim Fathers): but, here again, when a man expatriates himself for religion the old motives at least 'come in.' The immediate cause of his sailing for America is that authority, finding him obnoxious at home, makes the satisfaction of hunger, love and the parental instincts impossible for him save on condition of renouncing his faith, which he will not do.

Neither do I forget—indeed it will be my business, before I have done, to remind you—that hundreds of thousands of men have left home and country for the sake of learning. There lies the origin of the great universities. But here again you will find it hard to separate—at all events from the thirteenth century onward—the pure ardour of scholarship from the worldly advancement to which it led. Further, while men may migrate for the sake of learning I do not remember to have heard of their making war for it. On this point they content themselves with calling one another names.

To cut this part of the argument short—Of all the men you have known who went out to the Colonies, did not nine out of ten go to make money? Of all the women, did not nine out of ten go to marry, or to 'better themselves' by some less ambiguous process?

We are used to think of Marathon as a great victory won by a small enlightened Greek race over dense hordes of the obscurantist East; of Thermopylae as a pass held by the free mind of man against its would-be enslavers. But Herodotus does not see it so. Herodotus handles the whole quarrel as started and balanced on a trade dispute. Which was it first —East or West—that, coming in the way of trade, broke the rules of the game by stealing away a woman? Was Io that woman? Or was Europa? Jason sails to Colchis and carries off Medea, with the gold: Paris sails to Sparta and abducts Helen—both ladies consenting. Always at the root of the story, as Herodotus tells it, we find commerce, coast-wise trading, the game of marriage by capture: no silly notions about liberty, nationality, religion or the human intellect. It is open to us, of course, to believe that Troy was besieged for ten years for the sake of a woman, as it is pleasant to read in Homer of Helen watching the battlefield from the tower above the Skaian gates, while the old men of the city marvel at her beauty, saying one to another 'Small blame is it that for such a woman the Trojans and Achaeans should long suffer hardships.' But if you ask me, do I believe that the Trojan war happened so, I am constrained to answer that I do not:

I suspect there was money in it somewhere. There is a legend —I think in Suetonius, who to be sure had a nasty mind—that Caesar first invaded Britain for the sake of its pearls; a disease of which our oysters have creditably rid themselves. And even nowadays, when we happen to be fighting far abroad and our statesmen assure us that 'we seek no goldfields,' one murmurs the advice of Tennyson's Northern Farmer:

> Doänt thou marry for munny, but goä wheer munny is.

Money? Yes: but let your imagination play on these old trade-routes, and you will not only enhance your hold on the true springs of history; you will wonderfully seize the romance of it. You will see, as this little planet revolves back out of the shadow of night to meet the day, little threads pushing out over its black spaces—dotted ships on wide seas, crawling trains of emigrant waggons, pioneers, tribes on the trek, men extinguishing their camp-fires and shouldering their baggage for another day's march or piling it into canoes by untracked river sides, families loading their camels with figs and dates for Smyrna, villagers treading wine-vats, fishermen hauling nets, olive-gatherers, packers, waggoners, long trains of African porters, desert caravans with armed outriders, dahabeeyahs pushing up the Nile, busy rice-fields, puffs of smoke where the expresses run across Siberia, Canada, or northward from Cape-town, Greenland whalers, Newfoundland codfishers, trappers around Hudson's Bay. . . .

The main puzzle with these trade-routes is that while seas and rivers and river valleys last for ever, and roads for long, and even a railroad long enough to be called a 'permanent way,' the traffic along them is often curiously evanescent. Let me give you a couple of instances, one in quite recent times, the other of to-day, passing under our eyes.

A man invents a steam-engine. It promptly makes obsolete the stage-coaches, whose pace was the glory of England. Famous hostelries along the Great North Road put up their shutters; weeds begin to choke the canals; a whole nexus of national traffic is torn in shreds, dissipated. A few years pass,

and somebody invents the motor-car—locomotion by petrol.
Forthwith prosperity flows back along the old highways.
County Councils start re-metalling, tar-spraying; inns revive
under new custom: and your rich man is swept past a queer
wayside building, without ever a thought that here stood a
turnpike gate which Dick Turpin or John Nevinson had
to leap.

For a second change, which I have watched for a year or
two as it has passed under my own eyes at the foot of my garden
at home.—As you know, the trade of Europe from the West
Coast of America around the Horn is carried by large sailing-
vessels (the passage being too long for steamships without
coaling stations). One day America starts in earnest to cut
the Panama canal. Forthwith the provident British ship-
owner begins to get quit of these sailing-vessels: noble three-
and four-masters, almost all Clyde-built. He sells them to
Italian firms. Why to Italian firms? Because these ships
have considerable draught and are built of iron. Their
draught unfits them for general coasting trade; they could
not begin to navigate the Baltic, for instance. Now Italy has
deep-water harbours. But the Genoese firms (I am told) buy
these ships for the second reason, that they are of iron: because
while the Italian Government lays a crippling duty on ordinary
iron, broken-up ship-iron may enter free. So, after a coast-
wise voyage or two, it pays to rip their plates out, pass them
under the rollers and re-issue them for new iron; and thus for
a few months these beautiful things that used to wing it home,
five months without sighting land, and anchor under my garden,
eke out a new brief traffic until the last of them shall be towed
to the breakers' yard. Even in such unnoted ways grew,
thrived, passed, died, the commercial glories of Venice, Spain,
Holland.

II

Now I will ask you to consider something more transient,
more secret in operation, than ways of trade and barter—the
ways in which plants disseminate themselves or are spread and

acclimatized. For my pupils in Cambridge, the other day, I drew, as well as I could, in the Arts Lecture Theatre, the picture of an old Roman colonist in his villa in Britain, let us say in the fourth century—and you must remember that these Roman colonists inhabited Britain for a good four hundred years.[1] The owners of their villas (pavements and foundations of which the plough from time to time exhumes for us) were great acclimatizers in their generations; and upon Italy they could draw as a nursery into which the best fruits, trees, flowers of the world had been gathered after conquest and domesticated.

For beasts, it seems probable that they introduced the ass—with the mule as a consequence—the goat, certain new breeds of oxen; for birds, the peacock from India or Persia, the pheasant from Colchis, the Numidian 'guinea-fowl' (as we call it), the duck, the goose (defender of the Capitol), possibly the dove and the falcon. But we talk of plants. Britain swarmed with oak and beech, as with most of the trees of Gaul; but the Roman brought the small-leaved elm, ilex, cypress, laurel, myrtle, oriental plane, walnut; of fruits (among others) peach, apricot, cherry, probably the filbert; of vegetables, green peas (bless him!), cucumbers, onions, leeks; of flowers, some species of the rose (the China-rose, as we call it, for one), lilies, hyacinths, sweet-williams, lilacs, tulips.

But these were plants deliberately imported and tended. What of wild-flowers—the common blue speedwell, for instance? I am not botanist enough to say if the speedwell was indigenous in Britain: but, as a gardener in a small way, I know how it can travel! If the speedwell will not do, take some other seed that has lodged on his long tramp northward in the boot-sole of a common soldier in Vespasian's legion. The boot reaches Dover, plods on, wears out, is cast by the way, rots in a ditch. From it, next spring, Britain has gained a new flower.

[1] See pp. 28–30.

III

I come now to something more volatile, more fugacious yet —more secret and subtle and mysterious in operation even than the vagaries of seeds;.I come to the wanderings, alightings, fertilizings of man's thought.

Will you forgive my starting off with a small personal experience which (since we have just been talking of a very common weed) may here come in not inappropriately? I received a message the other day from an acquaintance, a young engineer in Vancouver. He had been constructing a large dam on the edge of a forest, himself the only European, with a gang of Japanese labourers. But the rains proved so torrential, washing down the sides of the dam as fast as they were heaped, and half drowning the diggers, that at length the whole party sought shelter in the woods. There, as he searched about, my young engineer came upon a log-shanty, doorless, abandoned, empty save for two pathetic objects left on the mud floor—the one a burst kettle, the other a 'soiled copy' (as the booksellers say) of one of my most unpopular novels. You see, there is no room for vanity in the narrative—a burst kettle and this book—the only two things not worth taking away! Yet I—who can neither make nor mend kettles—own to a thrill of pride to belong to a calling that can fling that *other thing* so far; and nurse a hope that the book did, in its hour, cheer rather than dispirit that unknown dweller in the wilderness.

But indeed—to come to more serious and less dead, though more ancient, authors—you never can tell how long this or that of theirs will lie dormant, then suddenly spring to life. Someone copies down a little poem on reed paper, on the back of a washing bill: the paper goes to wrap a mummy; long centuries pass; a tomb is laid bare of the covering sand, and from its dead ribs they unwind a passionate lyric of Sappho:

> Οἱ μὲν ἱππήων στρότον, οἱ δὲ πέσδων,
> οἱ δὲ νάων φαῖσ' ἐπὶ γᾶν μέλαιναν
> ἔμμεναι κάλλιστον· ἔγω δέ κῆν' ὅτ-
> τω τις ἔραται.

> Troops of horse-soldiers, regiments of footmen,
> Fleets in full sail—'What sight on earth so lovely?'
> Say you: but my heart far above them prizes
> Thee, my Belovèd.

I believe that this one was actually recovered from a rubbish-heap: but another such is unwrapped from the ribs of a mummy, of a woman thousands of years dead. Was it bound about them because her heart within them perchance had beaten to it?—wrapped by her desire—by the hands of a lover—or just by chance? As Sir Thomas Browne says:

> What song the syrens sang, or what name Achilles assumed when he hid himself among women, though puzzling questions, are not beyond all conjecture. What time the persons of these ossuaries entered the famous nations of the dead, and slept with princes and counsellors, might admit a wide solution. But who were the proprietaries of these bones, or what bodies these ashes made up, were a question above antiquarism.

IV

But these travels and resuscitations of the written or the printed word, though they may amuse our curiosity, are nothing to marvel at; we can account for them. I am coming to something far more mysterious.

A friend of mine, a far traveller, once assured me that if you wanted to find yourself in a real 'gossip shop'—as he put it—you should go to the Sahara. That desert, he informed me solemnly, 'is one great sounding-board. You scarcely dare to whisper a secret there. You cannot kill a man in the Algerian Sahara even so far south as Fort Mirabel but the news of it will be muttered abroad somewhere in the Libyan desert, say at Ain-el-Sheb, almost as soon as a telephone (if there were one, which there is not) could carry it.'

Well doubtless my friend overstated it. But how do you account for the folk-stories? Take any of the fairy-tales you know best. Take *Cinderella*, or *Red Riding Hood* or *Hop o' my Thumb*. How can you explain that these are common not only to widely scattered nations of the race we call Aryan, from Asia to Iceland, but common also to savages in Borneo and Zululand, the South Sea Islander, the American Indian? The missionaries did not bring them, but found them. There are tribal and local variations, but the tale itself cannot be mistaken. Shall we choose *Beauty and the Beast*? That is not only and plainly, as soon as you start to examine it, the Greek tale of *Cupid and Psyche*, preserved in Apuleius; not only a tale told by nurses in Norway and Hungary; not only a tale recognizable in the Rig-Veda: but a tale told by Bornuese and by Algonquin Indians. Shall we choose *The Wolf who ate the Six Kids while the Seventh was hidden in the Clock-case*? That again is negro as well as European: you may find it among the exploits of Brer Rabbit. Or shall we choose the story of the adventurous youth who lands on a shore commanded by a wizard, is made spell-bound and set to do heavy tasks, is helped by the wizard's pretty daughter and escapes with her aid. That is the story of Jason and Medea: you may find all the first half of it in Shakespeare's *The Tempest*: but you may also find it (as Andrew Lang sufficiently proved) 'in Japan, among the Eskimo, among the Bushmen, the Samoyeds and the Zulus, as well as in Hungarian, Magyar, Celtic and other European household tales.'

Well, I shall not give a guess, this evening, at the way in which these immemorial tales were carried and spread. As Emerson said:

> Long I followed happy guides,
> I could never reach their sides;
> Their step is forth, and, ere the day
> Breaks, up their leaguer, and away. . . .
> But no speed of mine avails
> To hunt upon their shining trails . . .
> On eastern hills I see their smokes,
> Mixed with mist by distant lochs.

But the camp-fires around which men told these old tales have been broken up for the next day's march, and the embers trodden out, centuries and centuries ago.

V

Now again, let us work back for a few minutes towards this inexplicable thing through something of which, though marvellous, we may catch at an understanding. In the beginning of the eighth century in the remote north of a barbarous tract of England, a monk called Bede founds a school. He is (I suppose) of all men in the world the least—as we should put it nowadays—self-advertising. He just labours there, in the cloisters of Jarrow, never leaving them, intent only on his page, for the love of scholarship. Between his solitary lamp and the continent of Europe stretches a belt of fens, of fog, of darkness, broad as two-thirds of England; beyond that, the Channel. Yet the light reaches across and over. As Portia beautifully says ·

> How far that little candle throws his beams!
> So shines a good deed in a naughty world.

Men on the continent have heard of Jarrow: eyes are watching; in due time Bede's best pupil, Alcuin of York, gets an invitation to come over to the court of Charlemagne, to be its educational adviser. So Alcuin leaves York, soon to be destroyed with its fine school and library by the Scandinavian raiders (for your true barbarian, even when he happens to be a pedantic one, always destroys a library. Louvain is his sign-manual) —Alcuin leaves York and crosses over to France with his learning. Very well: but how can you explain it, save by supposing a community of men in Europe alert for learning as merchants for gold, kept informed of where the best thing was to be had, and determined to have it?

Yes, and we are right in supposing this. For when light begins to glimmer, day to break, on the Dark Ages (as we call them, and thereby impute to them, I think, along with their own darkness no little of our own, much as the British seaman abroad has been heard to commiserate 'them poor ignorant foreigners')—when daylight begins to flow, wavering, and spreads for us over the Dark Ages, what is the first thing we see? I will tell you what is the first thing *I* see. It is the Roads.

VI

That is why—to your mild wonder, maybe—I began this lecture by talking of the old trade-routes. I see the Roads glimmer up out of that morning twilight with the many men, like ants, coming and going upón them; meeting, passing, overtaking; knights, merchants, carriers; justiciars with their trains, king's messengers riding post; afoot, friars—black, white and grey—pardoners, poor scholars, minstrels, beggar-men; pack-horses in files; pilgrims, bound for Walsingham, Canterbury, or to Southampton, to ship there for Compostella, Rome. For the moment let us limit our gaze to this little island. I see the old Roman roads—Watling Street, Ermine Street, Icknield Street, Akeman Street, the Fosse Way and the rest—hard-metalled, built in five layers, from the founda-tion or *pavimentum* of fine earth hard beaten in, through layers of large stones, small stones (both mixed with mortar), pounded *nucleus* of lime, clay or chalk, brick and tile, up to the paved surface, *summum dorsum*: one running north through York and branching, as Hadrian had diverted it, to point after point of the Great Wall; another coastwise towards Cornwall; a third for Chester and on to Anglesey, a fourth, embanked and ditched, through the Cambridgeshire fens: I see the minor network of cross-roads, the waterways with their slow freight. You may remember a certain chapter of Rabelais, concerning a certain Island of Odes in which the highways keep moving, moving of themselves; and another passage in Pascal in which the rivers are seen as roads themselves travelling with the travellers.[1] Well, I see it like that; and the by-roads where outlaws lurked; the eastern fens where a hunted man could hide for years, the lanes leading to sanctuary. Some years ago, in Cornwall, I took an old map and decided to walk by a certain road marked on it. My host averred there was no such road in the parish; his brother, a district councillor,

[1] It is observable how many of the great books of the world—the *Odyssey*, the *Aeneid*, *The Canterbury Tales*, *Don Quixote*, *The Pilgrim's Progress*, *Gil Blas*, *Pickwick* and *The Cloister and the Hearth*—are books of wayfaring.

agreed. Being obstinate, I followed the old map, and found that road. What is more, after tracking it for a quarter of a mile, stooping under thorns and elders and pushing through brambles, I came in the dusk upon a fire and a tramp cooking his pot over it. It is a question which of us two received the greater shock.

VII

In the Middle Ages, to keep these road in repair, and especially their bridges, was one of the first calls on godly piety: nor will you ever begin to understand these Middle Ages until you understand their charitable concern for all travellers. Turn to your Litany, and read:

> That it may please thee to preserve all that travel by land or by water, all women labouring of child, all sick persons, and young children; and to shew thy pity upon all prisoners and captives.

Read the evidence collected by Jusserand, and it will leave you with no doubt that the persons thus interceded for are not mixed together casually or carelessly; but that the keeping of the roads in repair was considered as a pious and meritorious work before God, of the same sort as attending the sick or caring for the poor, or comforting the prisoners. A religious order of Pontiffs (*Pontifices*, bridge-makers) built bridges in many countries of Europe. The famous Pont d'Avignon was one; Pont St. Esprit (still in use) was another. A bridge with a chapel on it was one of the most familiar features of mediaeval England—a chapel and a toll-gate—the church being no more averse then than now to 'taking up a collection.' Old London Bridge, with a chapel on it—Old London Bridge which for centuries was the marvel of England—Old London Bridge which (mind you) remained until the middle of the eighteenth century, until Dr. Johnson's day, the *only* bridge spanning the Thames—was begun in 1176, finished in 1209, with its twenty arches, by subscription of the charitable.

I have no time, this afternoon, to draw you separate portraits of the men and women travelling these roads: but mediaeval literature (and especially our Chaucer) teems with pictures of them—pictures which, if read with imagination will 'depict your chamber walls around' as with a moving frieze. I shall conclude by choosing one familiar figure and for a minute or two presenting him to you, with what he meant: the Wandering Scholar.

VIII

He is young, and poor, and careless. He tramps it on foot, and, when his pocket is empty, has no shame in begging: and men find a religious reward in doling him a penny: he being bound for one of the great universities, of whose learning the world has heard; for Oxford or Cambridge, or for Paris, or, farther yet, for Bologna, for Salerno. The roads of Europe are full of his like. No one quite knows how it has happened. The schools of Remigius and of William of Champeaux (we will say) have given Paris a certain prestige when a mysterious word, a rumour, spreads along the great routes, of a certain great teacher called Abelard whose voice will persuade a man's soul almost out of his body. The fame of it spreads almost as pollen is wafted on the wind: but spreads, and alights, and fertilizes. Forthwith, in all the far corners of Europe, young men are packing their knapsacks, bidding good-bye to their homes, waving back to the family at the gate, as they dare the great adventure and fare (say) for Paris, intellectual queen of Europe.

The desire of the moth for the star! The ineffable spell of those great names—Paris, Oxford, Cambridge, Bologna, Salamanca! These young men reach at length the city which has been shining in their imagination. The light fades down its visionary spires to a narrow noisome mediaeval street in which the new-comer is one of a crowd, a turbulent crowd of the wantonest morals. But youth is there, and friendship: to be kept green through the years of later life, when all this young blood is dispersed, and the boys have shaken hands, not to meet again, and nothing remains in common to Dick of York and Hans of Hungary but a memory of the old class-room where they blew on their fingers, and took notes by the light of unglazed windows, and shuffled their numb feet in the straw.

Let me instance one such scholar—William Dunbar, the great fifteenth-century poet of Scotland. He was born about 1460, went to St. Andrews and there graduated Master of Arts in 1479: at once became an Observantine Friar of the Franciscan Order, and started to travel: very likely took ship first from Leith to the Thames, but anyhow crossed to France —the little passenger ships of those days carrying a hundred besides their crew. Says the old ballad:

> Men may leve alle gamys,
> That saylen to seynt Jamys!

(that is, to St. James of Compostella)

> Ffor many a man hit gramys (vexes),
> When they begyn to sayle.

> Ffor when they have take the see,
> At Sandwyche, or at Wynchylsee,
> At Brystow, or where that hit bee,
> Theyr hertes begyn to fayle.

Then follows an extremely moving picture of the crowded sea-sickness on board. We will not dwell on it. Somehow, Dunbar gets to France; roves Picardy; is in Paris in 1491 and mingles with the scholars of the Sorbonne; returns home by way of London (and be it remembered that the kingdoms of England and his native Scotland were more often antagonistic than not in those days); on his way pauses to muse on London Bridge—that Bridge of which I spoke to you a few minutes ago—'lusty Brigge of pylers white' he calls it and breaks into this noble praise of our City:

> London, thou art of townes A per se.
>   Soveraign of cities, semeliest in sight,
> Of high renoun, riches and royaltie;
>   Of lordis, barons, and many a goodly knyght;

Of most delectable lusty ladies bright;
Of famous prelatis, in habitis clericall;
· Of merchauntis full of substaunce and of myght:
London, thou art the flour of Cities all.

.   .   .   .   .   •

Above all ryvers thy Ryver hath renowne,
  Whose beryall streamys, pleasaunt and preclare,
Under thy lusty wallys renneth down,
  Where many a swanne doth swymme with wyngis fair;
  Where many a barge doth saile, and row with are (oars);
Where many a ship doth rest with toppe-royall.
  O, towne of townes! patrone and not compare,
London, thou art the floure of Cities all.

My discourse, like many a better one, shall end with a moral.
I have often observed in life, and especially in matters of education—you too, doubtless, have observed—that what folks
get cheaply or for nothing they are disposed to undervalue.
Indeed I suspect we all like to think ourselves clever, and it
helps our sense of being clever to adjust the worth of a thing
to the price we have paid for it.   Now the mediaeval scholar
I have been trying to depict for you was poor, even bitterly
poor, yet bought his learning dear.   Listen to Chaucer's
account of him when he had attained to be a Clerk of Oxenford,
and to enough money to hire a horse:

As leené was his hors as is a rake,
And he nas nat right fat, I undertake,
But lookéd holwe, and ther-to sobrely;
Ful thredbare was his overeste courtepy;
For he hadde geten hym yet no benefice,
Ne was so worldly for to have office;
For hym was levere have at his beddes heed
Twénty bookés clad in blak or reed
Of Aristotle and his philosophie,
Than robés riche, or fithele, or gay sautrie:
But al be that he was a philosophre,
Yet haddé he but litel gold in cofre;
But al that he myghte of his freendés hente
On bookés and his lernynge he it spente,
And bisily gan for the soulés preye
Of hem that yaf hym wher-with to scoleye.

E 974

How happy would such a poor scholar deem us, who have printed books cheap and plenty, who have newspapers brought to our door for a groat, who can get in less than an hour and a half to Oxford, to Cambridge, in a very few hours to Paris, to Rome—cities of his desire, shining in a land that is very far off! Nevertheless I tell you, who have listened so kindly to me for an hour, that in the commerce and transmission of thought the true carrier is neither the linotype machine, nor the telegraph at the nearest post office, nor the telephone at your elbow, nor any such invented convenience: but even such a wind as carries the seed, 'it may chance of wheat, or of some other grain': the old, subtle, winding, caressing, omnipresent wind of man's aspiration. For the secret—which is also the reward—of all learning lies in the passion for the search.

A MIDSUMMER-NIGHT'S DREAM

I

DR. JOWETT, famous Master of Balliol—

But in the manner of Sterne I must break off, here at the outset, to recall that figure, so familiar to me in youth, as every morning he crossed the quad beneath my bedroom window in a contiguous college for an early trot around its garden; a noticeable figure, too—small, rotund, fresh of face as a cherub, yet with its darting gait and in its swallow-tailed coat curiously suggestive of a belated Puck surprised by dawn and hurrying to

> hang a pearl in every cowslip's ear

—Dr. Jowett used to maintain that after Shakespeare the next creative genius in our literature was Charles Dickens.

As everybody knows, Dickens left an unfinished novel behind him; and a number of ingenious writers from time to time have essayed to finish the story of *Edwin Drood*, constructing the whole from the fragment—yet not from the fragment only, since in the process they are forced into examining the plots of other novels of his; so into recognizing that his invention had certain trends—certain favourite stage-tricks, artifices, *clichés*—which it took almost predicably; and so to argue, from how he constructed by habit, how he probably would have constructed this tale.

I do not propose, in a paper on *A Midsummer-Night's Dream*, to attempt an ending for *Edwin Drood*, but I suggest that if inventive criticism, driven up against such an obstacle as *Drood*, turns perforce to examine Dickens's habitual trends of invention, his favourite artifices and *clichés*, the same process may be serviceable in studying the workmanship of the greater artist, Shakespeare.

For example, no careful reader of Dickens can fail to note his predilection for what I will call dénouement by masked

123

battery. At the critical point in story after story, and at a
moment when he believes himself secure, the villain is 'rounded
on' by a supposed confederate or a supposed dupe; a concealed
battery is opened, catches him unawares, levels him with his
machinations to the ground. Thus Monks brings about the
crisis of *Oliver Twist*; thus Ralph Nickleby and Uriah Heep
come to exposure; thus severally Jonas and Mr. Pecksniff in
Martin Chuzzlewit; thus Quilp and Brass in *The Old Curiosity
Shop*. Thus Haredale forces the conclusion of *Barnaby
Rudge*; thus in *Bleak House* Lady Dedlock (though she, to be
sure, cannot be reckoned among the villains) is hunted down.
Hunted Down, in fact, the name of one of Dickens's stories,
might serve for any other of a dozen. Sometimes the de-
nouncer—old Chuzzlewit, Mr. Micawber, Mr. Boffin—reaches
his moment after a quite incredibly long practice of dissimu-
lation. But always the pursuit is patient, hidden; always the
coup sudden, dramatic, enacted before witnesses; always the
trick is essentially the same—and the guilty one, after exposure, usually goes off and in one way or another commits
suicide.

I instance one only among Dickens's pet devices. But he
had a number of them: and so had Shakespeare.

Take the trick of the woman disguised in man's apparel.
It starts with Julia in *The Two Gentlemen of Verona*. It runs
(and good reason why it should, when we consider that all
women's parts were acted by boys) right through the comedies
and into *Cymbeline*. Portia, Nerissa, Jessica (these three in
one play); Rosalind, Viola, Imogen—each in turn masquerades
thus, and in circumstances that, unless we take stage convention on its own terms, beggar credulity.

> The bridegroom may forget the bride
> Was made his wedded wife yestreen,

but not in the sense that Bassanio and Gratiano forget. Is it
credible that Bassanio shall catch no accent, no vibration, to
touch, awaken, thrill his memory during all that long scene
in the Doge's court, or afterwards when challenged to part

with his ring? Translated into actual life, is it even conceivable?

Let us take another device—that of working the plot upon a shipwreck, shown or reported. (There is perhaps no better way of starting romantic adventures, misadventures, meetings, recognitions; as there is no better way to strip men more dramatically of all trappings that cover their native nobility or baseness.) *The Comedy of Errors* and *Pericles* are pivoted on shipwreck; by shipwreck Perdita in *The Winter's Tale* is abandoned on the magical seacoast of Bohemia. *Twelfth Night* takes its intrigue from shipwreck, and, for acting purposes, opens with Viola's casting-ashore:

Viola. What country, friends, is this?
Captain.   Illyria, lady.
Viola. And what should I do in Illyria?
        My brother he is in Elysium.
        Perchance he is not drown'd—what think you, sailors?
Captain. It is perchance that you yourself were sav'd.

The Tempest opens in the midst of shipwreck. In *The Comedy of Errors* and in *Twelfth Night* shipwreck leads on to another trick—that of mistaken identity. In *The Comedy of Errors* (again) and *Pericles* it leads on to the trick of a long-lost mother, supposed to have perished in shipwreck, revealed as living yet and loving. From shipwreck the fairy Prince lands to learn toil and through it to find his love, the delicate Princess to wear homespun and find her lover.

One might make a long list of these favourite themes; from Shakespeare's pet one of the jealous husband or lover and the woman foully misjudged (Hero, Desdemona, Hermione), to the trick of the potion which arrests life without slaying it (Juliet, Imogen), or the trick of the commanded murderer whose heart softens (Hubert, Leonine, Pisanio). But perhaps enough has been said to suggest an inquiry by which any reader may assure himself that Shakespeare, having once employed a stage device with some degree of success, had never the smallest scruple about using it again. Rather, I suppose that there was never a great author who repeated himself at once so lavishly and so economically, still husbanding his favourite themes while ever attempting new variations upon them. In the very wealth of this variation we find 'God's plenty,' of course. But so far as I dare to understand Shakespeare, I see him as a magnificently indolent man, not agonizing to invent new plots, taking old ones as clay to his hands, breathing life into that clay; anon unmaking, remoulding, reinspiring it. We know that he worked upon old plays, old chronicles, other men's romances. We know, too, that men in his time made small account of what we call plagiarism, and even now define it as a misdemeanour quite loosely and almost capriciously.[1] Shakespeare, who borrowed other men's inventions so royally, delighted in repeating and improving his own.

II

It has been pretty well established by scholars that the earlier comedies of Shakespeare run in the following chronological order: *Love's Labour's Lost*, *The Comedy of Errors*, *The Two Gentlemen of Verona*, *A Midsummer-Night's Dream*. It may, indeed, be argued that *The Comedy of Errors* came before *Love's Labour's Lost*, but whether it did or did not matters very little to us. So let us take the four in the order generally assigned by conjecture.

In the 1598 Quarto of *Love's Labour's Lost* we are informed that it was presented before her Highness this last Christmas and is now 'newly corrected and augmented by W. Shakespeare.' It was a court play, then, and indeed it bears every mark of one. It is an imitative performance, after the fashionable model of John Lyly, but it imitates with a high sense of humour and burlesques its model audaciously.

All young artists in drama are preoccupied with plot or

---

[1] For instance, any poet or dramatist may take the story of Tristram and Iseult and make what he can of it; whereas if I use a plot of Mr. Hall Caine's or of Mrs. Humphry Ward's, I am a branded thief. The reader will find an amusing attempt to delimit the offence of plagiarism in an appendix to Charles Reade's novel *The Wandering Heir*.

'construction.' 'Character' comes later. The plot of *Love's Labour's Lost* turns on 'confusion of identity,' the Princess and her ladies masking themselves to the perplexity of their masked lovers. For the rest, in its whole conception, as in its diction, the thing is consciously artificial and extravagant from first to last.

The Comedy of Errors is an experiment on a different model; not Lyly now, but Plautus, and Plautus out-Plautus'd. Again we have confusion of identity for the motive, but here confusion of identity does not merely turn the plot, as in *Love's Labour's Lost*; it means all the play, and the play means nothing else. Where Plautus had one pair of twin brothers so featured that they cannot be told apart, Shakespeare adds another pair, and the fun is drawn out with astonishing dexterity. Let four things, however, be observed: (1) The feat is achieved at a total sacrifice of character—and indeed he who starts out to confuse identity must, consciously or not, set himself the task of obliterating character. (2) Unless a convention of pasteboard be accepted as substitute for flesh and blood, the events are incredible. (3) On the stage of Plautus the convention of two men being like enough in feature to deceive even their wives might pass. It was *actually* a convention of pasteboard, since the players wore masks. Paint two masks alike, and (since masks muffle voices) the trick is done. But (4) Shakespeare, dispensing with the masks, doubled the confusion by tacking a pair of Dromios on to a pair of Antipholuses; and to double one situation so improbable is to multiply its improbability by the hundred.

It is all done, to be sure, with such theatrical resource that, were ingenuity of stagecraft the test of great drama, we might say, 'Here is a man who has little or nothing to learn.' But ingenuity of stagecraft is not the test of great drama; and in fact Shakespeare had more than a vast deal to learn. He had a vast deal to unlearn.

A dramatic author must start by mastering certain stage-mechanics. Having mastered them, he must—to be great—unlearn reliance on them, learn to cut them away as he grows to perceive that the secret of his art resides in playing human being against human being, man against woman, character against character, will against will—not in devising 'situations' or 'curtains' and operating puppets to produce these. His art touches climax when his 'situations' and 'curtains' so befall that we tell ourselves, 'It is wonderful—yet what else could have happened?' *Othello* is one of the cleverest stage plays ever written. What does it leave us to say but, in an awe of pity, 'This is most terrible, but it must have happened so'? In great art, as in life, character makes the bed it lies on, or dies on.

So in the next play, *The Two Gentlemen of Verona*, we find Shakespeare learning and, perhaps even more deliberately, unlearning. *The Two Gentlemen of Verona* is not a great play: but it is a curious one, and a very wardrobe of 'effects' in which Shakespeare afterwards dressed himself to better advantage.

In *The Two Gentlemen of Verona* Shakespeare is feeling for character, for real men and women. Tricks no longer satisfy him. Yet the old tricks haunt him. He must have again, as in *The Comedy of Errors*, two gentlemen with a servant apiece—though the opposition is discriminated and more cunningly weighted. For stage effect Proteus (supposed a friend and a gentleman) must suddenly behave with incredible baseness. For stage effect Valentine must surrender his true love to his false friend with mawkish generosity that deserves nothing so much as kicking:

> All that was mine in Silvia I give thee.

And what about Silvia? Where does Silvia come in? That devastating sentence may help the curtain. But it blows all character to the winds, and it leaves *no* gentlemen in Verona.

III

We come to *A Midsummer-Night's Dream*, and, with the three earlier comedies to guide us, will attempt to conjecture how the young playwright would face this new piece of work.

First we shall ask, 'What had he to *do*?'

Nobody knows precisely when, or precisely where, or precisely how, *A Midsummer-Night's Dream* was first produced. But it is evident to me that, like *Love's Labour's Lost* and *The Tempest*, it was written for performance at court; and that its particular occasion, like the occasion of *The Tempest*, was a court wedding. It has all the stigmata of a court play. Like *Love's Labour's Lost* and *The Tempest*, it contains an interlude; and that interlude—Bully Bottom's *Pyramus and Thisbe* —is designed, rehearsed, enacted, for a wedding. Can any one read the opening scene, or the closing speech of Theseus, and doubt that the occasion was a wedding? Be it remembered, moreover, how the fairies dominate this play; and how constantly and intimately fairies are associated with weddings in Elizabethan poetry, their genial favours invoked, their malign caprices prayed against. I take a stanza from Spenser's great *Epithalamion*:

> Let no deluding dreames, nor dreadfull sights
> Make sudden sad affrights;
> Ne let house-fyres, nor lightnings helpelesse harmes,
> *Ne let the Pouke, nor other evill sprights,*
> Ne let mischivous witches with theyr charmes,
> Ne let hob Goblins, names whose sence we see not,
> Fray us with things that be not:
> Let not the shriech Oule nor the Storke be heard,
> Nor the night Raven that still deadly yels;
> Nor damnèd ghosts, cald up with mighty spels,
> Nor griesly Vultures, make us once affeard,
> Ne let th' unpleasant Quyre of Frogs still croking
> Make us to wish theyr choking.
> Let none of these theyr drery accents sing;
> Ne let the woods them answer, nor theyr eccho ring.

And I compare this with the fairies' last pattering ditty in our play:

> Now the wasted brands do glow,
>   Whilst the screech-owl, screeching loud,
> Puts the wretch that lies in woe
>   In remembrance of a shroud.
> Now it is the time of night
>   That the graves, all gaping wide,

> Every one lets forth his sprite,
>   In the church-way paths to glide:
> And we fairies, that do run
>   By the triple Hecate's team,
> From the presence of the sun,
>   Following darkness like a dream,
> Now are frolic; not a mouse
> Shall disturb this hallow'd house;
> I am sent, with broom, before,
> To sweep the dust behind the door.
>
> .   .   .   .
>
> To the best bride-bed will we,
> Which by us shall blessèd be. . . .
>
> .   .   .   .
>
> And each several chamber bless,
> Through this palace, with sweet peace.

Can any one set these two passages together and doubt
A Midsummer-Night's Dream to be intended for a merry
κάθαρσις, a pretty purgation of those same goblin terrors which
Spenser would exorcise from the bridal chamber? For my
part, I make little doubt that Shakespeare had Spenser's very
words in mind as he wrote.

Here, then, we have a young playwright commissioned to
write a wedding play—a play to be presented at court. He is
naturally anxious to shine; and, moreover, though his fellow-
playwrights already pay him the compliment of being a little
jealous, he still has his spurs to win.

As I read the play and seek to divine its process of construction, I seem—and the reader must take this for what it is
worth — to see Shakespeare's mind working somewhat as
follows:

He turns out his repertory of notions, and takes stock.

'Lyly's model has had its day, and the bloom is off it; I
must not repeat the experiment of *Love's Labour's Lost*. . . .
I have shown that I can do great things with mistaken identity,
but I cannot possibly express the fun of that further than I did
in *The Comedy of Errors*; and the fun there was clever, but a
trifle hard, if not inhuman. . . . But here is a wedding; a

wedding should be human; a wedding calls for poetry—and
I long to fill a play with poetry. (For I *can* write poetry—
look at *Venus and Adonis*!) . . . Still, mistaken identity is a
trick I know, a trick in which I am known to shine. . . . If I
could only make it poetical! . . . A pair of lovers? For
mistaken identity that means two pairs of lovers. . . . Yet,
steady! We must not make it farcical. It was all very well
to make wives mistake their husbands. That has been funny
ever since the world began; that is as ancient as cuckoldry, or
almost. But this is a wedding play, and the sentiment must
be fresh. Lovers are not so easily mistaken as wives and
husbands—or ought not to be—in poetry.

'I like, too'—we fancy the young dramatist continuing—
'that situation of the scorned lady following her sweetheart.
. . . I did not quite bring it off in *The Two Gentlemen of
Verona*; but it is none the less a good situation, and I must use
it again.[1] . . . Lovers mistaking one another . . . scorned
lady following the scorner . . . wandering through a wood
(that is poetical, anyhow). . . . Yes, and by night; this play
has to be written for a bridal eve. . . . A night for lovers—a
summer's night—a midsummer's night—dewy thickets—the
moon. . . . The moon? Why, of course, the moon! Pitch-
darkness is for tragedy, moonlight for softer illusion. Lovers
can be pardonably mistaken—under the moon. . . . What
besides happens on a summer's night, in a woodland, under
the moon?

'Eh? . . . Oh, by Heaven! Fairies! Real Warwickshire
fairies! Fairies full of mischief—Robin Goodfellow and the
rest. Don't I know about *them*? Fairies full of mischief—
and for a wedding, too! How does that verse of Spenser's go?

Ne let the Pouke—

'Fairies, artificers and ministers of all illusion . . . the
fairy ointment, philters, pranks, "the little western flower"—

Before milk-white, now purple with Love's wounds,
And maidens call it Love-in-Idleness.

[1] And he did: not only here, but in *All's Well That Ends Well*, for
instance.

These and wandering lovers, a mistress scorned—why, we scarcely need the moon, after all!'

Then—for the man's fancy never started to work but it straightway teemed—we can watch it opening out new alleys of fun, weaving fresh delicacies upon this central invention. 'How, for a tangle, to get one of the fairies caught in the web they spin? Why not even the Fairy Queen herself? . . . Yes; but the mortal she falls in with? Shall he be one of the lovers? . . . Well, to say the truth, I haven't given any particular character to these lovers. The absolute jest would be to bring opposite extremes into the illusion, to make Queen Mab dote on a gross clown. . . . All very well, but I *haven't any clowns*. . . . The answer to that seems simple: if I haven't, I ought to have. . . . Stay! I have been forgetting the Interlude all this while. We must have an Interlude; our Interlude in *Love's Labour's Lost* proved the making of the play. . . . Now suppose we make a set of clowns perform the Interlude, as in *Love's Labour's Lost*, and get them chased by the fairies while they are rehearsing? Gross flesh and gossamer—that's an idea! If I cannot use it now, I certainly will some day.[1] . . . But I *can* use it now! What is that story in Ovid, about Midas and the ass's ears? Or am I confusing it with another story—which I read the other day, in that book about witches —of a man transformed into an ass?'

Enough! I am not, of course, suggesting that Shakespeare constructed *A Midsummer-Night's Dream* just in this way. (As the provincial mayor said to the eminent statesman, 'Aha, sir! that's more than you or me knows. That's *Latin*!') But I do suggest that we can immensely increase our delight in Shakespeare and strengthen our understanding of him if, as we read him again and again, we keep asking ourselves *how the thing was done*. I am sure that—hopeless as complete success must be—by this method we get far nearer to the τὸ τί ἦν εἶναι of a given play than be searching among 'sources' and 'origins,' by debating how much Shakespeare took from Chaucer's *Knight's Tale*, or how much he borrowed

[1] He did. See the last act of *The Merry Wives of Windsor*.

from Golding's *Ovid*, or how much Latin he learned at Stratford Grammar School, or how far he anticipated modern scientific discoveries, or why he gave the names 'Pease-blossom,' 'Cobweb,' 'Moth,' 'Mustard-Seed' to his fairies. I admit the idle fascination of some of these studies. A friend of mine—an old squire of Devon—used to demonstrate to me at great length that when Shakespeare wrote, in this play, of the moon looking 'with a watery eye'—

> And when she weeps, weeps every little flower,
> Lamenting some enforcèd chastity—

he anticipated our modern knowledge of plant-fertilization. Good man, he took 'enforced' to mean 'compulsory'; and I never dared to dash his enthusiasm by hinting that, as Shakespeare would use the word 'enforced,' an 'enforcèd chastity' meant a chastity violated.

IV

Let us note three or four things that promptly follow upon Shakespeare's discovering the fairies and pressing them into the service of this play.

(1) To begin with, Poetry follows. The springs of it in the author's *Venus and Adonis* are released, and for the first time he is able to pour it into drama:

> And never, since the middle summer's spring,
> Met we on hill, in dale, forest or mead,
> By pavèd fountain, or by rushy brook,
> Or in the beachèd margent of the sea
> To dance our ringlets to the whistling wind. . . .

> I know a bank whereon the wild thyme blows,
> Where oxlips, and the nodding violet grows,
> Quite over-canopied with lush woodbine,
> With sweet musk-roses, and with eglantine:
> There sleeps Titania some time of the night,
> Lull'd in these flowers. . . .

The honey-bags steal from the humble-bees,
And for night-tapers crop their waxen thighs,
And light them at the fiery glow-worm's eyes
To have my love to bed, and to arise:
And pluck the wings from painted butterflies
To fan the moonbeams from his sleeping eyes.

Never so weary, never so in woe,
Bedabbled with the dew and torn with briers—[1]

The overstrained wit of *Love's Labour's Lost*, the hard gymnastic wit of *The Comedy of Errors*, allowed no chance for this sort of writing. But the plot of *A Midsummer-Night's Dream* invites poetry, and poetry suffuses the play, as with potable moonlight.

(2) The logic-chopping wit of *Love's Labour's Lost* had almost excluded humour. Hard, dry wit had cased *The Comedy of Errors* against it. With Lance in *The Two Gentlemen of Verona* we have an incidental, tentative experiment in humour; but Lance is no part of the plot. Now, with Bottom and his men, we have humour let loose in a flood. In the last Act it ripples and dances over the other flood of poetry, until demurely hushed by the elves. The two greatest *natural* gifts of Shakespeare were poetry and humour; and in this play he first, and simultaneously, found scope for them.

(3) As I see it, this invention of the fairies—this trust in an imaginative world which he understands—suddenly, in *A Midsummer-Night's Dream*, eases and dissolves four-fifths of the difficulties Shakespeare has been finding with his plots. I remember reading, some years ago, a critique by Mr. Max Beerbohm on a performance of this play, and I wish I could remember his exact words, for his words are always worth exact quotation. But he said in effect, 'Here we have the Master, confident in his art, at ease with it as a man in his dressing-gown, kicking up a loose slipper and catching it on

---

[1] Echoed from *Venus and Adonis*:

> The bushes in the way
> Some catch her by the neck, some kiss her face,
> Some twine about her thigh to make her stay.

his toe.' *A Midsummer-Night's Dream* is the first play of Shakespeare's to show a really careless grace—the best grace of the Graces. By taking fairyland for granted, he comes into his inheritance; by assuming that we take it for granted, he achieves just that easy probability he had missed in several plays before trusting his imagination and ours.

(4) Lastly, let the reader note how the fairy business and the business of the clowns take charge of the play as it proceeds, in proportion as both of them are more real—that is, more really imagined—than the business of Lysander and Hermia, Demetrius and Helena. The play has three plots interwoven: (*a*) the main sentimental plot of the four Athenian lovers; (*b*) the fairy plot which complicates (*a*); and (*c*), the grotesque plot which complicates (*b*). Now when we think of the play the main plot (*a*) comes last in our minds, for in (*b*) and (*c*) Shakespeare has found himself.

V

I once discussed with a friend how, if given our will, we would have *A Midsummer-Night's Dream* presented. We agreed at length on this:

The set scene should represent a large Elizabethan hall, panelled, having a lofty oak-timbered roof and an enormous staircase. The cavity under the staircase, occupying in breadth two-thirds of the stage, should be fronted with folding or sliding doors, which, being opened, should reveal the wood, recessed, moonlit, with its trees upon a flat arras or tapestry. On this secondary remoter stage the lovers should wander through their adventures, the fairies now conspiring in the quiet hall under the lantern, anon withdrawing into the woodland to befool the mortals straying there. Then, for the last scene and the interlude of *Pyramus and Thisbe*, the hall should be filled with lights and company. That over, the bridal couples go up the great staircase. Last of all — and after a long pause, when the house is quiet, the lantern all but extinguished, the hall looking vast and eerie, lit only by a last flicker from the hearth—the fairies, announced by Puck, should come tripping back, swarming forth from cupboards and down curtains, somersaulting downstairs, sliding down the baluster rails; all hushed as they fall to work with their brooms— hushed, save for one little voice and a thin, small chorus scarcely more audible than the last dropping embers:

> Through this house give glimmering light,
>   By the dead and drowsy fire;
> Every elf and fairy sprite
>   Hop as light as bird from brier. . . .
> Hand in hand, with fairy grace,
> Will we sing and bless this place.

> Trip away,
> Make no stay,
> Meet me all by break of day.

MACBETH

I

I PROPOSE to take a single work of art, of admitted excellence, and consider its workmanship. I choose Shakespeare's tragedy of *Macbeth* as being eminently such a work: single or complete in itself, strongly imagined, simply constructed, and in its way excellent beyond any challenging.

There are, of course, many other aspects from which so unchallengeable a masterpiece deserves to be studied. We may seek, for example, and seek usefully, to fix its date and define its place in order of time among Shakespeare's writings; but this has been done for us, nearly enough. Or we may search it for light on Shakespeare, the man himself, and on his history, so obscure in the main, though here and there lit up by flashes of evidence, contemporary and convincing so far as they go. For my part, while admitting such curiosity to be human, and suffering myself now and again to be intrigued by it, I could never believe in it as a pursuit that really mattered. All literature must be personal: yet the artist—the great artist —dies into his work, and in that survives. What dread hand designed the Sphinx? What dread brain conceived its site, there, overlooking the desert? What sort of man was he who contrived Memnon, with a voice to answer the sunrise? What were the domestic or extra-domestic habits of Pheidias? Whom did Villon rob or Cellini cheat or Molière mock? Why did Shakespeare bequeath to his wife his second-best bed? These are questions which, as Sir Thomas Browne would say, admit a wide solution, and I allow some of them to be fascinating. 'Men are we,' and must needs wonder, a little wistfully, concerning the forerunners, our kinsmen who, having achieved certain things we despair to improve or even to rival, have gone their way, leaving so much to be guessed. 'How splendid,' we say, 'to have known them! Let us delve back and discover all we can about them!'

Brave lads in olden musical centuries
Sang, night by night, adorable choruses,
    Sat late by alehouse doors in April,
Chaunting in joy as the moon was rising.

Moon-seen and merry, under the trellises,
Flush-faced they played with old polysyllables;
    Spring scents inspired, old wine diluted,
Love and Apollo were there to chorus.

Now these, the songs, remain to eternity,
Those, only those, the bountiful choristers
    Gone—those are gone, those unremembered
Sleep and are silent in earth for ever.

No: it is no ignoble quarrel we hold with Time over these men. But, after all, the moral of it is but summed up in a set of verses ascribed to Homer, in which he addresses the Delian Women. 'Farewell to you all,' he says, 'and remember me in time to come: and when any one of men on earth, a stranger from afar, shall inquire of you, "O maidens, who is the sweetest of minstrels here about? and in whom do you most delight?" then make answer modestly, "Sir, it is a blind man, and he lives· in steep Chios."'

But the shutters are up at *The Mermaid*: and, after all, it is the masterpiece that matters—the Sphinx herself, the *Iliad*, the Parthenon, the Perseus, the song of the Old Héaulmière, *Tartuffe*, *Macbeth*.

Lastly, I shall not attempt a *general* criticism of *Macbeth*, because that work has been done, exquisitely and (I think) perdurably, by Dr. Bradley, in his published *Lectures on Shakespearean Tragedy*, a book which I can hardly start to praise without using the language of extravagance: a book which I hold to belong to the first order of criticism, to be a true ornament of our times. Here and there, to be sure, I cannot accept Dr. Bradley's judgement: but it would profit my readers little to be taken point by point through these smaller questions at issue, and (what is more) I have not the necessary self-confidence.

If, however, we spend a little while in considering *Macbeth* as a *piece of workmanship* (or artistry, if you prefer it), we shall be following a new road which seems worth a trial—perhaps better worth a trial just because it lies off the trodden way; and whether it happen or not to lead us out upon some fresh and lively view of this particular drama, it will at least help us by the way to clear our thoughts upon dramatic writing and its method: while I shall not be false to my belief in the virtue of starting upon any chosen work of literature *absolutely*, with minds intent on discovering just that upon which the author's mind was intent.

I shall assume that *Macbeth* is an eminently effective play; that, by consent, it produces a great, and intended, impression on the mind. It is the shortest of Shakespeare's plays, save only *The Comedy of Errors*. It is told in just under 2,000 lines —scarcely more than half the length of Hamlet. We may attribute this brevity in part—and we shall attribute it rightly [1] —to its simplicity of plot, but that does not matter; or, rather, it goes all to *Macbeth's* credit. The half of artistry consists in learning to make one stroke better than two. The more simply, economically, you produce the impression aimed at, the better workman you may call yourself.

Now what had Shakespeare to *do*? He—a tried and competent dramatist—had to write a play: and if it be answered that everybody knew this without my telling it, I reply that it is the first thing some commentators forget. This play had to be an 'acting play': by which of course I mean a play to succeed on the boards and entertain, for three hours or so,[2] an audience which had paid to be entertained. This differentiates it at once from a literary composition meant to be read by the fireside, where the kettle does all the hissing. Therefore, to understand what Shakespeare as a workman was driving at, we must in imagination seat ourselves amid the audience he had in mind as he worked.

---

[1] I am, of course, aware of other (conjectural) explanations of its brevity.
[2] In the Prologue to *Romeo and Juliet* Shakespeare talks of 'the two hours' traffic of our stage.' But the actual performance must have taken longer than two hours.

Moreover we must imagine ourselves in the Globe Theatre, Southwark, different in so many respects from the playhouses we know: because at every point of difference we meet with some condition of which Shakespeare had to take account. The stage, raised pretty much as it is nowadays, was bare and ran out for some way into the auditorium, the central area of which was unroofed. Thus—the fashionable time for the theatre being the afternoon—the action, or a part of it, took place in daylight. When daylight waned, lanterns were called in, and some may agree with me, after studying Shakespeare's sense of darkness and its artistic value, that it were worth while, with this in mind, to tabulate the times of year, so far as we can ascertain them, at which his several plays were first performed. For my part, I am pretty sure that, among other conditions, he worked with an eye on the almanac.

To return to the stage of the Globe Theatre.—Not only did it run out into the auditorium: the audience returned the compliment by overflowing *it*. Stools, ranged along either side of it, were much in demand by young gentlemen who wished to show off their fine clothes. These young gentlemen smoked —or, as they put it, 'drank'—tobacco in clay pipes. So the atmosphere was free and easy; in its way (I suspect) not much unlike that of the old music-halls I frequented in graceless days, where a corpulent chairman called for drinks for which, if privileged to know him and sit beside him, you subsequently paid; where all joined companionably in a chorus; where a wink from the singer would travel—I know not how—around four-fifths of a complete circle.

The Elizabethan theatre had no painted scenery; [1] or little, and that of the rudest. At the back of the stage, at some little height above the heads of the players, projected a narrow gallery, or platform, with (as I suppose) a small doorway

---

[1] 'The Elizabethan Stage,' 'the Elizabethan Drama,' are terms which actually cover a considerable period of time. It is certain that—say between 1550 and.1620—the theatre enormously improved its apparatus: upon the masques, as we know, very large sums of money were spent; and I make no doubt that before the close of Shakespeare's theatrical career, painted scenes and tapestries were the fashion.

behind it, and a 'practicable' ladder to give access to it or
be removed, as occasion demanded. Fix the ladder, and it
became the stairway leading to Duncan's sleeping-chamber:
take it away, and the gallery became the battlements of Dunsinane, or Juliet's balcony, or Brabantio's window, or Shy-
lock's from which Jessica drops the coffer, or Cleopatra's up
to which she hales dying Antony. From the floor of this
gallery to the floor of the stage depended draperies which, as
they were drawn close or opened, gave you the arras behind
which Falstaff was discovered in slumber, or Polonius stabbed,
the tomb of Juliet, Desdemona's bed, the stage for the play-
scenes in *Hamlet* and the *Midsummer-Night's Dream*, the cave
of Prospero or of Hecate.

To right and left of this draped alcove, beyond the pillars
supporting the gallery, were two doors giving on the back and
the green-room—*mimorum aedes*—for the entrances and exits
of the players.

Such was the Elizabethan theatre, with an audience so
disposed that, as Sir Walter Raleigh puts it, 'the groups of
players were seen from many points of view, and had to aim at
statuesque rather than pictorial effect.' When we take the
arrangements into account with the daylight and the lack of
scenic background, we at once realize that it *must* have been so,
and that these were the conditions under which Shakespeare
wrought for success.

I must add another, though without asking it to be taken
into account just here. I must add it because, the more we
consider it, the more we are likely to count it the heaviest
handicap of all. All female parts were taken by boys. Reflect
upon this, and listen to Lady Macbeth:

> I have given suck, and know
> How tender 'tis to love the babe that milks me:
> I would, while it was smiling in my face,
> Have pluck'd my nipple from his boneless gums
> And dash'd the brains out, had I so sworn as you
> Have done to this.

That in the mouth of a boy! Shakespeare's triumph over

this condition will remain a wonder, however closely it be studied. Nevertheless, there it was: a condition which, having to lay account with it, he magnificently over-rode.

It were pedantic, of course, to lay upon a modern man the strain of constantly visualizing that old theatre on the Bankside when reading Shakespeare, or, when seeing him acted, of perpetually reminding himself, 'He did not write it for *this*.' He did not, to be sure. But so potent was his genius that it has carried his work past the conditions of his own age to reincarnate it in unabated vigour in later ages and under new conditions, even as the *Iliad* has survived the harp and the warriors' feast. This adaptable vitality is the test of first-rate genius; and, save Shakespeare's, few dramas even of the great Elizabethan age have passed it. But, as for Shakespeare, I verily believe that, could his large masculine spirit revisit London, it would—whatever the *dilettante* and the superior person may say—rejoice in what has been done to amplify that cage against which we have his own word that he fretted, and would be proud of the care his countrymen, after three centuries, take to interpret him worthily; and this although I seem to catch, together with a faint smell of brimstone, his comments on the 'star' performer of these days, with the lime-light following him about the stage and analysing the rainbow upon his glittering eye. These things, however, Shakespeare could not foresee: and we must seek back to the limitations of *his* theatre for our present purpose, to understand what a workman he was.

II

We pass, then, from the *conditions* under which he built his plays to the *material* out of which he had to build this particular one. The material of *Macbeth*, as we know, he found in Raphael Holinshed's *Chronicles of Scotland*, first published in 1578 (but he appears to have read the second edition, of 1587). It lies scattered about in various passages in the separate chronicles of King Duncan, King Duff, King Kenneth, King Macbeth; but we get the gist of it in two passages from the *Chronicle of King Duncan*. There is no need to quote them in full: but the purport of the first may be gathered from its opening:

Shortly after happened a strange and uncouth wonder. . . . It fortuned as Macbeth and Banquho journeyed towards Fores, where the king as then lay, they went sporting by the way together without other companie save only themselves, passing through the woodes and fieldes, when sodenly, in the middes of a launde, there met them 3 women in strange and ferly apparell, resembling creatures of an elder worlde; whom they attentively behelde, wondering much at the sight.

Then follow the prophecies: 'All hayle, Macbeth, Thane of Glamis,' etc., with the promise to Banquho that 'contrarily thou in deede shall not reigne at all, but of thee shall be borne which shall governe the Scottish Kingdome by long order of continuall descent.' I pause on that for a moment, merely because it gives a reason, if a secondary one, why the story should attract Shakespeare: for James I, a descendant of Banquho, had come to be King of England: actors and playwrights have ever an eye for 'topical' opportunity, and value that opportunity none the less if it be one to flatter a reigning house.

I take up the quotation at a later point:

The same night at supper Banquho jested with him and sayde, Nowe Makbeth thou hast obtayned those things which the two former sisters prophesied, there remayneth onely for thee to purchase that which the thyrd sayd should come to passe. Whereupon Makbeth, revolving the thing in his mind even then, began to devise how he mighte attayne to the kingdome.

Next we read that Duncan, by appointing his young son, Malcolm, Prince of Cumberland, 'as it were thereby to appoint him his successor in the Kingdome,' sorely troubled Macbeth's ambition, insomuch that he now began to think of usurping the kingdom by force. The *Chronicle* goes on:

The wordes of the three weird sisters also (of whome before ye have heard) greatly encouraged him hereunto, but specially his wife lay sore upon him to attempt the thing, as she that was very ambitious burning in unquenchable desire to beare the name of a Queene. At length, therefore, communicating his proposed intent with his trustie friendes, amongst whom Banquho was the chiefest, upon confidence of their promised ayde, he slewe the king at Envernes (or as some say at Botgosuane) in the VI year of his reygne.

The *Chronicle* proceeds to tell how Macbeth had himself crowned at Scone; how he reigned (actually for a considerable time); how he got rid of Banquho; how Banquho's son escaped; how Birnam Wood came to Dunsinane, with much more that is handled in the tragedy; and ends (so far as we are concerned) as the play ends:

But Makduffe . . . answered (with his naked sworde in his hande) saying: it is true, Makbeth, and now shall thine insatiable crueltie have an ende, for I am even he that thy wysards have tolde thee of, who was never borne of my mother, but ripped out of her wombe: therewithall he stept unto him, and slue him in the place. Then cutting his heade from the shoulders, he set it upon a poll, and brought it into Malcolme. This was the end of Makbeth, after he had reigned XVII years over the Scottish-men. In the beginning of his raigne he accomplished many worthie actes, right profitable to the common wealth (as ye have heard), but afterwards, by illusion of the Divell, he defamed the same with most horrible crueltie.

There, in brief, we have Shakespeare's material: and patently it holds one element on which an artist's mind (if I understand the artistic mind) would by attraction at once inevitably seize. I mean the element of the supernatural. It is the element which almost every commentator, almost every critic, has done his best to belittle. I shall recur to it, and recur with stress upon it; because, writing as diffidently as a man may who has spent thirty years of his life in learning to understand how stories are begotten, and being old enough to desire to communicate what of knowledge, though too late for me, may yet profit others, I can make affidavit that what first arrested Shakespeare's mind as he read the *Chronicles* was that passage concerning the 'three weird sisters'—'All hayle, Makbeth, Thane of Glamis!' and the rest.

Let us consider the *Chronicle* with this supernatural element left out, and what have we? An ordinary sordid story of a disloyal general murdering his king, usurping the throne, reigning with cruelty for seventeen years, and being overcome at length amid every one's approval. There is no material for tragedy in that. 'Had Zimri peace, who slew his master?' Well (if we exclude the supernatural in the *Chronicle*), yes, he had; and for seventeen years: which, for a bloody tyrant, is no short run.

Still, let us exclude the supernatural for a moment. Having excluded it, we shall straightway perceive that the story of the *Chronicle* has one fatal defect as a theme of tragedy. For tragedy demands some sympathy with the fortunes of its hero: but where is there room for sympathy in the fortunes of a disloyal, self-seeking murderer?

Just there lay Shakespeare's capital difficulty.

III

Before we follow his genius in coming to grips with it, let us realize the importance as well as the magnitude of that difficulty. 'Tragedy [says Aristotle] is the imitation of an action: and an action implies personal agents, who necessarily possess certain qualities both of character and thought. It is these that determine the qualities of actions themselves: these —thought and character—are the two natural causes from which actions spring: on these causes, again, all success or failure depends.' [1]

But it comes to this—the success or failure of a tragedy depends on what sort of person we represent; and principally, of course, on what sort of person we make our chief tragic figure, our protagonist. Everything depends really on our protagonist: and it was his true critical insight that directed

---

[1] I quote from Butcher's rendering, which gives the sense clearly enough; though, actually, Aristotle's language is simpler, and for 'thought' I should substitute 'understanding' as a translation of διάνοια.

Dr. Bradley, examining the substance of Shakespearian tragedy, to lead off with these words:

> Such a tragedy brings before us a considerable number of persons (many more than the persons in a Greek play, unless the members of the Chorus are reckoned among them); but it is pre-eminently the story of one person, the 'hero,' or at most of two, the 'hero' and 'heroine.' Moreover, it is only in the love-tragedies, *Romeo and Juliet, Antony and Cleopatra*, that the heroine is as much the centre of the action as the hero. The rest, including *Macbeth*, are single stars. So that, having noticed the peculiarity of these two dramas, we may henceforth, for the sake of brevity, ignore it, and may speak of the tragic story as being concerned primarily with one person.

So, it makes no difference to this essential of tragedy whether we write our play for an audience of Athenians or of Londoners gathered in the Globe Theatre, Southwark: whether we crowd our *dramatis personae* or are content with a cast of three or four. There must be one central figure (or at most two), and on this figure, as the story unfolds itself, we must concentrate the spectators' emotions of pity or terror, or both.

Now, I am going, for handiness, to quote Aristotle again, because he lays down very succinctly some rules concerning this 'hero' or protagonist, or central figure (call him what we will—I shall use the word 'hero' merely because it is the shortest). But let us understand that though these so-called 'rules' of Aristotle are marvellously enforced—though their wisdom is marvellously confirmed—by Dr. Bradley's examination of the 'rules' which Shakespeare consciously or unconsciously obeyed, they do no more than turn into precept certain inductions drawn by Aristotle from the approved masterpieces of his time. There is no reason to suppose that Shakespeare had ever heard of them; rather, there is good reason to suppose that he had not.

But Aristotle says this concerning the hero, or protagonist, of tragic drama, and Shakespeare's practice at every point supports him:

> (1) A Tragedy must not be the spectacle of a perfectly good man brought from prosperity to adversity. For this merely shocks us.

(2) Nor, of course, must it be that of a bad man passing from adversity to prosperity: for that is not tragedy at all, but the perversion of tragedy, and revolts the moral sense.

(3) Nor, again, should it exhibit the downfall of an utter villain: since pity is aroused by undeserved misfortunes, terror by misfortunes befalling a man like ourselves.

(4) There remains, then, as the only proper subject for Tragedy, the spectacle of a man not absolutely or eminently good or wise, who is brought to disaster not by sheer depravity but by some error or frailty.

(5) Lastly, this man must be highly renowned and prosperous— an Oedipus, a Thyestes, or some other illustrious person.

Before dealing with the others, let us get this last rule out of the way; for, to begin with, it presents no difficulty in *Macbeth*, since in the original—in Holinshed's *Chronicles*— Macbeth is an illustrious warrior who makes himself a king; and moreover the rule is patently a secondary one, of artistic expediency rather than of artistic right or wrong. It amounts but to this, that the more eminent we make our persons in Tragedy, the more evident we make the disaster—the dizzier the height, the longer way to fall, and the greater shock on our audience's mind. Dr. Bradley goes further, and remarks, 'The pangs of despised love and the anguish of remorse, we say, are the same in a peasant and a prince: but (not to insist that they cannot be so when the prince is really a prince) the story of the prince, the triumvir, or the general, has a greatness and dignity of its own. His fate affects the welfare of a whole; and when he falls suddenly from the height of earthly greatness to the dust, his fall produces a sense of contrast, of the powerlessness of man, and of the omnipotence—perhaps the caprice —of Fortune or Fate, which no tale of private life can possibly rival.' In this wider view Dr. Bradley may be right, though some modern dramatists would disagree with him. But we are dealing more humbly with Shakespeare as a *workman*; and for our purpose it is more economical, as well as sufficient, to say that downfall from a high eminence is more spectacular than downfall from a low one; that Shakespeare, who knew most of the tricks of his art, knew this as well as ever did

Aristotle, and those who adduce to us Shakespeare's constant selection of kings and princes for his *dramatis personae*, as evidence of his having been a 'snob,' might as triumphantly prove it snobbish in a Greek tragedian to write of Agamemnon and Clytemnestra, or of Cadmus and Harmonia, because

> The gods had to their marriage come,
> And at the banquet all the Muses sang.

But, touching the other and more essential rules laid down by Aristotle, let me—very fearfully, knowing how temerarious it is, how imprudent to offer to condense so great and close a thinker—suggest that, after all, they work down into one: that a hero of Tragic Drama must, whatever else he miss, engage our sympathy; that, however gross his error or grievous his frailty, it must not exclude our feeling that he is a man like ourselves; that, sitting in the audience, we must know in our hearts that what is befalling him might conceivably in the circumstances have befallen us, and say in our hearts, 'There, but for the grace of God, go I.'

I think, anticipating a little, I can drive this point home by a single illustration. When the ghost of Banquo seats itself at that dreadful supper, who sees it? Not the company. Not even Lady Macbeth. Whom does it accuse? Not the company, and, again, not even Lady Macbeth. Those who see it are Macbeth and you and I. Those into whom it strikes terror are Macbeth and you and I. Those whom it accuses are Macbeth and you and I. And what it accuses is what, of Macbeth, you and I are hiding in our own breasts.

So, if this be granted, I come back upon the capital difficulty that faced Shakespeare as an artist.

(1) It was not to make Macbeth a grandiose or a conspicuous figure. He was already that in the *Chronicle*.

(2) It was not to clothe him in something to illude us with the appearance of real greatness. Shakespeare, with his command of majestic poetical speech, had that in his work-bag surely enough, and knew it. When a writer can make an imaginary person talk like this:

> She should have died hereafter;
> There would have been a time for such a word.
> To-morrow, and to-morrow, and to-morrow
> Creeps in this petty pace from day to day
> To the last syllable of recorded time;
> And all our yesterdays have lighted fools
> The way to dusty death— *

I say, when a man knows he can make his Macbeth talk like that, he needs not distrust his power to drape his Macbeth in an illusion of greatness.

But (here lies the crux) how could he make us sympathize with him—make us, sitting or standing in the Globe Theatre some time (say) in the year 1610, feel that Macbeth was even such a man as you or I? He was a murderer, and a murderer for his private profit—a combination which does not appeal to most of us, to unlock the flood-gates of sympathy or (I hope) as striking home upon any private and pardonable frailties. The *Chronicle* does, indeed, allow just one loop-hole for pardon. It hints that Duncan, nominating his boy to succeed him, thereby cut off Macbeth from a reasonable hope of the crown, which he thereupon (and not until then) by process of murder usurped, 'having,' says Holinshed, 'a juste quarrell so to do (as he took the matter).'

Did Shakespeare use that one hint, enlarge that loop-hole? He did not.

The more we study Shakespeare as an artist, the more we must worship the splendid audacity of what he did, just here, in this play of *Macbeth*.

Instead of using a paltry chance to condone Macbeth's guilt, he seized on it and plunged it threefold deeper, so that it might verily

> the multitudinous seas incarnadine.

Think of it:

He made this man, a sworn soldier, murder Duncan, his liege-lord.

He made this man, a host, murder Duncan, a guest within his gates.

He made this man, strong and hale, murder Duncan, old, weak, asleep and defenceless.

He made this man commit murder for nothing but his own advancement.

He made this man murder Duncan, who had steadily advanced him hitherto, who had never been aught but trustful, and who (that no detail of reproach might be wanting) had that very night, as he retired, sent, in most kindly thought, the gift of a diamond to his hostess.

To sum up: instead of extenuating Macbeth's criminality, Shakespeare doubles and redoubles it. Deliberately this magnificent artist locks every door on condonation, plunges the guilt deep as hell, and then—tucks up his sleeves.

There was once another man, called John Milton, a Cambridge man of Christ's College; and, as most of us know, he once thought of rewriting this very story of Macbeth. The evidence that he thought of it—the entry in Milton's handwriting—may be examined in the library of Trinity College, Cambridge.

Milton did not eventually write a play on the story of Macbeth. Eventually he preferred to write an epic upon the Fall of Man, and of that poem critics have been found to say that Satan, 'enemy of mankind,' is in fact the hero and the personage that most claims our sympathy.

Now (still bearing in mind how the subject of Macbeth attracted Milton) let us open *Paradise Lost* at Book IV upon the soliloquy of Satan, which between lines 32 and 113 admittedly holds the *clou* of the poem:

> O! thou that, with surpassing glory crown'd .

Still thinking of Shakespeare and of Milton—of Satan and of Macbeth—let us ponder every line: but especially these:

> Lifted up so high,
> I 'sdain'd subjection, and thought one step higher
> Would set me highest, and in a moment quit
> The debt immense of endless gratitude,

> So burdensome, still paying, still to owe:
> Forgetful what from him I still receiv'd;
> And understood not that a grateful mind
> By owing owes not, but still pays at once
> Indebted and discharg'd. . . .

And yet more especially this:

> Farewell, remorse! All good to me is lost:
> *Evil, be thou my good.*

IV

How then could it lie within the compass even of Shakespeare, master-workman though he was and lord of all noble persuasive language, to make a tragic hero of this Macbeth— traitor to his king, murderer of his sleeping guest, breaker of most sacred trust, ingrate, self-seeker, false kinsman, perjured soldier? Why, it is sin of this quality that in *Hamlet*, for example, outlaws the guilty wretch beyond range of pardon— our pardon, if not God's.

> Upon my secure hour thy uncle stole. . . .

Why, so did Macbeth upon Duncan's. Hear Claudius himself on his knees:

> Forgive me my foul murder?
> That cannot be; since I am still possess'd
> Of those effects for which I did the murder . . .

Why, so was Macbeth. Hear Claudius again:

> O bosom black as death!
> O limèd soul, that, struggling to be free,
> Art more engag'd!

How could Shakespeare make his audience feel pity or terror for such a man? Not for the deed, not for Duncan; but for Macbeth, doer of the deed; how make them sympathize, saying inwardly, 'There, but for the grace of God, might you go, or I'?

He could, by majesty of diction, make them feel that Macbeth

was somehow a great man: and this he did. He could con-
ciliate their sympathy at the start by presenting Macbeth as a
brave and victorious soldier: and this he did. He could show
him drawn to the deed, against will and conscience, by persuasion of another, a woman: and this—though it is extremely
dangerous, since all submission of will forfeits something of
manliness, lying apparently on the side of cowardice, and ever
so little of cowardice forfeits sympathy—this, too, Shakespeare
did. He could trace the desperate act to ambition, 'last
infirmity of noble mind': and this again he did. All these
artifices, and more, Shakespeare used. But yet are they
artifices and little more. They do not begin—they do not
pretend—to surmount the main difficulty which I have indicated, How of such a criminal to make a hero?

Shakespeare did it: *solutum est agendo.* How?

There is (I suppose) only one possible way, which is Aristotle's: to make our hero—supposed great, supposed brave,
supposed of certain winning natural gifts—proceed to his crime
under some fatal hallucination. It must not be an hallucination
of mere madness: for that merely revolts. In our treatment
of lunatics we have come to be far tenderer than the Elizabethans. (We recall Malvolio in the dark cellar.) Still, to us
madness remains unaccountable; a human breakdown, out
of which anything may happen. No: the hallucination, the
dreadful mistake, must be one that can seize on a mind yet
powerful and lead it logically to a doom that we, seated in the
audience, understand, awfully forbode, yet cannot arrest—
unless by breaking through the whole illusion heroically.

Further, such an hallucination once established upon a
strong mind, the more forcibly that mind reasons the more
desperate will be the conclusion of its error; the more powerful
is the will, or combination of wills, the more irreparable must
be the deed to which it drives, as with the more anguish we
shall follow the once-noble soul step by step to its ruin.

Now, of all forms of human error, which is the most fatal?
Surely that of exchanging Moral Order, Righteousness, the
Will of God (call it what we will) for something directly

opposed to it: in other words, of assigning the soul to Satan's terrible resolve, 'Evil, be thou my good.'

By a great soul such a resolve cannot be taken save under hallucination. But if Shakespeare could fix that hallucination upon Macbeth and plausibly establish him in it, he held the key to unlock his difficulty. I have no doubt at all where he found it, or how he grasped it.

V

What is Witchcraft? Or rather let us ask, What *was* Witchcraft?

Well, to begin with, it was something in which the mass of any given audience in the Globe Theatre devoutly believed; and of the educated few less than one in ten, perhaps, utterly disbelieved. I shall not here inquire if Shakespeare believed in it; or, if at all, how far: but if Shakespeare did utterly disbelieve when he wrote (if he wrote) the First Part of *Henry VI*, then it adds — what we could thankfully spare — one more feature of disgrace to his treatment of Joan of Arc.

Women were burnt for witches in Shakespeare's time, and throughout the seventeenth century and some way on into the eighteenth. We may read (and soon have our fill) in the pious abominable works of Cotton and Increase Mather of what these poor women suffered publicly, in New England and Massachusetts, at the hands of Puritan Fathers. We may find in Sinclair's *Satan's Invisible World Discovered* more than any Christian should bargain for concerning our home - grown beldames, and specially those of Scotland. To go right back to Shakespeare's time, we may study the prevalent, almost general, belief in Reginald Scot's *Discovery of Witchcraft* (1584). To the Elizabethans witchcraft was an accepted thing: their drama reeks of it. We need only call to mind Marlowe's *Faustus*, Greene's *Friar Bacon*, Middleton's *Witch*, Dekker's *Witch of Edmonton*.

I shall not labour this, because it has been seized on by

Dr. Johnson with his usual straight insight and expounded with his usual common sense. This play of *Macbeth* peculiarly attracted him. In 1745, long before he annotated the complete Shakespeare, he put forth a pamphlet entitled *Miscellaneous Observations on the Tragedy of Macbeth, with Remarks on Sir T. H.'s* (Sir Thomas Hanmer's) *Edition of Shakespeare.* To that pamphlet (says Boswell) he affixed proposals for a new edition of his own: and though no copy survives which contains them, he had certainly advertised his intention somehow and somewhere. As all the world knows, twenty years elapsed before, in October 1765, his constitutional lethargy at length overcome, there appeared his edition of Shakespeare in eight volumes.

Now what has Johnson to tell us of this his favourite play?

He begins on Act I, Scene ɪ, line 1—nay, before it: on the stage direction, 'Enter Three Witches.' Says he:

> In order to make a true estimate of the abilities and merits of a writer, it is always necessary to examine the spirit of his age and the opinions of his contemporaries. A poet who should now make the whole action of his tragedy depend upon enchantment, and produce the chief events by the assistance of supernatural spirits, would be censored as transgressing the bounds of probability, be banished from the theatre to the nursery, and condemned to write fairy-tales instead of tragedies.

Here I submit that Johnson talks too loudly. I may not actually believe in Jove or Apollo or Venus, 'mother of the Aeneid race divine,' any more than I believe in Puck or in Oberon, or in ghosts as vulgarly conceived. Yet Jove, Apollo and Venus remain for me symbols of things in which I do firmly and even passionately believe: of things for which neither Christian doctrine nor modern Natural Science provides me with symbols that are equivalent or even begin to be comparable. Tradition has consecrated them: and an author to-day may invoke these names of gods once authentic; as an author to-day may employ ghosts, fairies, even witches, to convey a spiritual truth, without being suspected by any one, not a fool, of literal belief in his machinery, of practising

Walpurgis or Corybantic dances in his closet or drenching his garden at night with the blood of black goats.

But a survey [proceeds Johnson] of the notions that prevailed at the time when this play was written, will prove that Shakespeare was in no danger of such censors, since he only turned the system that was then universal to his advantage, and was far from over-burthening the credulity of his audience.

Some learned observations follow, on the Dark Ages and their credence in witchcraft; among which is introduced a story from Olympiodorus, of a wizard, one Libanius, who promised the Empress Placidia to defeat her enemies without aid of soldiery, and was promptly on his promise put to death by that strong-minded lady: 'who,' adds Johnson, 'shewed some kindness in her anger, by cutting him off at a time so convenient for his reputation.'

He continues:

The Reformation did not immediately arrive at its meridian, and tho' day was gradually increasing upon us, the goblins of witchcraft still continued to hover in the twilight. In the time of Queen Elizabeth was the remarkable trial of the witches of Warbois, whose conviction is still commemorated in an annual sermon at *Huntingdon.* But in the reign of King *James,* in which this tragedy was written, many circumstances concurred to propagate and confirm this opinion. The King, who was much celebrated for his knowledge, had, before his arrival in *England,* not only examined in person a woman accused of witchcraft, but had given a very formal account of the practices and illusions of evil spirits, the compacts of witches, the ceremonies used by them, the manner of detecting them, and the justice of punishing them, in his Dialogues of *Daemonologie,* written in the Scottish dialect, and published at *Edinburgh.* This book was, soon after his accession, reprinted in London, and as the ready way to gain King James's favour was to flatter his speculations, the system of *Daemonologie* was immediately adopted by all who desired either to gain preferment or not to lose it. Thus the doctrine of witchcraft was very powerfully inculcated; and as the greatest part of mankind have no other reason for their opinions than that they are in fashion, it cannot be doubted but this persuasion made a rapid progress, since vanity and credulity co-operated in its favour. The infection soon reached the parliament, who in the first year of King *James,* made a law by which it was enacted, chap. xii, that 'if any person shall use any invocation or conjuration of any evil or wicked spirit;

2, or shall consult, covenant with, entertain, employ, fee or reward any evil or cursed spirit to or for any intent or purpose; 3, or take up any dead man, woman or child out of the grave—or the skin, bone, or any part of the dead person—to be employed or used in any manner of witchcraft, sorcery, charm, or enchantment; 4, or shall use, practise or exercise any sort of witchcraft, sorcery, charm, or enchantment; 5, whereby any person shall be destroyed, killed, wasted, consumed, pined, or lamed in any part of the body; 6, that every such person being convicted shall suffer death.' This law was repealed in our own time.

Thus, in the time of Shakespeare, was the doctrine of witchcraft at once established by law and by the fashion, and it became not only unpolite, but criminal, to doubt it.

Upon this general infatuation *Shakespeare* might be easily allowed to found a play, especially since he has followed with great exactness such histories as were then thought true; nor can it be doubted that the scenes of enchantment, however they may now be ridiculed, were both by himself and his audience thought awful and affecting.

Thus wrote Johnson in the middle of the eighteenth century, 'the age of reason'; and, assuming that he talks sense, I put the further, more important question: 'What is, or was, Witchcraft?' 'What did men hold it, essentially and precisely, to mean?'

It meant, essentially and precisely, that the person who embraced witchcraft sold his soul to the devil, to become his servitor; that, for a price, he committed himself to direct reversal of the moral order; that he consented to say, 'Evil, be thou my good.' 'Satan, be thou my God.' It meant this, and nothing short of this.

Now let us return to Holinshed. The *Chronicle* relates that Macbeth and Banquo 'went sporting by the way together without other companie save only themselves, passing the woodes and fieldes, when sodenly, in the middes of a launde there met them 3 women in strange and ferly apparell, resembling creatures of an elder world': and it adds that by common opinion these women 'were eyther the weird sisters, that is (as ye would say) ye Goddesses of destinee, or else some Nimphes or Faieries.' I have already announced my readiness to make affidavit that Shakespeare's mind, as he read, seized on this passage at once. Following this up, I will suggest (as a diversion from my main argument) a process—rough indeed, yet practical—by which a dramatist's mind would operate.

He would say to himself, 'I have to treat of a murder; which is, of its nature, a deed of darkness. Here to my hand is a passage which, whether I can find or not in it the motive of my plot, already drapes it in the supernatural, and so in mystery, which is next door to darkness.'

Let us pause here and remind ourselves how constantly Shakespeare uses darkness to aid the effect of his tragedies upon the spectator. To omit *Romeo and Juliet*—of which the tragic action really starts under a moonlit balcony and ends in a vaulted tomb—of the four tragedies in popular esteem preferred as greatest, *Hamlet* opens on the dark battlements of Elsinore, with a colloquy in whispers, such as night constrains, between sentinels who report a ghost visiting their watch: *Othello* opens with the mutter of voices in a dark street, and ends by the bedside lit by one candle: the total impression of *Lear* is of a dark heath upon which three or four men wander blindly, lit only at intervals by flashes from the dark elements; and the physical blindness of Kent (the one morally sane character in the piece) enhances our sense of impotent moral groping. Of *Macbeth* I cannot do better than quote Dr. Bradley:

Darkness, we may even say blackness, broods over this tragedy. It is remarkable that almost all the scenes which at once recur to the memory take place either at night or in some dark spot. The vision of the dagger, the murder of Duncan, the murder of Banquo, the sleep-walking of Lady Macbeth, all come in night-scenes. The witches dance in the thick air of a storm, or 'black and midnight hags' receive Macbeth in a cavern. The blackness of night is to the hero a thing of fear, even of horror; and that which he feels becomes the spirit of the play. The faint glimmerings of the western sky at twilight are here menacing: it is the hour when the traveller hastens to reach safety in his inn, and when Banquo rides homeward to meet his assassins: the hour when 'light thickens,' when 'night's black agents to their prey do rouse,' when the wolf begins to howl, and the owl to scream, and withered murder steals forth to his work. Macbeth bids the stars hide their fires that his 'black' desires may be concealed: Lady Macbeth calls on thick night to come, palled in the dunnest smoke of hell. The moon is down and no stars shine when Banquo, dreading the dreams of the coming night, goes unwillingly to bed, and leaves Macbeth to wait for the summons of the little bell. When the next day should dawn, its light is 'strangled' and 'darkness does the face of earth entomb.' In the whole drama the sun seems to shine only twice: first, in the beautiful but ironical passage where Duncan sees the swallows flitting round the castle of death; and afterwards, when at the close the avenging army gathers to rid the earth of its shame. Of the many slighter touches which deepen this effect I notice only one. The failure of nature in Lady Macbeth is marked by her fear of darkness; 'she has light by her continually.' And in the one phrase of fear that escapes her lips even in sleep, it is of the darkness of the place of torment that she speaks.

'Hell is murky.' Yes, and upon the crucial test of the guilty king's soul in *Hamlet*—the play-scene—what is the cry?

> *King.* Give me some light—away!
> *All.* Lights, lights, lights!

What, again, is the scene that gives quality to *Julius Caesar* but the brooding night in Brutus' garden? What, again (to go back among the plays), retrieves *The Merchant of Venice* from tragedy—from the surcharged air of the trial scene—to comedy, but the Fifth Act, with placid night shimmering towards dawn, and the birds starting to sing in the shrubberies, as Portia, mistress of the house and the play, says in four words what concludes all?—

> It is almost morning.

It may well be that Shakespeare, as a stage-manager, had means of employing darkness at will, say by a curtain pulled overhead across the auditorium, or part of it. If he had not— and the first account of the play by a spectator is by one Dr. Forman, an astrologer, who paid for his seat in the Globe on Saturday, April 20th, 1610—that is, at a time of year when the sky over the theatre would be day-lit—I frankly confess my ignorance of how it was managed. But that Shakespeare saw the play in darkness, no one who has studied it can have any doubt at all.

He saw the whole thing in darkness, or at best in the murk

light of the Scottish highlands. He saw it (as the play proves)
a thing of night. Now, always and everlastingly, amongst
men, as day typifies sight and sanity, night typifies blindness
and evil. In the night-time murder stalks, witches ride, men
doubt of God in their dreams—doubt even, lying awake—and
wait for dawn to bring reassurance.

In darkness—in a horror of darkness only—can one mistake
and purchase evil for good.

So, as I reason, Shakespeare saw his chance. I am weary,
and over-weary, of commentators who dispute whether his
witches were real witches or fates or what-not. Schiller, as all
know, adapted *Macbeth*; and Schiller was a poet: but Schiller
was no Shakespeare, and by philosophizing Shakespeare's
witches, as by other means, he produced a *Macbeth* remarkably
unlike Shakespeare's *Macbeth*. Why, when he came to the
knocking at the gate, Schiller omitted the Porter—in deference
(I believe) to the genteel taste of his age—and substituted a
Watchman, with a song to the rising dawn; and a charming
song, too, with the one drawback that it ruins the great dramatic
moment of the play. Schlegel rates Schiller roundly for his
witches; and Gervinus says that Schlegel's censure is not a
half-pennyworth too harsh. But Schlegel proceeds to evolve
out of his inner consciousness a new kind of witch of his own;
and this too has the merit of being a witch of Schlegel's own
with the defect of being as much like Shakespeare's as any other
camel. Thereupon starts up Gervinus, and says that Schlegel
'gives throughout an opposite idea of Shakespeare's meaning';
and forthwith proceeds in his turn to evolve his own camel,
leading off with the observation that 'the poet, in the actual
text of the play, calls these beings "witches" only derogatorily:
they call themselves weird sisters.' Profoundly true!—and has
any one, by the way, ever known a usurer who called himself a
usurer, or a receiver of stolen goods who called himself a
receiver, or a pander who called himself a pander, or a swindler
who called himself anything but a victim of circumstances? A
few days ago, some enterprising firm sent me a letter which
began (as I thought with gratuitous abruptness), 'We are not

money-lenders'—and went on to suggest that if, however, I should need 'temporary financial accommodation,' they were prepared to advance any sum between £5 and £50,000.

But, as everybody knows who has studied the etiquette of traffic with Satan, it is the rule never to mention names. If Professor Gervinus had never, to ponder it, studied the tale of *Rumpelstiltskin*, he might at any rate have remembered the answer given to Macbeth's salutation in Act IV, Scene 1:

> *Macbeth.* How now, you secret, black, and midnight hags!
>   What is 't you do?
> *All.*   A deed without a name.

—and if the deed be nameless, why not the doer? But if the reader insist on my being definite, when a lady wears a beard on her chin, and sails to Aleppo in a sieve, and sits at midnight boiling a *ragoût* of poisoned entrails, newt's eyes, frog's toes, liver of blaspheming Jew, nose of Turk and Tartar's lips, finger of birth-strangled babe, to make a gruel thick and slab for a charm of powerful trouble—I say, if he insist on my giving that lady a name, I for one am content with that given in the stage-direction, and to call her 'witch.'

But if these philosophizing critics would leave their talk about Northern Fates, Norns, Valkyries—beings of which it is even possible that, save for the hint in Holinshed, Shakespeare had never heard, and certain that not one in ten of the Globe audience had ever heard—and would turn their learned attention to what Shakespeare as a workman *had to do*, could they miss seeing that a part of his very secret of success lay in leaving these creatures vague, the full extent of their influence dreadfully indeterminate? Coleridge on this, as not seldom, has the right word:

> The Weird Sisters are as true a creation of Shakespeare's as his Ariel and Caliban—fates, furies, and materializing witches being the *elements*. They are wholly different from any representation of witches in the contemporary writers, and yet presented a sufficient external resemblance to the creatures of vulgar prejudice to act immediately on the audience. Their character consists in the imaginative disconnected from the good; they are the shadowy

obscure and fearfully anomalous of physical nature, the lawless of human nature—elemental avengers without sex or kin.

> 'Fair is foul, and foul is fair;
> Hover through the fog and filthy air.'

I will put it in another way. Suppose that Shakespeare as a workman had never improved on what Marlowe taught. Suppose, having to make Macbeth choose evil for good, he had introduced Satan, definite, incarnate, as Marlowe did. Suppose he had made the man assign his soul, by deed or gift, on a piece of parchment and sign it with his blood, as Marlowe made Faustus do. What sort of play would *Macbeth* be?

But we know, and Shakespeare has helped to teach us, that the very soul of horror lies in the vague, the impalpable: that nothing in the world or out of it can so daunt and cow us as the dread of *we know not what*. Of darkness, again—of such darkness as this tragedy is cast in—we know that its menace lies in *suggestion* of the hooded eye watching us, the hand feeling to clutch us by the hair. No; Shakespeare knew what he was about when he left his witches vague.

Can we not see that very vagueness operating on Macbeth's soul? For a certainty, standing near in succession to the throne, he has, before ever the action begins, let his mind run on his chances. We need not say, with Coleridge, that 'he who wishes a temporal end for itself does in truth will the means': but at least Macbeth has let his mind toy with the means. He has been on the stage scarce two minutes when, at the Third Witch's salutation—'All hail, Macbeth, thou shalt be king hereafter'—he starts,

> betrayed by what is false within.

'Good sir,' says Banquo,

> 'why do you start, and seem to fear
> Things that do sound so fair?'

If we read and ponder Macbeth's letter to his wife; if we read and ponder what they say—yes, and specially ponder what they *omit* to say—when she greets his return; we see beyond shadow of doubt that certain things are understood between them. They had talked of the chance, even if, until this moment, they had forborne to speak of the way to it. These are things which, until the necessary moment arrives—the moment that summons action, now or never—cannot be uttered aloud, even between husband and wife.

Let us pause here, on the brink of the deed, and summarize:

(1) Shakespeare, as artificer of this play, meant the Witches, with their suggestions, to be of capital importance.

(2) Shakespeare, as a workman, purposely left vague the extent of their influence; purposely left vague the proportions in which they and Macbeth's own guilty promptings, his own acceptance of the hallucination, contribute to persuade him; vague as the penumbra about him in which—for he is a man of imagination—he sees that visionary dagger. For (let us remember) it is not on Macbeth alone that this horrible dubiety has to be produced; but on us also, seated in the audience. We see what he does not see, and yearn to warn him; but we also see what he sees—the dagger, Banquo's ghost—and understand why he doubts.

(3) As witchcraft implies a direct reversal of the moral order, so the sight and remembrance of the witches, with the strange fulfilment of the Second Witch's prophecy, constantly impose the hallucination upon him—'Fair is foul, and foul is fair.' 'Evil, be thou my good.'

VI

And now let us mark the daring of the great workman! So far he has carefully piled up shadows, doubts, darkness, half-meanings upon the distraught mind of Macbeth. Now, of a sudden, he confronts him with a will that has no doubts at all, but is all for evil: this in his wife, his 'dearest partner of greatness.' She, poor soul, is to suffer hereafter: but for the moment she sees the way—which is the evil way—with absolute conviction.

So before the First Act closes—for actually, though our

reluctant horror drags upon it, the action moves with a curious (nay, for an Elizabethan drama, with a singular) rapidity—the hallucination is established, the scene is set, and we behold this man and this woman groping their road to certain doom. So cunningly has Shakespeare, to heighten our interest in these, flattened down the other figures in the drama that none of them really matter to us. Duncan's murder matters, but not Duncan. He sleeps, and anon after life's fitful fever he is to sleep well: but the only fever *we* feel burns or shivers in that tremendous pair. The thick walls of Inverness Castle fence in the stealthy, damnable work. The gate is closed, barred. Around and outside broods darkness; yet even this is aware of something monstrous at work within. An owl screams: 'there 's husbandry in heaven': the stars, 'as troubled by man's act,' dare but peer through it as through slits in a covering blanket: in the stables the horses catch a panic and gnaw each other's flesh in their madness. For within, up the stair, past the snoring grooms, a murderer creeps to his deed, a woman prompting. In part, no doubt—mostly, if we will—themselves have betrayed themselves: but the powers of evil have their way and reign in that horrible house.

So! and so—when it is done—as Lady Macbeth takes the dagger and Macbeth still stares at his bloody hands, the hour strikes and the word is spoken.

What word? It is the critical word of the drama: and yet no voice utters it. As befits the horrible, impalpable, enclosing darkness, it is no articulate word at all. What is it?

It is this: *Knock! knock! knock! knock!*

A knocking at the gate—but *who* knocks? Can we suppose it is Macduff or Lennox? Who cares more than a farthing for Macduff? Who cares even less than a farthing for Lennox?

Then *who* is it—or, shall I say, *what* is it—stands without, on the other side of the gate, in the breaking dawn, clamouring to be admitted? What hand is on the hammer? Whose step on the threshold?

It is, if we will, God. It is, if we will, the Moral Order. It is, whatever be our religion, that which holds humankind together by law of sanity and righteousness. It is all that this man and this woman have outraged. It is daylight, revealing things as they are and evil different from good. It is the tread of vengeance, *pede claudo*, marching on the house. Macbeth is king, or is to be. But that knock insists on what his soul now begins to know, too surely. Evil is *not* good; and from this moment the moral order asserts itself to roll back the crime to its last expiation.

Knock, knock! 'Here's a knocking indeed!' growls the Porter as he tumbles out. 'If a man were porter of hell-gate, he should have old turning the key. . . .' 'Ay, my good fellow: *and that is precisely what you are!*'

VII

We have examined at some length the means by which Shakespeare overcame his main difficulty—that of reconciling Macbeth as hero or protagonist with the 'deep damnation' of Duncan's taking-off. I do not think we have extenuated that damnation, as I am sure that Shakespeare has not extenuated it. Rather—to use a favourite word of Johnson's—he has 'inspissated' it, like a strong man glorying in his strength. If now we see how, accepting the murder, and all the murder, he has forced us into terrified sympathy—into actual *fellow-feeling* with the murderer—we hold the artistic secret of the drama.

I propose next to take some specimens of his workmanship in this play and attempt to show how excellent it is in detail; not pretending to be exhaustive; choosing more or less at random from the heap of excellence, seeing that 'here is God's plenty.'

Nevertheless let us preserve the semblance of good order by starting afresh just where we left off—with the knocking at the gate.

Embedded in the works of De Quincey you may find a little

paper six pages long, and prolix at that, which contains the last word of criticism on this knocking at the gate.

De Quincey starts by confessing that from his boyish days this knocking produced an effect on his mind for which he could never account. 'The effect was, that it reflected back upon the murderer a peculiar awfulness and depth of solemnity.' He goes on to tell us (as he told us elsewhere, in his *Murder Considered as One of the Fine Arts*) how in the dreadful business of the murders in the Ratcliffe Highway—a series of crimes so fiendish that nothing like them again thrilled London until the days of Jack the Ripper—there did actually happen what the genius of Shakespeare had invented two hundred years before. The murderer, one Williams, who had entered the house of the Marrs and locked the door behind him, was startled, right on the close of his bloody work, as he had butchered the last member of the family, by the knocking of a poor little servant-girl, the Marrs' maid-of-all-work, who had been sent out on an errand. De Quincey draws a wonderful picture of these two, one on either side of that thin street door, breathing close and listening: the little maid on the pavement, the stealthy devil in the passage, with his hand on the key, which, mercifully, he did not turn.

And here let us note, in parenthesis, how fashionable this effect of the closed door has since become with dramatists. If we study Maeterlinck, for example, we shall find it his favourite master-trick. It is the whole secret of *L'Intruse*, of *The Death of Tintagiles*—the door with something dark, uncanny, foreboding, something that threatens doom on the other side. Maeterlinck has variants, to be sure. In *Les Aveugles* he makes it the shutter of physical darkness in a company of old people, all blind. Sometimes, as in *Intérieur* and *Les Sept Princesses*, he rarefies the partition to a glass screen through which one set of characters, held powerless to interfere, watches another set unconscious of observation. But in one way or another always the dramatic effect hangs on our sense of this barrier, whether impalpable or solid, whether transparent as glass or dense as a door of oak, locked, bolted, barred.

Now let De Quincey go on. In what happened to the Marrs' murderer he says he found the solution of what had always puzzled him—the effect wrought on his feelings by the knocking in *Macbeth*. A murderer—even such a murderer as a poet will condescend to—exhibits human nature in its most abject and humiliating attitude. Yet if, as in *Macbeth*, the murderer is to be the protagonist, upon him our interest *must* be thrown. But how?

In *Macbeth*, for the sake of gratifying his own enormous and teeming faculty of creation, Shakespeare has introduced two murderers: and, as usual in his hands, they are remarkably discriminated; but, though in Macbeth the strife of mind is greater than in his wife, the tiger spirit not so awake, and his feelings caught chiefly by contagion from her—yet, as both were finally involved in the guilt of murder, the murderous mind of necessity is finally to be presumed in both. This was to be expressed. . . . And, as this effect is marvellously accomplished in the *dialogues* and *soliloquies* themselves, so it is finally consummated by the expedient under consideration; and it is to this that I now solicit the reader's attention. If the reader has ever witnessed a wife, daughter, or sister in a fainting-fit, he may chance to have observed that the most affecting moment in such a spectacle is that in which a sigh and a stirring announce the recommencement of suspended life. Or, if the reader has ever been present in a vast metropolis on the day when some great national idol was carried in funeral pomp to his grave, and, chancing to walk near the course through which it passed, has felt powerfully in the silence and desertion of the streets, and in the stagnation of ordinary business, the deep interest which at that moment was possessing the heart of man—if, all at once, he should hear the death-like stillness broken up by the sound of wheels rattling away from the scene, and making known that the transitory vision was dissolved, he will be aware that at no moment was his sense of the complete suspension and pause in ordinary human concerns so full and affecting as at that moment when the suspension ceases, and the goings-on of human life are suddenly resumed. All action in any direction is best expounded, measured, and made apprehensible, by reaction. Now apply this to the case in *Macbeth*. Here, as I have said, the retiring of the human heart, and the entrance of the fiendish heart, was to be expressed and made sensible. Another world has stept in; and the murderers are taken out of the region of human beings, human purposes, human desires. Macbeth has forgot that he was born of woman; both are conformed to the image of devils; and the world of devils is suddenly revealed. But how shall this be conveyed and made palpable? In order that a new world may step in, this world must for a time disappear. The murderers and the murder must be insulated—cut off by an immeasurable gulf from the ordinary tide and succession of human affairs—locked up and sequestered in some deep recess; we must be made sensible that the world of ordinary life is suddenly arrested—laid aside—tranced—racked into a dread armistice. Time must be annihilated; relation to things without abolished; and all must pass self-withdrawn into a deep syncope and suspension of earthly passion. Hence it is that when the deed is done, when the work of darkness is perfect, then the world of darkness passes away like a pageantry in the clouds: the knocking at the gate is heard; and it makes known audibly that the reaction has commenced; the human has made its reflux upon the fiendish; the pulses of life are beginning to beat again; and the re-establishment of the goings-on of the world in which we live first makes us profoundly sensible of the awful parenthesis that had suspended them.

We perceive, then, with how right an artistry Shakespeare throws all the effect of this knocking upon the souls *within*. Suppose an inferior artist at work writing a play on this theme. Suppose he sets the scene on the outside of the door. Suppose Macduff and Lennox to arrive in the dawn, after the night of tempest, and to stand there, Macduff with his hand on the knocker, the pair chatting lightly before they ask admission. That were a situation with no little of tragic irony in it, since we, the spectators, know upon what they are to knock. Suppose the door to open upon a sudden cry and the sight of Duncan's body borne down by his sons into the daylight of the courtyard. That were a 'situation' indeed; yet how flat in comparison with Shakespeare's!

Let me give a special reason, too, why it would have been flat: for this also illustrates workmanship. It is that, excepting only Banquo (and I am to talk of Banquo), he has deliberately flattened down every other character to throw up Macbeth and Lady Macbeth into high relief. For why? Because he had, against odds, to interest us in them, and only in them. As I demanded before, who cares more than a farthing for Macduff or even less than a farthing for Lennox? Says Dr. Bradley of the Macduffs, 'Neither they, nor Duncan, nor

Malcolm, nor even Banquo himself have been imagined intensely, and therefore they do not produce that sense of unique personality which Shakespeare could convey in a much smaller number of lines than he gives to most of them.   And this is, of course, even more the case with persons like Ross, Angus and Lennox, though each of these has distinguishable features. I doubt if any other great play of Shakespeare's contains so many speeches which a student of the play, if they were quoted to him, would be puzzled to assign to the speakers.   Let the reader turn, for instance, to the Second Scene of the Fifth Act, and ask himself why the names of the persons should not be interchanged in all the ways mathematically possible.'   To be sure they could: because Shakespeare was taking good care all the time that not one of these puppets should engage our interest, to compete in it for one moment with the two great figures of guilt in whom (as I have tried to show) he had so jealously to keep us absorbed.

VIII

Let us pursue a little further this effect of flattening (as I call it) the subsidiary characters.   But first let me deal with the Porter, and so get this business of the knocking out of the way.

There are critics who find the Porter's humour offensive and irrelevant: who complain that it is a low humour and ordinary.   For answer (if answer be seriously required) I would refer them to a play entitled *Hamlet, Prince of Denmark*, written about the same time as *Macbeth*, and invite them to explain why Hamlet, after an agonizing colloquy with his father's ghost, should break out into shouting back on it, 'Art thou there, true-penny?'   'Well said, old mole!' and swearing his comrades to secrecy upon the profound remark that

> 'There 's ne'er a villain dwelling in all Denmark
> But he 's an arrant knave.'

This is the laughter in which surcharged hysteria breaks and expends itself. I have scarce patience to enlarge that explanation. Some who read these lines are too young, perhaps, to have yet suffered a great tension such as must sooner or later befall every man, though his life be ever so happy. He who has not known that tension stretched maybe over weeks, say by the almost desperate illness of a wife or a child, cannot know upon what sheer craziness the delivered soul recoils. Yet he may *guess*, as, alas! he will assuredly *learn*, and as Shakespeare *knew*.

To be brief, the Porter's speech is just such a discharge, vicarious, of the spectator's overwrought emotion; and it is quite accurately cast into low, everyday language, because that which knocks at the gate is not any dark terrific doom— for all the darkness, all the terror, is cooped within—but the sane, clear, broad, ordinary, common workaday order of the world reasserting itself, and none the more relentlessly for being workaday, and common, and ordinary, and broad, clear, sane.

Let us now return to Shakespeare's clever—as it seems to me, his immensely clever—flattening of the virtuous characters in this play. I have suggested the word for them—your Rosses and Lennoxes. They are ordinary, and of purpose ordinary.

If we consider this carefully, we shall see that one or two consequences flow from it.

To begin with a very practical piece of workmanship—the Elizabethan stage, as I have remarked, had not a straight-drawn front, with footlights, but thrust forward from its broad platform a sort of horn upon the auditorium. Along this horn, or isthmus, a player who had some specially fine passage to declaim advanced and began, laying his hand to his heart—

> 'All the world 's a stage . . .'

or

> 'The quality of mercy is not strained . . .'

or (raising his hand to his brow)

> 'To be, or not to be: that is the question'—

and, having delivered himself, pressed his hand to his heart again, bowed to the discriminating applause, and retired into the frame of the play. An Elizabethan audience loved these bravuras of conscious rhetoric, and in most of his plays Shakespeare was careful to provide opportunities for them. But we shall hardly find any in Macbeth. Here, by flattening the virtuous characters almost to figures on tapestry, Shakespeare flattened back his whole stage. Obviously, neither Macbeth nor his lady, with their known antecedents, were the kind of persons to stalk forward and spout virtue: and the virtuous receive no chance, because virtue has all the while to be kept uninteresting.

Further, this flattening of the virtuous characters gives *Macbeth* (already Greek in its simplicity of plot) a further resemblance to Greek tragedy in its sense of fatality. I reiterate that nobody can care more than a farthing for Macduff on his own account. He had, to be sure, an unusual start in the world; but he has not quite lived up to it. His escape, which leaves his wife and children at Macbeth's merciless mercy, is (to say the least) unheroic. Here again I suggest that Shakespeare's workmanship was sure. By effecting Macbeth's discomfiture through such men of straw, he impresses on us the conviction—or, rather, he leaves us no room for anything but the conviction—that Heaven has taken charge over the work of retribution; and the process of retribution is made the more imposing as its agents are seen in themselves to be naught.

I come now to Banquo, who really *has* individual character: and the more we study Banquo (limned for us in a very few strokes, by the way), the more, I think, we find cause to wonder at Shakespeare as a workman. The *Chronicle* makes Banquo guilty as an accomplice before the fact. Here are Holinshed's words:

> At length therefore communicating his purposed intent with his trustie friendes, amongst whom Banquho was the chiefest, upon confidence of theyr promised ayde, he (Macbeth) slewe the King at Envernes, etc.

Now, in the play, on the eve of the murder, Macbeth does seem to hang for a moment on the edge of hinting at his purpose to Banquo, who has just brought him the King's diamond. 'I dreamt,' says Banquo,

> 'I dreamt last night of the three weird sisters—
> To you they have showed much truth.'

Macbeth returns:

> 'I think not of them:
> Yet, when we can entreat an hour to serve,
> We would spend it in some words upon this business,
> If you would grant the time.'

And Banquo replies:

> 'At your kindest leisure.'

His leisure! Macbeth's 'kindest leisure' at that moment! Let the reader remember it when I come to say a word on the all-pervading irony of this play. The dialogue goes on:

> *Macbeth.* If you shall cleave to my consent, when 'tis,
>   It shall make honour for you.
> *Banquo.*   So I lose none
>   In seeking to augment it, but still keep
>   My bosom franchis'd and allegiance clear,
>   I shall be counsell'd.
> *Macbeth.*   Good repose the while!
> *Banquo.* Thanks, sir: the like to you!

Now, why did Shakespeare avoid the *Chronicle* at this point and send Banquo to bed with a clear conscience? The commentators are ready, as usual. 'Why, don't you see? Banquo was to be father to a line of kings, the last of whom, in 1603, had inherited the throne of England also, "and two-fold balls and treble sceptres swayed." It would never do, in a play written some time before 1610 for performance by His Majesty's Servants, to depict His Majesty's Scottish forbear as an accomplice in treason.'

O Tweedledum! O Tweedledee! how near we came to forget something so profoundly true! Yet, though profoundly true, and even illuminating in its way, it scarcely illustrates

the way in which dramatic masterpieces are constructed. At
least, I think not.

Let us try again, and we shall find two most potent artistic
reasons—one simple, the other subtler, but both (as I say)
potent—why Shakespeare did not involve Banquo in Macbeth's
guilt.

In the first place, it is surely obvious that by sharing the plot
up with Banquo and other 'trustie friendes' (in Holinshed's
phrase) Shakespeare would have destroyed the impressiveness
of Macbeth and his wife. In proportion as he dragged in
that crowd, and just so far, would he have shortened the
stature, blurred the outlines, marred the effect of that tremendous pair, who, as it is, command us by the very isolation
of their grandeur in guilt.

The second reason is subtler, though scarcely less strong.
In all great literature there is always a sense of the norm.
Even in Shakespeare's most terrific and seismic inventions—
when, as in *Hamlet* or in *Lear*, he seems to be breaking up the
solid earth under our feet—there is always some point and
standard of sanity to which all enormities and passionate
errors are referred by us, albeit unconsciously, for correction;
on which the agitated mind of the spectator settles back as
upon its centre of gravity.

It was Coventry Patmore who first taught me to see this
clearly, in his little book *Principle in Art*. He calls it the
punctum indifferens, or Point of Rest. In a painting (he shows)
it may be—often is—something apparently insignificant: a
sawn-off stump in a landscape of Constable's; in the Dresden
Madonna of Raphael, the heel of the Infant—which yet, as we
know, was to bruise, yea, to crush, the Serpent's head. 'Cover
these from sight,' says he, 'and, to the moderately sensitive
and cultivated eye, the whole life of the picture will be found
to have been lowered.' But, he continues, it is

in the most elaborate plays of Shakespeare that we find this device
in its fullest value; and it is from two or three of these that I shall
draw my main illustration of a little noticed but very important
principle of art. In *King Lear* it is by the character of Kent; in

Romeo and Juliet by Friar Laurence; in *Hamlet* by Horatio; in *Othello* by Cassio, and in *The Merchant of Venice* by Bassanio,[1] that the point of rest is supplied. . . . Thus Horatio is the exact *punctum indifferens* between the opposite excesses of the characters of Hamlet and Laertes — over-reasoning inaction and unreasoning action — between which extremes the whole interest of the play vibrates. The unobtrusive character of Kent is, as it were, the eye of the tragic storm which rages round it; and the departure, in various directions, of every character more or less from moderation, rectitude or sanity, is the more clearly understood or felt from our more or less conscious reference to him. So with the central and comparatively unimpressive characters in many other plays—characters unimpressive on account of their facing the exciting and trying circumstances of the drama with the regard of pure reason, justice, and virtue. Each of these characters is a peaceful focus radiating the calm of moral solution throughout all the difficulties and disasters of surrounding fate; a vital centre, which, like that of a great wheel, has little motion in itself, but which at once transmits and controls the fierce revolution of the circumference.

Now in *Macbeth* Banquo supplies this Point of Rest. He is —though on an enlarged scale, having to stand beside the 'hero'—the Ordinary Man. Like Macbeth, he is a thane, a general, a gallant soldier. The two have fought side by side for the same liege-lord and, without jealousy, have helped one another to conquer. They are brought upon the stage together, two equal friends returning from victory. To Banquo as to Macbeth the witches' predictions are offered. Macbeth shall be King of Scotland: Banquo shall beget kings. But whereas Macbeth, taking evil for good and under persuasion of his wife as well as of the supernatural, grasps at the immediate means to the end, Banquo, like an ordinary, well-meaning, sensible fellow, *doesn't do it*, and therefore on the fatal night can go like an honest man to his dreams.

This is not to say that Banquo did not feel the temptation.

To be sure he did: and Shakespeare would not have been Shakespeare if he had not made Banquo feel it. The point is that, feeling it (I do not say strongly—it may have been lethargically, as ordinary decent men *do* feel the spur to emprises which mean the casting-off of honour), Banquo did not yield

But no: by Antonio surely.—A. Q.-C.

to it: and (as it seems to me) Dr. Bradley wastes a great deal of subtlety in trying to show him an accessory after the event, since he apparently acquiesces in Macbeth's attainment of the crown, while suspecting his guilt. For or against this I shall only quote Banquo's own words when the murder is discovered:

> 'Fears and scruples shake us:
> In the great hand of God I stand, and thence
> Against the undivulged pretence I fight
> Of treasonous malice'

—and leave the reader to determine. For what does it matter? What *does* matter is that, of the two soldiers, one is tempted and yields, the other is tempted but does not yield.

And it matters in this way: that from the moment Macbeth yields and apparently succeeds, Banquo, who has not yielded, becomes a living reproach to him. He is the shadowiest of *dangers*, but a very actual *reproach*: and therefore Macbeth's first instinct is by removing Banquo to obliterate the standard of decency, of loyalty—if that loyalty were partial only, why, then, the more credit for obeying it—which survives to accuse him. So Banquo becomes naturally the first sacrifice to be paid to a guilty conscience, and Banquo is murdered.

But now let us mark this: We are scarcely yet midway in Act III: a half of the play has to come and we have done away with the one man who, on the principle we have been examining, is the touchstone to test the wrong from the reasonably right. All the other characters are mere shadows of men, painted on the flat. Macduff survives to be the avenger, but he is to be the avenger by no strength of his own, and he survives (as we have seen) by a pretty base action; fleeing the country and leaving his wife and children behind, unprotected.

The answer is that Banquo survives in his ghost: and that the accusing sanity is still carried forward in the next victim, little Macduff—one of those gallant, precocious, straight-talking children in whom Shakespeare delighted—it may be because he had lost such a son, at just such an age. Be it noted how this boy is introduced close after Macbeth's purposed visit to the Witches—*he* seeking *them*, this time. (Another

touch of insight: it is always the Devil who first accosts, and
the lost soul that later pays the visits, seeking ways of escape.)

Straight upon that foul scene in the cavern light breaks, for
the last time in the drama, in the sunny wisdom of a child.
Good gospel, too, as I take it—

> 'Was my father a traitor, mother?'
> 'Ay, that he was.'
> 'What *is* a traitor?'

—and so on.   'Now God help thee, poor monkey!' says his
mother at length (irony again), even while the Murderer is at
the gate, being admitted.

'Where is your husband? . . . He's a traitor,' are the words
in the Murderer's mouth.

'Thou liest, thou shag-hair'd villain,' answers up the proud,
plucky boy, a moment before he is stabbed.

All these pretty ones end tragically in Shakespeare: but
surely this one in this play lives his few moments not wholly
in vain.

The counterpoise of will and character between Macbeth
and his wife has been so often and on the whole so well discussed that I shall take leave to say very little about it, on the
understanding that there, at any rate, the marvels of the workmanship are accepted.   But two brief notes I will make:

(1) Looking into the matter historically, I cannot find that
criticism even began to do Lady Macbeth justice until Mrs.
Siddons taught them.   Johnson, for example, wrote that
'Lady Macbeth is merely detested.'   An amazing judgment,
truly, to one who saw Ellen Terry rehearsing the part, and sat
and watched John Sargent painting her, in her green robe of
beetles' wings, as she stood in the act of lifting the crown to
her brow!

Exquisitely chosen moment!   For, reading the play carefully, let us observe how, for her, everything ends in that
achievement.   Up to it, hers has been the tiger nature, with
every faculty glued, tense on the purpose, on the prey: her
husband but a half-hearted accomplice.   The end achieved, it

would seem that the spring of action somehow breaks within her. It is Macbeth who, like a man, shoulders the weight of moral vengeance. *She* almost fades out. She is always the great lady; and while she can, she helps. They are both great: never one vulgar word of reproach or recrimination passes between them. But they drift apart. Macbeth no longer relies on her. Uncounselled by her he seeks the Witches again; solitary he pursues his way; and *her* mental anguish is left to be watched by a Doctor and a Gentlewoman. It is but reported to her husband. When the wail of the waiting-woman announces her death, he is busy arming himself for his doom. All he finds to say on the word 'dead' is:

> 'She should have died hereafter:
> *There* would have been a time for such a word.'

Through its strong simplicity of plot, its flattening of the stage as of all the subsidiary characters, its working out of vengeance by agents who are carefully kept as mere puppets in the hand of Heaven, *Macbeth* bears a resemblance unique among Shakespeare's writings to Greek Tragedy; nor can it by accident be full of that irony in which the Greek tragedians —say Sophocles—delighted.

But it is to be observed that the irony most prevalent in *Macbeth* is, if not an invention of Shakespeare's own, at least different from the usual tragic irony, that consists in making the protagonist utter words which, coming on the momentary occasion to his lips, convey to the audience (who know what he does not) a secondary, sinister, prophetic meaning.

There is, to be sure, some of this traditional tragic irony in *Macbeth*: but its *peculiar* irony is retrospective rather than prophetic. It does not prepare the spectator for what is to come; but rather, when it comes, reminds him as by an echo that it has been coming all the while. Thus, when Macbeth and Lady Macbeth stare—how differently!—at their bloodied fingers, *he* says,

> 'Will all great Neptune's ocean wash this blood
> Clean from my hand?'

She says confidently,

> 'A little water clears us of this deed.'

The irony is not yet. It comes in after-echo, in the sleep-walking scene, when (*he* having passed beyond account of it) *she* says, 'Here's the smell of blood still! All the perfumes of Arabia will not sweeten this little hand.'

So when the ghost of Banquo seats itself at the feast, we catch, as by echo, the insistent invitation,

> 'Fail not at our feast,'

with the promise,

> 'My lord, I will not':

as, when Macbeth calls out on the same ghost,

> 'What man dares, I dare:
> Take any shape but that!'

we hear again,

> 'I dare do all that may become a man:
> Who dares do more is none.'

Again, when Birnam Wood comes to Dunsinane, do we not catch again the whisper,

> 'Stones have been known to move and trees to speak'?

The whole play, as it were a corridor of dark Inverness Castle, resounds with such echoes: and I know no other tragedy that so teems with these peculiar whispers (as I will call them) of reminiscent irony.

Macbeth (as I have said and as others have said before me) curiously resembles Greek tragedy in a dozen ways, of which I will mention but one more.

Though it is full of blood and images of blood, the important blood-shedding is hidden, removed from the spectator's sight. There is, to be sure, a set scene for Banquo's murder: but it can be omitted without detriment to the play, and, in fact, always is omitted. Duncan is murdered off the stage; so is little Macduff: Lady Macbeth dies off the stage; Macbeth makes his final exit fighting, to be killed off the stage. There is nothing here like the blood-boltered culmination of *Hamlet*.

Lastly—for there is no space left to argue it—I must proclaim my conviction that this tragedy, so curiously resembling classical tragedy, does, in fact overpass in its bold workmanship any classical tragedy.

As we remember, Milton once proposed to rewrite *Macbeth*. The entry in his list of projects runs: '*Macbeth*, beginning at the arrival of Malcolm at Macduff. The matter of Duncan may be expressed by the appearing of his ghost.'

Milton, in effect, wished to cast *Macbeth* in the strict form of classical tragedy, as he afterwards cast *Samson Agonistes*. And another Cambridge man, Professor Richard Moulton, has actually taken Shakespeare's *Macbeth* and, by one of the most brilliant *tours de force* in modern criticism, recast it, with a Chorus and all, step by step back into a Greek tragedy.

Yes, and he uses scarcely anything that cannot be found in Shakespeare. It is an uncannily clever performance. But his permanent scene is, of course, Dunsinane Castle, not Inverness. That is to say, the play begins when all but the slow retribution —all that we first think of in *Macbeth*—is concluded.

'I have done the deed. Didst thou not hear a noise?'

'Infirm of purpose,
Give me the daggers.'

(*Knock, knock, knock.*)

ANTONY AND CLEOPATRA

I

IF examinations were rightly conducted, to test your acquaintance with the methods by which great artists make great
literature, and that understanding of them which is the true
and capital and joyous reward of critical study, where can we
find a drama more illustrative than this *Antony and Cleopatra*?
For we have to our hand in North's *Plutarch* the very page that
gave Shakespeare his material; the life of Marcus Antonius
out of which he built this play (and not this play only, but a
part of *Julius Caesar*); the very words that Shakespeare took
and transmuted into poetry, often by the most economical
touch. If you happen to know Greek, you have the earlier
pleasure of watching how North turns the prose of Plutarch
into English no less charming: but you need no Greek for the
deeper, subtler and withal more instructive pleasure of assisting
while Shakespeare conjures sound English prose into superb
English poetry under your eyes.

Let me first take the famous account of Cleopatra's first
meeting with Antony. Here is North's version of Plutarch:

For Caesar and Pompey knew her when she was but a young
thing, and knew not then what the world meant: but now she went
to Antonius at the age when a woman's beauty is at the prime, and
she also of best judgement. So, she furnished her self with a world
of gifts, store of gold and silver, and of riches and other sumptuous
ornaments, as is credible enough she might bring from so great a
house, and from so wealthy and rich a realm as Egypt was. But yet
she carried nothing with her wherein she trusted more than in her
self, and in the charms and enchantment of her passing beauty and
grace. Therefore when she was sent unto by divers letters, both
from Antonius himself, and also from his friends, she made so light
of it and mocked Antonius so much, that she disdained to set forward
otherwise, but to take her barge in the river of Cydnus, the poop
whereof was of gold, the sails of purple, and the oars of silver, which
kept stroke in rowing after the sound of the music of flutes, howboys,
citherns. viols, and such other instruments as they played upon in
the barge.

Let us halt here, for a moment, to note something the commentators miss. In the play Enobarbus omits the opening sentence of this passage, because it has already, in an earlier scene, been dramatically suggested by Cleopatra herself, who is shameless in private talk with her servants Iras, Charmian and the young man Alexas:

> Did I, Charmian,
> Ever love Caesar so? . . .
> My salad days,
> When I was green in judgement: cold in blood,
> To say as I said then!

Enobarbus has but to give a description; and this is how he begins it:

> I will tell you. .
> The barge she sat in, like a burnish'd throne,
> Burn'd on the water: the poop was beaten gold;
> Purple the sails, and so perfumèd that
> The winds were love-sick with them; the oars were silver,
> Which to the tune of flutes kept stroke and made
> The water which they beat to follow faster,
> As amorous of their strokes.

Let Plutarch and North resume:

And now for the person of her self: she was laid under a pavilion of cloth of gold of tissue, apparelled and attired like the goddess Venus, commonly drawn in picture: and hard by her, on either hand of her, pretty fair boys apparelled as painters do set forth God Cupid, with little fans in their hands, with the which they fanned wind upon her. Her ladies and gentlewomen also, the fairest of them were apparelled like the nymphs nereids (which are the mermaids of the waters) and like the Graces, some steering the helm, others tending the tackle and ropes of the barge, out of the which there came a wonderful passing sweet savour of perfumes, that perfumed the wharf's side, pestered with innumerable multitudes of people. Some of them followed the barge all alongst the river-side: others also ran out of the city to see her coming in. So that in the end there ran such multitudes of people one after another to see her, that Antonius was left post alone in the market-place, in his imperial seat to give audience: and there went a rumour in the people's mouths, that the goddess Venus was come to play with the god Bacchus, for the general good of all Asia.

Now let us see how this goes into verse—

> For her own person,
> It beggar'd all description; she did lie
> In her pavilion, cloth-of-gold of tissue,
> O'er-picturing that Venus where we see
> The fancy outwork nature: on each side her
> Stood pretty dimpled boys, like smiling Cupids,
> With divers-colour'd fans, whose wind did seem
> To glow the delicate cheeks which they did cool,
> And what they undid did.

Agrippa.   O, rare for Antony!
Enobarbus. Her gentlewomen, like the Nereides,
> So many mermaids, tended her i' the eyes,
> And made their bends adornings: at the helm
> A seeming mermaid steers: the silken tackle
> Swells with the touches of those flower-soft hands,
> That yarely frame the office.   From the barge
> A strange invisible perfume hits the sense
> Of the adjacent wharfs.   The city cast
> Her people out upon her; and Antony,
> Enthroned i' the market-place, did sit alone,
> Whistling to the air; which, but for vacancy,
> Had gone to gaze on Cleopatra too,
> And made a gap in nature.

Let me pause for a moment upon this passage, and a good example of a paradox constantly observable in Shakespeare's fitting together of description and thought.

The paradox is this.   In handling a thought he ever inclines to put it in the concretest form; as conversely, his most vivid visualizations are ever shading off into thought.   For an instance or two—'Sleep that knits up the ravell'd sleave of care,' or,

> Golden lads and girls all must,
> As chimney-sweepers, come to dust

or

> And unregarded age in corners thrown

or

> And all our yesterdays have lighted fools
> The way to dusty death.   Out, out, brief candle!

—or, in this play,

> 'Tis paltry to be Caesar;
> Not being Fortune, he 's but Fortune's knave

> A minister of her will: and it is great
> To do that thing that ends all other deeds;
> Which shackles accidents and bolts up change;
> Which sleeps, and never palates more the dug,
> The beggar's nurse and Caesar's.

I say it is the great paradox in Shakespeare's handling of language that while he never touches a generalization but he must visualize it and force us to see it thus in concrete images, he scarce ever describes a thing but, where other describers would hold to particulars, he shades us off into a thought, or tells the actual thing and straightway glides to some image of it; reflected in the mind as it were glassed on water, 'following darkness like a dream.'

So here, in this famous passage of Cleopatra upon Cydnus, her sails perfume the air as in Plutarch, but so (as not in Plutarch) that the winds were love-sick with them: and again the silver oars keep time, as in Plutarch, but so (as not in Plutarch) they made

> The water which they beat to follow faster,
> As amorous of their strokes.

Still all this is descriptive writing—a purple patch in a drama —and, after all, not so much better than Plutarch's, and, anyhow and however well executed, not the real test of a *dramatist's* quality. If you ask my opinion, I say that North is even a trifle better than Shakespeare — prose against verse — in describing the approach of the barge with the attendants:

Some steering the helm, others tending the tackle and ropes of the barge, out of the which there came a wonderful passing sweet savour of perfumes, that perfumed the wharf's side, pestered with innumerable multitudes of people.

Again, if you will, we will call it a draw between the prose which leaves Antony 'post alone in the market-place, in his imperial seat to give audience,' and the verse which so graphically sets him and leaves him enthroned, whistling to the air which

> but for vacancy,
> Had gone to gaze on Cleopatra too,
> And made a gap in nature

—and so does not, after all, treat Antony any better than does the crowd, but, like the crowd, edges off to follow a curiosity and a conceit.

It is not, I say, upon *description* that we can test a dramatist. His traffic lies not in word-pictures, though he may use them profitably now and again, to lift his play. He deals rather— as Aristotle pointed out—with men and women in action, *doing* things: and it is in a passage concerned with action that we must properly seek a dramatic artist, to judge his handling of his material.

Here then, is the material supplied by Plutarch and North as preliminary to Antony's self-slaughter:

When Antonius saw that his men did forsake him, and yielded unto Caesar, and that his footmen were broken and overthrown: he then fled into the city, crying out that Cleopatra had betrayed him unto them, with whom he had made war for her sake. Then she being afraid of his fury, fled into the tomb which she had caused to be made, and there locked the doors upon her, and shut all the springs of the locks with great bolts, and in the meantime sent unto Antonius to tell him that she was dead. Antonius believing it, said unto himself: What dost thou look for further, Antonius, sith spiteful fortune hath taken from thee the only joy thou hadst, for whom thou yet reservedst thy life? when he had said these words, he went into a chamber and unarmed himself, and being naked said thus: 'O Cleopatra, it grieveth me not that I have lost thy company, for I will not be long from thee: but I am sorry, that having been so great a captain and emperor, I am indeed condemned to be judged of less courage and noble mind, than a woman!' Now he had a man of his called Eros, whom he loved and trusted much, and whom he had long before caused to swear unto him, that he should kill him when he did command him: and then he willed him to keep his promise. His man drawing his sword, lift it up as though he had meant to have stricken his master: but turning his head at one side, he thrust his sword into himself, and fell down dead at his master's foot.

As prose this passage has many merits. Every non-inflected language finds trouble over its pronouns: and our Elizabethans inclined (perhaps wisely) to let that trouble take care of itself. We should be shy, nowadays, of writing 'whom he had long before caused to swear unto him, that he should kill

him when he did command him'; but the meaning is perfectly
plain and easy and no more ambiguous (say) than the meaning
of St. Matthew xxvii. 43, in the Authorized Version—'He
trusted in God; let him deliver him now, if he will have him.'
North, following Plutarch, tells the story straightforwardly, with
liveliness and some simple dignity.

Now watch the poet. His eye travels down the page and,
first of all, lights on the two commanding words—the name of
the servant, Eros, and the word 'unarmed'—'he went into a
chamber and unarmed himself.' Was it glorious chance that
Antony's body-servant bore the name Eros, name also of the
god of Love?—For what is the theme of our play but human
ambition, imperial greatness, cast away for love, slain in the
end for love and by love? *All for Love: or The World Well
Lost*—Dryden, though he wrote a much inferior play on this
very theme and model, packed the secret into his title. We
have come—Antony has come—to the very moment of realizing
all: yes, all: for he believes Cleopatra to be dead, as all else is
broken. The battle has been for love: it is lost; and now Love
(Eros) shall strip and slay him. I suppose it in the last degree
unlikely that Shakespeare ever read the *Pervigilium Veneris*, the
first printed edition of which appeared in Paris in 1577. He
has the gift by this time—notably in *Antony and Cleopatra* he
has the gift—of charging his words with overtones and under-
tones so that they mean, or we feel them to mean, far more
than they actually say. Still there, in the *Pervigilium* stands
the line:

> Totus est inermis idem quando nudus est Amor.
>
> Love naked, love unarmed, is armed complete.
>
> —Totus est inermis idem quando nudus est—Eros.

'Eros,' 'unarmed'—Shakespeare catches these two notes
together, adds a third of his own, and strikes the magnificent
chord. The Eunuch Mardian has delivered his false news.

Antony.   Dead, then?
Mardian.   Dead.

Antony. Unarm, Eros: the long day's task is done,
And we must sleep . . .
                    Off, pluck off:
                    . . . Apace, Eros, apace!
No more a soldier. Bruised pieces, go:
You have been nobly borne. From me awhile.

                              [*Exit Eros.*

I will o'ertake thee, Cleopatra, and
Weep for my pardon. So it must be, for now
All length is torture: since the torch is out,
Lie down and stray no farther: now all labour
Mars what it does; yea, very force entangles
Itself with strength: seal then, and all is done.
Eros!—I come, my queen. Eros!—Stay for me:
Where souls do couch on flowers, we 'll hand in hand,
And with our sprightly port make the ghosts gaze:
Dido and her Aeneas shall want troops,
And all the haunt be ours. Come, Eros, Eros!

                    Re-enter Eros.

Eros. What would my lord?
Antony.   Since Cleopatra died
I have lived in such dishonour that the gods
Detest my baseness. I, that with my sword
Quarter'd the world, and o'er green Neptune's back
With ships made cities, condemn myself to lack
The courage of a woman; less noble mind
Than she which by her death our Caesar tells
'I am conqueror of myself.' Thou art sworn, Eros,
That, when the exigent should come—which now
Is come indeed—when I should see behind me
The inevitable prosecution of
Disgrace and horror, that, on my command,
Thou then wouldst kill me: do 't; the time is come:
Thou strikest not me, 'tis Caesar thou defeat'st.
Put colour in thy cheek.
Eros.   The gods withhold me!
Shall I do that which all the Parthian darts,
Though enemy, lost aim and could not?
Antony.   Eros,
Wouldst thou be window'd in great Rome, and see
Thy master thus with pleach'd arms, bending down
His corrigible neck, his face subdued
To penetrative shame, whilst the wheel'd seat

          Of fortunate Caesar, drawn before him, branded
          His baseness that ensued?
Eros.   I would not see 't.
Antony.   Come, then: for with a wound I must be cured. . . .

Enough: but here you have it—the amazing process in operation under your eyes.

II

I do most ardently desire this play to be reckoned—as it has never been reckoned yet, but I am sure it deserves to be— among the very greatest, and in some ways the most wonderful, of Shakespeare's triumphs.   I want it to stand at length—in your estimation at any rate—as a compeer of *Hamlet, Macbeth, Lear, Othello*: no less.

'Wonderful' is at any rate the word; and Coleridge gives it to me.   'The highest praise,' he says, 'or rather form of praise, of this play

which I can offer in my own mind, is the doubt which the perusal always occasions in me, whether the *Antony and Cleopatra* is not, in all exhibitions of a giant power in its strength and vigour of maturity, a formidable rival of *Macbeth, Lear, Hamlet* and *Othello. Feliciter audax* is the motto for its style comparatively with that of Shakespeare's other works, even as it is the general motto of all his works compared with those of other poets.   Be it remembered, too, that this happy valiancy of style is but the representative and result of all the material excellencies so expressed.'

He goes on:

'Of all Shakespeare's historical plays, *Antony and Cleopatra* is by far the most wonderful.   There is not one in which he has followed history so minutely, and yet there are few in which he impresses the notion of angelic strength so much;—perhaps none in which he impresses it more strongly.   This is greatly owing to the manner in which the fiery force is sustained throughout, and to the numerous momentary flashes of nature counteracting the historic abstraction. As a wonderful specimen of the way in which Shakespeare lives up to the very end of this play, read the last part of the concluding scene.   And if you would feel the judgment as well as the genius of Shakespeare in your heart's core, compare this astonishing drama with Dryden's *All for Love*.'

Now, when Coleridge wrote, Dryden's *All for Love* had been acted at least ten times to *Antony and Cleopatra's* once. And so we may forgive him that, groping toward the truth by instinct, he hesitates and just misses to declare it. 'The highest praise . . . which I can offer in my own mind, is the doubt which the perusal always occasions in me.' 'Of all Shakespeare's *historical* plays, *Antony and Cleopatra* is by far the most wonderful.' Upon that he pauses. After admitting that the audacity of its style distinguishes it above Shakespeare's other works, even as that audacity is Shakespeare's general distinction above other poets, he trails off to admit the 'numerous momentary flashes of nature counteracting the historic abstraction.' Wnat he means by 'historic abstraction' heaven knows. History is not abstract, but particular; as Aristotle long ago pointed out. It narrates what Alcibiades did or suffered. Coleridge is talking cotton-wool. Hazlitt shows himself no less cautious:

This is a very noble play. Though not in the first class of Shakespeare's productions, it stands next to them, and is, we think, the finest of his *historical* plays. . . .

He goes on 'What he has added to the actual story, is on a par with it,' but promptly admits that which really means everything—

His genius was, as it were [why 'as it were'?], a match for history as well as nature, and could grapple at will with either. The play is full of that pervading comprehensive power by which the poet could always make himself master of time and circumstances—

and, with that, Hazlitt too, having like them that dwelt in Zebulon and the land of Naphtali seen a glimmer, wanders off to remark 'The character of Cleopatra is a master-piece. What an extreme contrast it affords to Imogen!' O yes—and as the Victorian lady in the stalls observed to her companion when Sir Herbert Tree presented this very play, 'How different, my dear, from the home life of *our* beloved Queen!'

And then comes along Gervinus, solemnly between his little finger and his enormous useful thumb measuring out the play against history and condemning it. 'The crowd of matter,' murmurs Gervinus, checking it, 'creates a crowd of ideas.' Vengeance on a crowd of ideas!

'A wanton multiplicity of incidents and personages pass before our eyes; political and warlike occurrences run parallel with the most intimate affairs of domestic life and of the affections': and, as if all this were not sufficiently shocking, 'the interest is fettered to the passion of a single pair, and yet the scene of it is the wide world from Parthia to Cape Misenum.'

But if you are setting out to show how the passion between one man and one woman can crack the pillars of a wide world and bring down the roof in ruin (which is precisely what this play does), surely the grander the sense of that world's extent you can induce upon your audience's mind, the grander your effect! Surely for dramatic purpose Shakespeare could have extended Parthia to China and Cape Misenum to Peru, and with advantage, if those remoter regions had happened just then to be discovered and included in the Roman Empire.

III

In a previous lecture, speaking to you of Aristotle's dictum that the tragic hero in drama should preferably be a person of high worldly estate, I suggested that the chief reason for this was a very simple one, and indeed none other than Newton's Law of Gravitation—the higher the eminence from which a man falls the harder he hits the ground—and our imagination. I believe this to be true and yet not all the truth: for as Dr. Bradley says, quoting the end of Chaucer's *Monk's Tale*:

> An-hangèd was Cresus, the proudè kyng:
> His roial tronè myghte hym nat availle.
> Tragédie is noon other maner thyng.

The pangs of despised love and the anguish of remorse, we say, are the same in a peasant and a prince; yet, not to insist that they cannot be so when the prince is really a prince, the story of the prince, the triumvir, or the general, has a greatness and dignity of its own. His fate affects the welfare of a whole nation or empire;

and when he falls suddenly from the height of earthly greatness to the dust, his fall produces a sense of contrast, of the powerlessness of man, and of the omnipotence—perhaps the caprice—of Fortune or Fate, which no tale of private life can possibly rival.

We must not press this too far, or in every play. For, as Sir Walter Raleigh points out, in *Hamlet* (for example) the issue of the events upon the state of Denmark scarcely concerns us. 'The State of Denmark,' says he, 'is not regarded at all, except as a topical and picturesque interest. The tragedy is a tragedy of private life, made conspicuous by the royal station of the chief actors in it.' Yes: but in all *historical* drama, maybe, and in *Antony and Cleopatra* most certainly, most eminently, the sense of reacting far-reaching issues *is* a necessary part of our concern. We are not sympathetic merely to the extent of having our emotions swayed by Cleopatra and Antony in turn. We are the world, the stake this pair are dicing away. We watch not only for their catastrophe but for ours, involved in it. Philo gives the thematic phrase in the twelfth and thirteenth lines of the first scene of the first Act:

> The triple pillar of the world transform'd
> Into a strumpet's fool.

—Every word important, and 'world' not the least important, since, if and when the pillar cracks, the roof of a world must fall. I put it to you that any one insensitive to this dominant, struck by Shakespeare so early in the play and insistent to the end through all that crowding of great affairs which so afflicts the good Gervinus, must miss, roughly speaking, some two-thirds of its meaning. For Gervinus, 'by these too numerous and discordant interruptions that psychical continuity is destroyed which is necessary to the development of such a remarkable connection of the innermost affections as that between Antony and Cleopatra.'

Pro-digious!

But indeed the theme itself is overpoweringly too much for our poor commentator. For it is of Love: not the pretty amorous ritual played, on a time, by troubadours and courtiers:

not the delicate sighing languishment which the Elizabethans called Fancy; not the business as understood by eighteenth century sentimentalists: but Love the invincible destroyer—*'Ἔρως ἀνίκατε μάχαν*—destroying the world for itself—itself, too, at the last: Love voluptuous, savage, perfidious, true to itself though rooted in dishonour, extreme, wild, divine, merciless as a panther on its prey. With this Love, wayward, untameable, Shakespeare here dares to traffic, and with the end of it—the latest dream—'on the cold hill side'—

> I saw pale kings and princes too,
>   Pale warriors, death-pale were they all;
> Who cry'd—'La belle Dame sans Merci
>   Hath thee in thrall!'

Yet—why do I seek farther than Shakespeare's own writ?—

> Yon sometime famous princes, like thyself,
> Drawn by report, adventurous by desire,
> Tell thee, with speechless tongues and semblance pale,
> That without covering, save yon field of stars,
> Here they stand martyrs, slain in Cupid's wars;
> And with dead cheeks advise thee to desist
> For going on death's net. . . .

Though he have never read Sappho, how ignorant is he of this world's history who knows not that at any moment a woman may turn—nay, has turned—the whole of it upside down by turning a man inside out: as Herodotus, 'father of history,' starts—as the Book of Genesis itself starts—each with a woman at the bottom of the whole mischief!

What matters her name? Eve, or Helen of Troy, or La Belle Dame sans Merci, or Cleopatra? She is our common mother, and she is that which makes Troilus turn incredulous to Diomed and gasp 'Think, we had mothers.' And it is she who warns—

> If thou love me, take heed of loving me!

—as it is she who hears—

> Thou art the grave where buried love doth live,
> Hung with the trophies of my lovers gone.

She is the Universal in the particular. She is the woman who

cried on the wall of Troy, 'Yonder goeth one son of Atreus,
wide-ruling Agamemnon, goodly king and mighty spearsman:
and he was husband's brother to me,—bitch that I am.'
Saying this, she yet wears

> . . . the face that launched a thousand ships
> And burnt the topless towers of Ilium.

She is 'royal Egypt'; and withal

> but e'en a woman, and commanded
> By such poor passion as the maid that n. lks
> And does the meanest chares. . . .

She is the woman Pater saw in the dep*' of La Gioconda's
smile. 'She is older than the rocks ar ig which she sits;
like the vampire she has been dead many times, and learned
the secrets of the grave; and has been a diver in deep seas, and
keeps their fallen day about her; and trafficked for strange
webs with Eastern merchants . . . and all this has been to
her but as the sound of lyres and flutes . . .'   Yes, and 'her
feet go down to death; her steps take hold on hell; her ways
are moveable that thou canst not know them.'   Comely she
is as Jerusalem, terrible as an army with banners.   She is Eve,
she is Rahab, she is Helen; but most of all she is Cleopatra,
'my serpent of old Nile': for if a serpent betrayed the first
woman, into this one he has insinuated himself, and works,
and dies in the end of his own bite.

> Charmian.   O eastern star!
> Cleopatra.   Peace, peace!
> Dost thou not see my baby at my breast,
> That sucks the nurse asleep?

Let me here interpose a word which, though it will·at first
seem to you a mere *obiter dictum* and irrelevant, has some
bearing on our subject.

They have now done away with compulsory Greek at Oxford,
as well as here: and I have no great objection to that; because
my own instinct abhors every kind of compulsion, but specially
any compulsion practised on the human mind.   If we cannot
induce young Englishmen to want to know Greek for its own
sake, for the ineffable beauty of its literature and the inestimable

worth of its content: if we have taught it so stupidly, fenced about its wells and streams, its green walks and whispering recesses, with deserts of grammar and frontiers of syntax so arid that few any longer desire to learn Greek, pant to learn Greek—why then we have been, in this as in other things, fools in our generation, and Greek is too good for us. Nor have I, keeping a sense of humour amid the strokes and discouragements of life, any serious quarrel with those who, voting down compulsory Greek in the name of 'liberty,' use the very moment as an occasion, and this liberty as a cloak, to substitute another form of compulsion more to their mind. Almost always this happens. The Pilgrim Fathers braved the Atlantic in the name of Religious Liberty; and promptly planted, on the other side, a religious tyranny of their own, at least as harsh, at least as cruel, as the one they had left at home, and by several degrees uglier.

People say that, since our universities have ceased to make Greek compulsory, the study of Greek will die out of the land. I do not myself believe this. But, say that it is so. Then I warn my countrymen—and will cite two great examples for proof—that gracious as the old Greek spirit is, and, apt to be despised because it comes jingling no money in its pocket, using no art but intellectual persuasion, they had wiselier, if only for their skins' sake, keep it a friend than exile or cage it. For, embodying the free spirit of man, it is bound to break out sooner or later, to re-invade: and this guest, so genial when we entreat it kindly, is—like its most representative god, Phoebus Apollo—a deadly archer when it breaks prison and the great bow-string starts to twang:

> ὣς ἔφατ᾽ εὐχόμενος, τοῦ δ᾽ ἔκλυε Φοῖβος Ἀπόλλων,
> βῆ δὲ κατ᾽ Οὐλύμποιο καρήνων χωόμενος κῆρ . .

So spake he in prayer, and Phoebus Apollo heard him, and came down from the peaks of Olympus wroth at heart, bearing on his shoulders his bow and covered quiver. And the arrows rattled upon his shoulder in his wrath, as the god moved: and he descended like to night. Then he sat him aloof from the ships and let an arrow fly; and the silver bow clanged, and the sound was terror. First he shot down the mules, and the dogs as they ran: then he turned and, aiming his barb on men, he smote; and the pyres of the dead burned continually in multitudes.

You may think this a fancy: but I warn you, it is no fancy. Twice the imprisoned spirit has broken loose upon Europe. The first time it slew over half of Europe an enthroned religion; the second time it slew an idea of monarchy. Its first access made, through the Renascence, a Reformation: its second made the French Revolution. And it made the French Revolution very largely (as any one who cares may assure himself by reading the memoirs of that time) by a simple translation of a Greek book—Plutarch's *Lives*. Now Plutarch is not, as we estimate ancient authors, one of the first rank. A late Greek, you may call him, an ancient

> musical at close of day:

an easy garrulous tale-teller. That but weights the warning. If Plutarch, being such a man, could sway as he did the men who made the French Revolution, what will happen to our Church and State in the day when a Plato comes along to probe and test the foundations of both with his Socratic irony? Were this the last word I ever spoke, in my time here, I would bid any lover of compulsory 'Natural Science'—our new tyranny—to beware that day.

IV

Paulo minora canamus. Amyot translated Plutarch in his free way, and North translated Plutarch out of Amyot, and Shakespeare read North and (there is no doubt of it) was fascinated by this translation at a double remove. 'About the year 1600,' says Mr. Frank Harris truly, 'Shakespeare seems to have steeped himself in Plutarch. For the next five or six years, whenever he thinks of suicide, the Roman way of looking at it occurs to him.' This is equally true of Macbeth's

> Why should I play the Roman fool, and die
> On mine own sword?

*G 974

of Laertes'—

> I am more an antique Roman than a Dane,

of Antony's—

> The miserable change now at my end
> Lament nor sorrow at, but please your thoughts
> In feeding them with those my former fortunes
> Wherein I lived, the greatest prince o' the world,
> The noblest, and do now not basely die,
> Not cowardly put off my helmet to
> My countryman, a Roman by a Roman
> Valiantly vanquish'd.

Lastly, of Cleopatra's echo:

> Good sirs, take heart:
> We 'll bury him; and then, what 's brave, what 's noble,
> Let 's do it after the high Roman fashion,
> And make death proud to take us.

And I would have you note by the way, and even though it lead us off our track for a moment, that the future fate of the world—whether the West should conquer the East, or the East the West—did actually and historically hang on the embraces of Cleopatra and Antony, as delicately as it had once hung balanced on the issue of Marathon. I do not urge that we are, any of us, the better off because the cold priggish mind of Octavius prevailed over the splendid whoredoms of Egypt: though I think it probable. But it was—for the second time—a great crisis between Europe and Asia; and again, in the second bout, as in the first, Europe won. And I do not say that Shakespeare realized the full weight of the argument that rested on his 'triple pillar of the world, or that he realized what a stupendous roof came down with its fall. I only note here that Shakespeare, with superlative skill, sets all this fate of a world rocking in the embrace of one man and one woman, both fatally loving: and I note that this idea of the high Roman fashion steadily, in Cleopatra's own thought, conquers her whose magnificent wantonness has challenged Rome and the West. Her victory in death is her defeat. She dies *as a Roman*: the more a Roman because death will deliver her, sensitive, from the eyes of Rome which her own eyes have never seen. But she has imagination to see, to shudder from the very streets of it, and their populace, and the spectacle of her naked self dragged through this capital.

> Now, Iras, what think'st thou?
> Thou, an Egyptian puppet, shalt be shown
> In Rome, as well as I: mechanic slaves
> With greasy aprons, rules and hammers, shall
> Uplift us to the view: in their thick breaths,
> Rank of gross diet, shall we be enclouded
> And forced to drink their vapours.
>
> *Iras.*   The gods forbid!
> *Cleopatra.* Nay, 'tis most certain, Iras: saucy lictors
> Will catch at us like strumpets, and scald rhymers
> Ballad us out o' tune: the quick comedians
> Extemporally will stage us and present
> Our Alexandrian revels; Antony
> Shall be brought drunken forth, and I shall see
> Some squeaking Cleopatra boy my greatness
> I' the posture of a whore.
>
> *Iras.*   O the good gods!
> *Cleopatra.* Nay, that 's certain.
> *Iras.*   I 'll never see 't.

But that is what *had* to be seen. And the East—that is, Cleopatra—has, above its turbulent passions, very clear eyes.

V

It sees, and shudders from, the cold calculating politics of the West, to which it has to succumb. The calm policy of Octavia's self-sacrifice lies outside its understanding as outside its morals. To marry—to give yourself to a man so coldly, on a sense of honour, for any State! Octavia is, be it acknowledged, after her own lights an extremely noble woman: but are hers the true lights, after all?

Let us get back to Plutarch. He, good fellow, simply tells the story. That is his gift: he gives it to us, and there is an end. Cleopatra's beauty, says he, was not so passing, as unmatchable of other women. That is no explanation. Indeed

it would seem by every report collected that Cleopatra was by
no means an absolutely lovely woman—that is to say, a woman
absolutely lovely when, or if, seen (as the phrase is) 'in repose':
and perhaps one may dare to say, not cynically, that a certain
sort of woman may often look her best in a certain kind of
repose.   As Antony puts it, of his wife Fulvia, in this very
play—

> She 's good, being gone.

But even Plutarch makes us feel that, somehow, Cleopatra
was miraculously winning.   Here we come face to face with
Shakespeare's main difficulty, which he deliberately, in the
very first speech and before the play is two minutes old,
thrusts upon us:

> Look, where they come:
> Take but good note, and you shall see in him
> The triple pillar of the world transform'd
> Into a strumpet's fool.

Now I would have you note that Shakespeare, when he has a
dramatic miracle to work, never—I think I am accurate in
saying *never*—hides the difficulty from himself or from us.
At any rate he does not in this play.   Philo's words are
spoken in no rhetorical extravagance, but as the sad verdict
of a man of the world, a soldier, a friend who, without sentimentality, loves Antony passing well.   And we feel it to be
the just verdict: the *punctum indifferens* or standard of the
normal man which Shakespeare is ever careful to set in his
tragedies.   What Horatio is to the feverish cerebration of
Hamlet, Philo is in less than a dozen words to the passionate
excess of this play.   What Rome reports in scandalous gossip
he sorrowfully confirms: and when he has spoken it, we know
that it is so.   How then, of such a pair, shall Shakespeare
make a tragedy of high seriousness? how can he compel us to
follow either of such a pair—nay, but he will have us follow
both—sympathetically?   How can he bring them both to
end so nobly that, all contempt forgotten, even our pity is
purged into a sense of human majesty?   How from the orts

and ravages of this sensual banquet shall he dismiss us with 'an awed surmise' that man is, after all, master of circumstance and far greater than he knows?

Shakespeare had Plutarch: and Plutarch has the story: but with Shakespeare the story is never the secret. He will take, in his own large indolent way, any man's story and make it his property; nor does he care how the facts may seem to damn hero or heroine, so only that he have the handling of their motives. Many excellent persons profess themselves shocked by the scene where, close on the end, Cleopatra plays the cheat, handing Caesar a false schedule of her wealth, and is detected in the lie. Here is the narrative in Plutarch:

Then she suddenly altered her speech, and prayed him [Caesar] to pardon her, as though she were affrayed to die and desirous to live.

At length, she gave him a brief and memorial of all the ready money and treasure she had. But by chance there stood Seleucus by, one of her treasurers, who to seem a good servant, came straight to Caesar, to disprove Cleopatra, that she had not set in all, but kept many things back of purpose. Cleopatra was in such a rage with him that she flew upon him, and took him by the hair of the head, and boxed him well-favouredly.

Shakespeare found this in Plutarch and used it, because it is truth; nor mere truth of fact, but truth of that universal quality which (as Aristotle noted) makes Poetry a more philosophical thing than History. Cleopatra did not tell that falsehood by chance. She told it naturally, because she was courtesan in grain: born a liar and born also royal Egypt, she cannot sentimentalize one half of her character away at the end, to catch our tears. We must accept her, without paltering, for the naked, conscienceless, absolute, royal she-animal that she is. Cover the courtesan in mistaken charity, and by so much you hide out of sight the secret of her majesty—with her no secret at all, for she is regnant, rather, by virtue of being shameless.

With such a woman our excellent Plutarch can make no weather at all. 'Now her beauty,' he reports, 'was not so passing, as unmatchable of other women, nor yet such, as upon present view did enamour men with her; but so sweet was her company and conversation, that a man could not possibly but be taken. And besides her beauty, the good grace she had to talk and discourse, her courteous nature that tempered her words and deeds, was a spur that pricked to the quick. Furthermore, besides all these, her voice and words were marvellous pleasant: for her tongue was an instrument of music to divers sports and pastimes, the which she easily turned to any language that pleased her,' etc. All of which is all very well, but we feel (do we not?) that Plutarch might continue in this strain for twenty years without explaining Cleopatra or her charm to us. It is all description, and of a being we know by instinct to be indescribable.

Shakespeare can get plenty of description out of Plutarch to help the impression of Cleopatra's magnificent luxury. I started by quoting the famous description of her barge upon Cydnus. But all that is *description*: of externals, accessories; helpful but quite undramatic. Getting nearer to the woman, he can make an observer tell us, and truly, that

> Age cannot wither her, nor custom stale
> Her infinite variety: other women cloy
> The appetites they feed, but she makes hungry
> Where most she satisfies.

That is superbly said: we turn back to it as to a last word. But, still, it is somebody's description. It is not the flashing, the revealing, word, that can only, in a drama, be spoken by the person, spoken here by Cleopatra herself.

The witch lives in the very words she first utters. Grand doting was never more subtly played with:

Cleopatra. If it be love indeed, tell me how much.
Antony.   There's beggary in the love that can be reckon'd.
Cleopatra. I'll set a bourn how far to be beloved.
Antony.   Then must thou needs find out new heaven, new earth.

Enter an Attendant.

Attendant. News, my good lord, from Rome.

Antony.   Grates me: the sum.
Cleopatra. Nay, hear them, Antony:
          Fulvia perchance is angry; or, who knows
          If the scarce-bearded Caesar have not sent
          His powerful mandate to you, 'Do this, or this;
          Take in that kingdom, and enfranchise that;
          Perform 't, or else we damn thee.'
Antony.   How, my love?
Cleopatra. Perchance! nay, and most like:
          You must not stay here longer, your dismission
          Is come from Caesar; therefore hear it, Antony.
          Where 's Fulvia's process? Caesar's I would say? both?
          Call in the messengers.   As I am Egypt's queen,
          Thou blushest, Antony, and that blood of thine
          Is Caesar's homager: else so thy cheek pays shame
          When shrill-tongued Fulvia scolds.   The messengers!
Antony.   Let Rome in Tiber melt, and the wide arch
          Of the ranged empire fall!   Here is my space.
          Kingdoms are clay: our dungy earth alike
          Feeds beast as man: the nobleness of life
          Is to do thus; when such a mutual pair
          And such a twain can do 't.

There you have the lists set, and the play not forty lines gone!
Into those forty lines is already compressed the issue as the world
sees it, critical but well-wishing, through the eyes of Philo:
the issue as Antony sees it:

                    Here is my space.
          Kingdoms are clay . . .

and the hints of half-a-dozen coils through which, entangled
in jealousies, Cleopatra's mind is working.

                              VI

   I shall say nothing of the minor characters of the play save
this—that the true normal, or *punctum indifferens*—which you
always find somewhere in any tragedy of Shakespeare's—is to
be sought, not in Octavius, but in some spectator such as
Philo or even the loose-moralled Enobarbus.   Octavius Caesar
represents rather the cool enemy, blameless, priggish, who, as

this world is ordered, inevitably overthrows Armida's palace
—but is none the more lovable for the feat. His character
has already been given us, ineffaceably, in a single line of
Julius Caesar. He and Antony dispute which is to command
the right, and which the left, of the army before Philippi.
'Why,' demands Antony, 'why do you cross me in this exigent?'
To which Octavius responds with that serene stupidity only
granted to a young egoist that he may prevail:

> I do not cross you: but I will do so.

The whole point of Octavius—and of Octavia (upon whom
Gervinus, recognizing the abstract German housewife in a
wilderness of Latins, expends so many tears)—is that they are
ministers of fate precisely because incapable of understanding
what it is all *about*. Precisely because he has not the ghost of
a notion of any one's being such a fool as to lose the world
for love, we see this politician predestined to win. Nor—the
beauty of it!—will he ever divine the sting in Cleopatra's word
to the asp, as she applies it to her breast—

> O, couldst thou speak,
> That I might hear thee call great Caesar ass
> Unpolicied!

It is not only, of course, by direct representation of Cleopatra
in her gusts of passion — now real, now simulated — that
Shakespeare weaves the spell. The talk exchanged among
Iras, Charmian, Alexas and the Soothsayer is as deft and witty
an introduction to Venusberg as ever playwright could invent:
and, after that, 'Let Rome in Tiber melt!' 'Melt Egypt into
Nile!'

Gervinus writes out a long laboured estimate of Antony's
character. It is all idle; because, the lists being those of
passion, all we want is, of Antony that he should be generous
and lusty and great; all we want of Cleopatra is that she shall
be subtle and lustful and great: both lustful, both unmistakably
great. With all his detailed portraiture of 'my serpent of old
Nile' Shakespeare triumphs in this play, the closer you examine

it, by a very sublime simplicity: he triumphs by making this
pair royal *because* elemental; *because* they obey impulses
greater even than Rome, though it stretch from Parthia to
Cape Misenum. I do not deny that Shakespeare has spent
pains in making Mark Antony lovable to us, so that Dryden
and every playwright who makes him a soft voluptuary must
necessarily fail. But truly this is a woman's play, in which the
man has to be noble in order that the woman may win a high
triumph and perish in it. I would even call it the paradox of
Antony and Cleopatra that it at once is the most wayward of
Shakespeare's tragedies, dependent from scene to scene on the
will of a wanton, and withal one of the most heavily charged
with fate and the expectancy of fate. Who can forget the
hushed talk of the guards and the low rumbling of earth under-
foot that preludes the arming of Antony, when Cleopatra
misarrays him?

Antony.   Eros! mine armour, Eros!
Cleopatra.   Sleep a little.
Antony.   No, my chuck.   Eros, come; mine armour, Eros!

                    Enter Eros *with armour.*

            Come, good fellow, put mine iron on:
            If fortune be not ours to-day, it is
            Because we brave her: come.
Cleopatra.   Nay, I 'll help too.
            What 's this for?
Antony.   Ah, let be, let be! thou art
            The armourer of my heart: false, false; this, this . . .

and if any object that the supernatural prelude to this is out
of place in tragedy, I am content to answer him with a word
from an early page of Plutarch. 'There be some,' says Plutarch, 'who think these things to be but fables and tales devised
of pleasure. But methinks, for all that, they are not to be
rejected or discredited, if we will consider Fortune's strange
effects upon times, and of the greatness also of the Roman
empire; which had never achieved to her present possessed
power and authority if the gods had not from the beginning

been workers of the same, and if there had not also been some strange cause and wonderful foundation.'

But I marvel in this play most of all, and whenever I read it, at the incomparable life-likeness of Cleopatra, which follows her through every bewildering trick and turn, caprice or gust of passion, equally when she queens it, or fools it, modulates her voice to true or to false passion, or beats her servants and curses like a drab—and she can do all within any given two minutes. It is not lime-lantern that follows Cleopatra about the stage: she carries everywhere with her the light—her own light—of a convincing if almost blinding realism. I am not, as you know, over fond of those critics who read Mary Fitton, or some other 'dark lady' into everything Shakespeare wrote: but I must make them the handsome admission that if Shakespeare did not take some actual particular woman for his Cleopatra, I am clean at a loss to imagine how he created this wonder.

It surprises me—to take up a small point—that the most insistent of these critics, Mr. Frank Harris, should boggle, all of a sudden, over Cleopatra's

> Here 's sport indeed!

when she and her women are drawing Antony aloft. This, says Mr. Harris,

seems to me a terrible fault, an inexcusable lapse of taste. I should like to think it a misprint, or a misreading; but it is unfortunately like Shakespeare in a certain mood, possible to him, here as elsewhere.

Yes, yes, Mr. Harris! It is shockingly bad taste. But it seems to me mighty fine hysteria.

Let me read the whole passage as leading up to a word upon which I shall conclude because it seems to me the *last* word upon this play.

> *Enter, below,* Antony, *borne by the* Guard.

Cleopatra.   O sun,
>   Burn the great sphere thou movest in! darkling stand
>   The varying shore o' the world. O Antony,
>   Antony, Antony! Help, Charmian, help, Iras, help;
>   Help, friends below; let 's draw him hither.

Antony.   Peace!
Not Caesar's valour hath o'erthrown Antony,
But Antony's hath triumph'd on itself.

Cleopatra. So it should be, that none but Antony
Should conquer Antony; but woe 'tis so!

Antony. I am dying, Egypt, dying; only
I here importune death awhile, until
Of many thousand kisses the poor last
I lay upon thy lips.

Cleopatra.   I dare not, dear,
Dear my lord, pardon, I dare not,
Lest I be taken: not the imperious show
Of the full-fortuned Caesar ever shall
Be brooch'd with me; if knife, drugs, serpents, have
Edge, sting, or operation, I am safe:
Your wife Octavia, with her modest eyes
And still conclusion, shall acquire no honour
Demuring upon me.   But come, come, Antony,—
Help me, my women,—we must draw thee up;
Assist, good friends.

Antony.   O, quick, or I am gone.

Cleopatra. Here 's sport indeed!   How heavy weighs my lord!
Our strength is all gone into heaviness;
That makes the weight.   Had I great Juno's power,
The strong-wing'd Mercury should fetch thee up
And set thee by Jove's side.   Yet come a little—
Wishers were ever fools—O, come, come, come;
                    [*They heave Antony aloft to Cleopatra.*
And welcome, welcome! die where thou hast lived:
Quicken with kissing: had my lips that power,
Thus would I wear them out.

All.   A heavy sight!

Antony. I am dying, Egypt, dying:
Give me some wine, and let me speak a little.

Cleopatra. No, let me speak, and let me rail so high,
That the false housewife Fortune break her wheel,
Provoked by my offence.

Antony.   One word, sweet queen:
Of Caesar seek your honour, with your safety.   O!

Cleopatra. They do not go together.

Antony.   Gentle, hear me:
None about Caesar trust but Proculeius.

Cleopatra. My resolution and my hands I 'll trust;
None about Caesar.

Antony. The miserable change now at my end

Lament nor sorrow at, but please your thoughts
In feeding them with those my former fortunes
Wherein I lived, the greatest prince o' the world,
The noblest, and do now not basely die,
Not cowardly put off my helmet to
My countryman, a Roman by a Roman
Valiantly vanquish'd.   Now my spirit is going;
I can no more.

Cleopatra.   Noblest of men, woo't die?
Hast thou no care of me? shall I abide
In this dull world, which in thy absence is
No better than a sty?   O, see, my women,   [*Antony dies.*
The crown o' the earth doth melt.   My lord!
O, wither'd is the garland of the war,
The soldier's pole is fall'n: young boys and girls
Are level now with men; the odds is gone,
And there is nothing left remarkable
Beneath the visiting moon.   [*Faints.*

Charmian.   O, quietness, lady!
Iras.   She 's dead too, our sovereign.
Charmian.   Lady!
Iras.   Madam!
Charmian. O madam, madam, madam!
Iras.   Royal Egypt,
      Empress!
Charmian.   Peace, peace, Iras!
Cleopatra. No more, but e'en a woman, and commanded
By such poor passion as the maid that milks
And does the meanest chares.   It were for me
To throw my sceptre at the injurious gods,
To tell them that this world did equal theirs
Till they had stol'n our jewel.   All 's but naught;
Patience is sottish, and impatience does
Become a dog that 's mad: then is it sin
To rush into the secret house of death,
Ere death dare come to us?   How do you, women?
What, what! good cheer!   Why, how now, Charmian!
My noble girls!   Ah, women, women, look,
Our lamp is spent, it 's out!   Good sirs, take heart:
We 'll bury him; and then, what 's brave, what 's noble,
Let 's do it after the high Roman fashion,
And make death proud to take us.

VII

After that will you refuse to consent with me that the last word upon this play should be of its greatness? All these people, whatever of righteousness they lack, are great. They have the very aura of greatness.

And they are great, of course, not in their dealing with affairs, with the destinies of Rome or of Egypt—for it is by their neglect or misprision or mishandling of these that they come to misfortune and allow meaner men, calculators, to rise by their downfall: but great as the gods are great, high-heartedly, carelessly.   Note how finely, when the whole stake has been thrown and lost, they sit down to their last earthly banquet. They seem in their passion to stand remote above circumstance. They are indifferent to consistency. Says Enobarbus, when Antony will leave for Rome:

Under a compelling occasion let women die: it were pity to cast them away for nothing; though, between them and a great cause, they should be esteemed nothing.   Cleopatra, catching but the least noise of this, dies instantly; I have seen her die twenty times upon far poorer moment. . . .

Yet she plays as largely with real death.   She

hath pursued conclusions infinite
Of easy ways to die.

—and the way she finally chooses is most regal. Like the gods too, these people are exempt of shame: as absolutely above it as Zeus, father of gods and men, who could be ridiculous enough in his amours and yet, when all is said, remains a very grand gentleman.   They are heroic souls in this disorderly house of Alexandria—even to pretty mischievous Charmian. Hear her, as she closes Cleopatra's eyes and stands up herself, as the Guard bursts in, to take the stroke. Hear her and mark her last word:

Charmian.   So, fare thee well.
Now boast thee, death, in thy possession lies
A lass unparallel'd. Downy windows, close;

And golden Phoebus never be beheld
Of eyes again so royal!   Your crown's awry;
I 'll mend it, and then play.

Enter the Guard, *rushing in.*

First Guard.   Where is the queen?
Charmian.   Speak softly, wake her not.
First Guard.   Caesar hath sent—
Charmian.   Too slow a messenger.
                                   [*Applies an asp.*
O, come apace, dispatch: I partly feel thee.
First Guard.   Approach, ho!   All 's not well: Caesar 's beguiled.
Second Guard. There 's Dolabella sent from Caesar; call him.
First Guard.   What work is here!   Charmian, is this well done?
Charmian.   It is well done, and fitting for a princess
                      Descended of so many royal kings.
                      Ah, soldier!   [*Dies.*

MILTON

I

WHAT is the word that comes uppermost when we think of Milton, the man and his work together? Suppose that, for a start, I passed around a number of slips of paper, inviting each of you to write down the one epithet which seemed to him most characteristic, most compendious, and at the same time most nearly expressive. How would the votes go?

Well, I dare say 'sublime' would carry the day: either that or 'harmonious' (or some other word expressive of majestic verbal music). A few might hit on 'prophetic.' All these are good, and I shall recur to them. But I hope that one or two papers, being opened, would agree with mine and reveal the word '*solitary*.'

I believe that *loneliness*, if neither uppermost nor least impressive, must be the common denominator with all of us in our conceptions of Milton and of the poetry in which he reflects himself. What is Wordsworth's first word of him?

> Thy soul was like a Star, and dwelt apart. . . .

We deceive ourselves, even if, acknowledging this, we trace it to our pity for his later blindness and exile. These throw their shadows back on his earlier work: but that earlier work dwells somehow in its own lonely shadow and throws it forward:

> Or let my Lamp at midnight hour
> Be seen in som high lonely Towr,
> Where I may oft out-watch the *Bear*,
> With thrice great *Hermes*, or unsphear
> The spirit of *Plato* to unfold
> What Worlds, or what vast Regions hold
> The immortal mind that hath forsook
> Her mansion in this fleshly nook.

Now I ask you, still for a start upon our subject, to move your thought onward to the time when, blindness having overtaken

him, he begins upon *Paradise Lost*.　What is he about to essay?
He tells us.　It is an

> adventurous Song
> That with no middle flight intends to soar
> Above the *Aonian* Mount, while it pursues
> Things unattempted yet in Prose or Rhime.

His blindness apart, how can we separate sublimity from
solitariness here?　As an eagle, flying towards the sun above
all other birds, is alone, so a poet must be determined to be
solitary as part of his intention to soar above the Helicon of
others and to pursue in an upper aether

> Things unattempted yet in Prose or Rhime.

Let us move on to the passage where, almost alone in this great
impersonal epic, the personal man breaks forth—breaks out
of conscious physical blindness and, on the very strength of its
weakness, challenges a light unendurable by happier normal
eyes.　I mean of course the famous Invocation to Light which
opens the Third Book of *Paradise Lost*.　Every one knows it:
many of you, I doubt not, have it by heart: the most of you, I
dare say, have felt not only its intrinsic beauty, but its exquisite
appropriateness, coming just where it does.　Throughout the
first two Books the poet has been trafficking with his theme
through the mirk of Hell, and thereafter through the profounder dark of Chaos and Night, out of which, heartened by
promise, Satan—the apostate Angel—Lucifer

> Springs upward, like a pyramid of fire,

aloft through glimmering dawn, dubious twilight, into the
Upper Universe all radiant with light streaming from the battlements of Heaven.　As the poet and his readers follow him
aloft and front it too, 'it is but natural,' says Masson, they
should 'feel the novelty of the blaze and be delayed by the
strange sensation.'

　　I cannot offer to read that passage to you as it should be
read.　I shall merely try to repeat it for my purpose; indicating
by pauses (if I can) how chosen qualities—sublimity, majesty,

music, prophecy—nay, physical blindness itself —are one by
one subsumed into this great dignity of solitude.

> Hail, holy light, ofspring of Heav'n first-born!
> Or of th' Eternal Coeternal beam
> May I express thee unblam'd?   Since God is light,
> And never but in unapproachèd light
> Dwelt from Eternitie, dwelt then in thee,
> Bright effluence of bright essence increate!
> Or hear'st thou rather pure Ethereal stream,
> Whose Fountain who shall tell? before the Sun,
> Before the Heavens thou wert, and at the voice
> Of God as with a Mantle didst invest
> The rising world of waters dark and deep
> Won from the void and formless infinite.
>
> Thee I re-visit now with bolder wing,
> Escapt the *Stygian* Pool, though long detain'd
> In that obscure sojourn, while in my flight
> Through utter and through middle darkness borne
> With other notes then to th' *Orphean* Lyre
> I sung of *Chaos* and *Eternal Night*,
> Taught by the heav'nly Muse to venture down
> The dark descent and up to reascend,
> Though hard and rare: thee I revisit safe,
> And feel thy sovran vital Lamp; but thou
> Revisit'st not these eyes, that rowle in vain
> To find thy piercing ray, and find no dawn;
> So thick a drop serene hath quencht thir Orbs,
> Or dim suffusion veild.
>   Yet not the more
> Cease I to wander where the Muses haunt
> Cleer Spring, or shadie Grove, or sunnie Hill,
> Smit with the love of sacred song; but chief
> Thee *Sion*, and the flowrie Brooks beneath
> That wash thy hallowd feet, and warbling flow,
> Nightly I visit: nor sometimes forget
> Those other two equal'd with me in Fate.
> So were I equal'd with them in renown,
> Blind *Thamyris* and blind *Maeonides*,
> And *Tiresias* and *Phineus* Prophets old;
> Then feed on thoughts, that voluntarie move
> Harmonious numbers; as the wakeful Bird
> Sings darkling, and in shadiest Covert hid
> Tunes her nocturnal Note.

                    Thus with the Year
Seasons return, but not to me returns
Day, or the sweet approach of Ev'n or Morn,
Or sight of vernal bloom, or Summers Rose,
Or flocks, or herds, or human face divine;
But cloud in stead, and ever-during dark
Surrounds me, from the chearful waies of men
Cut off, and for the Book of knowledg fair
Presented with a Universal blanc
Of Nature's works to mee expung'd and ras'd,
And wisdome at one entrance quite shut out.

So much the rather thou Celestial light
Shine inward, and the mind through all her powers
Irradiate, there plant eyes, all mist from thence
Purge and disperse, that I may see and tell
Of things invisible to mortal sight.

The main word, you perceive, is of blindness; of blindness
groping, aching, back toward light remembered. But consider how melody—melody of Sion's brooks, melody of the
hidden 'darkling bird'—melts into it; consider how prophecy,
through Tiresias and Phineus, is compelled into it: consider
how all these at the end compressed back upon the inner soul,
there find the light to match the divine light, sublimity to
challenge sublimity. It is only in solitude or darkness that the
brightest light can be read, as it is only through smoked spec-
tacles that our eyes can endure the extreme flames of astronomy.
Hear, for illustration, Shelley's word on the apprehensive genius
of Coleridge, palsied between vision and fleshly weakness—

        You will see Coleridge—he who sits obscure
        In the exceeding lustre and the pure
        Intense irradiation of a mind,
        Which, with its own internal lightning blind,
        Flags wearily through darkness and despair—
        A cloud-encircled meteor of the air,
        A hooded eagle among blinking owls

—the difference, of course, between Milton and Coleridge
being that the one conquered and put forth his strength, that
the other failed of will, and sank. But the moral of both is
Blanco White's famous sonnet—that only the hooded eye

can speculate on intensest light, as only when dark draws in
upon him can man even surmise the stars.

> Mysterious Night! when our first parent knew
>   Thee from report divine, and heard thy name,
>   Did he not tremble for this lovely frame,
> This glorious canopy of light and blue?
> Yet 'neath a curtain of translucent dew,
>   Bathed in the rays of the great setting flame,
>   Hesperus with the host of heaven came,
> And lo! Creation widened in man's view.
>
> Who could have thought such darkness lay concealed
>   Within thy beams, O Sun! or who could find,
> Whilst flow'r and leaf, and insect stood revealed,
>   That to such countless orbs thou mad'st us blind!
> Why do we then shun Death with anxious strife?
> If Light can thus deceive, wherefore not Life?

II

When I was of your age, Gentlemen—an undergraduate at
the sister University—I sat sometimes in a Lecture Theatre
less comfortable (as I remember) than this, but in many respects
so similar that the recollection of it has daunted me, more than
once or twice, on entering by the door yonder.   For I came to
hear, and I sat and listened to, the very voice of a man who
might (I say it with conviction) not presumptuously have compared himself with Milton, as Milton compared himself with
blind Maeonides—

> equal'd with me in Fate,
> So were I equal'd with [him] in renown.

Fate, even in these few years, has so juggled with the fame of
John Ruskin that the teachings for which he was then worshipped but a little this side of idolatry seem forgotten as a
flame up a chimney, whereas those which his contemporaries
merely derided, accounting him a crank, astray and wandering
from his mission—the gospel he preached in *Unto This Last*,
for instance—burn on to-day as a fire that slowly eats into the
core of a great log on the hearth.   After such vicissitudes,
such oscillation of valuing in so brief a while, no one can say

precisely where men's judgment of John Ruskin will finally set up its rest. And prose is prose: poetry is poetry. For that reason, if for no other, John Ruskin will never be estimated alongside of John Milton. But I avow to you that in many ways he was even such a man; that essentially he was a comparable man; and that fate (if not renown) so nearly equalled the two as to invite, and excuse, a brief comparison.

For a comparison, then, somewhat in the manner of Plutarch:

John Ruskin was born in London—at 54, Hunter Street, Brunswick Square—on February 8th, 1819; his father being a well-to-do wine-merchant of Scottish descent, by his own exertions well-educated, valuing literature and the arts. This worthy man had married a cousin somewhat older than himself and of his own straitish evangelical sect; and this woman, being with child, vowed the vow of Hannah—'Lord . . . if thou wilt . . . remember me, and not forget thine handmaid, but wilt give unto thine handmaid a man child, then I will give him unto the Lord all the days of his life.' So a man child was born to her, and (the appetite growing by what it feeds on) in her exaltation she hoped that he would live to be a bishop.

This prayer was not granted, or not literally: although the child, denied childish toys, rekindled the hope from time to time by mounting a chair and preaching sermons to his parents across the back of it. Very soon there supervened a tendency to compose verses. The parents shifted their hopes: he might, *faute de mieux*, live to be a great poet. They whipped him sometimes, just as often as they thought it good for him: to the child it appeared a puzzle that they should keep a good table (which they could well afford) and fare richly, while inflicting so much self-denial upon him. It was not greed in him, but a genuine intellectual puzzle. He loved them devotedly: he failed in no filial duty throughout his life, and was nursing his mother when she died at the age of ninety.

How often, looking around, is one moved to cry out upon parents, 'God! why, after feeding their children and making them happy, cannot they leave them alone!' But the Ruskins with aching care were all the while protecting and preparing

this sacrificial urchin.   They were 'giving' him—their only one
—and making him meet to be given.   Their worldly prosperity
increasing, they moved out to Herne Hill, where he played
alone in a fine garden, and was (as the phrase goes) privately
educated.   You may read all the sad story in *Praeterita*.   The
father's culture inclining to a connoisseurship of drawings in
water colour, the child is set to acquire this art under tuition of
Copley Fielding and Harding: 'to wash colours smoothly in
successive tints, to shade cobalt through pink madder into
yellow ochre for skies,' etc.   He is taken for an annual holiday
with his Papa and Mamma, at first about Great Britain on the
wine-selling business, afterwards abroad.   He goes through
the callow love-fever incident to sheltered youth.   He is at
length launched upon Christ Church, Oxford, and from Oxford
upon the 'grand tour' of Italy.   The trouble is, that this dedicated son, instead of being the mere clod or the vain prig on
which his parents' practice would have worked little harm one
way or another, turns out to be a real prophet of genius.   He
comes back—eager to accomplish, and sensitive—to wrestle
with the world of which he sees the evil, without having learnt
—without having even surmised—that understanding which
many an ordinary boy pricks up by genial converse with his
father's stablemen.   He came home to face and fight a real
world in which he had to be tortured and beaten, praised for
that which he accounted of no worth, and, as soon as his
argument came to seriousness, laughed at by every soul he
strove to save.   So, having spent a large patrimony in poor
service of his fellows, he lingered out his last days in a life's
defeat, and died, most lonely, in the chair in which he had
stood to delight his parents with childish sermons.   This was
in 1900: but the real agony of his life had been passed some
years before I heard him.   It had actually ended some eleven
or twelve years before, in 1878; when on the verge of a serious
mental sickness, having to write a note on an exhibition of
Turner's in Bond Street, the desolate man penned this:

Oh, that someone had told me, in my youth, when all my heart
seemed to be set on these colours and clouds, that appear for a little

while and then vanish away, how little my love of them would serve me, when the silence of lawn and wood in the dews of morning should be completed; and all my thoughts should be of those whom, by neither, I was to meet more!

Now will you mark the parallel and forgive the length to which I have drawn the lower line?

John Milton, like Ruskin, was a Londoner and very much of a Londoner: born well within sound of Bow Bells and almost beneath the shadow of the belfry—the date, December 9th, 1608. His father, too, like John Ruskin's, was

> a citizen
> Of credit and renown,

doing prosperously as a scrivener at the sign of the Spread Eagle in Bread Street, Cheapside, and dwelling comfortably above and behind his place of business. (A scrivener's business, one may explain, consisted partly in the drawing up of wills, marriage settlements, deeds, and the like, partly—and, one suspects, more profitably—in arranging loans upon mortgage.)

John Milton the father had lofty designs for John Milton the son, even as John Ruskin the father had lofty designs for John Ruskin the son. 'From the first'—to quote Masson—'there is proof that his heart is bound up in his son John, and that he had conceived the highest expectations of what that son would turn out to be. A portrait of the poet, as a sweet, serious round-headed boy at the age of ten'—I suppose 'round-headed' here to be purely descriptive and void of any proleptic intention—'still exists, which his father caused to be done by the foreign painter then most in fashion, and which hung on the wall of one of the rooms in the house in Bread Street. Both father and mother doted on the boy and were proud of his promise.' They planned him for Holy Orders and to become a bishop.

John Milton anticipated John Ruskin again in being given a good sober Scottish tutor; from whose supervision he passed to St. Paul's School, then located hard by Bread Street. From St. Paul's, at sixteen, he came up here, to Christ's College, and here he abode seven years.

There was no hurry in the preparation of John Milton. It is uncertain at what date he disappointed his parents by announcing that he would have none of Holy Orders. The decision, whenever taken, showed wisdom: for those were the days of Archbishop Laud; and under Laud's church-rule the temper of Milton, never docile, could have found no place. But although he will have no eye on any episcopate,[1] he is by this time as sure as ever his parents had been, and even surer, that a high destiny awaits him. He is shaping himself to it. He intends, in fine, to be a great Poet. For what has Ben Jonson said?—'Every beggarly Corporation affoords the State a Mayor, or two Bailiffs, yearly: but'—quoting Petronius— '*Solus Rex aut Poeta non quotannis nascitur*'—'the King and the Poet, these two, cannot be raised by annual husbandry.' And what has Tasso said, that proud bard? '*Non c' è in mondo chi merita nome di creatore, se non Iddio ed il Poeta*'— 'in this Universe is no one deserving the name Creator save God himself and the Poet.'

So, at twenty-three, our poet goes down from Cambridge, admired by all and nicknamed *The Lady* 'on account of his fair complexion, feminine and graceful appearance, and a certain haughty delicacy in his tastes and morals'; carrying great expectations, but not to be hurried towards realizing them, albeit this fine deliberation be attended by some private misgivings. We may read it all confessed, the misgivings together with the proud conscious claim, in the sonnet he wrote on leaving Cambridge:

> How soon hath Time, the subtle thief of youth,
>   Stoln on his wing my three-and-twentith year!
>   My hasting dayes flie on with full career,
> But my late spring no bud or blossom shew'th.
> Perhaps my semblance might deceive the truth
>   That I to manhood am arriv'd so near;
>   And inward ripenes doth much less appear,
> That som more timely-happy spirits indu'th.

---

[1] Save a dour one. Let us remind ourselves of *Lycidas* and its angry derangement of metaphors:

> Blind mouthes! that scarce themselves know how to hold
> A Sheep-hook. . . .

> Yet, be it less or more, or soon or slow,
>> It shall be still in strictest measure eev'n
>> To that same lot, however mean, or high,
> Toward which Time leads me, and the will of Heav'n.
>> All is, if I have grace to use it so,
>> As ever in my great task Master's eye.

His father, having retired from London and business (in or about 1632, in his seventieth year), had taken a country house at Horton in Buckinghamshire. Thither our doubly dedicated young man withdrew, and there, for another five years and eight months (July 1632—April 1638), he went on strictly meditating the apparently thankless Muse. This was all very well; but even a destined Isaiah has to start in practice sooner or later. He was, in fact, beginning to write gloriously: but to cold appearance, he was nearing his thirtieth year and, so far, had not done a hand's turn of verifiable work. His Cambridge friends began to grow impatient for some fulfilment of the promise on which they had pinned belief; and so, and yet more naturally, did the father. We know that even before leaving Cambridge, Milton had written the Ode *On the Morning of Christ's Nativity*, and that to these meditative years belong *L'Allegro, Il Penseroso, At a Solemn Music, Comus, Lycidas*—things imperishable. But these were not published—although *Comus* had been acted, winning great favour—and he aspired far beyond these. Meanwhile he continued 'wholly intent, through a period of absolute leisure, on a steady perusal of the Greek and Latin writers, but still so that occasionally I exchanged the country for the city, either for the purpose of buying books or for that of learning anything new in Mathematics or in Music, in which I then took delight.' These, you will agree, were innocent purposes to take a young man of his age up to London. But I cannot doubt that the account is strictly truthful.

If you consider the lines in *L'Allegro*:

> Towred Cities please us then,
> And the busie humm of men,
> Where throngs of Knights and Barons bold
> In weeds of Peace high triumphs hold,

> With store of Ladies, whose bright eyes
> Rain influence, and judge the prize
> Of Wit, or Arms. . . .

I think you will almost certainly adjudge this to be second-hand experience derived from books; remoter, even, than the banquet which in *Paradise Regained* Satan spread for Christ, obviously combining recollections of Petronius with personal reminiscences of a Lord Mayor's feast in London Guildhall.

I make no doubt that you will find the true Milton rather in the youth acquainted with our Chapel of King's College and aspiring in *Il Penseroso*:

> But let my due feet never fail
> To walk the studious Cloysters pale,
> And love the high embowèd Roof
> With antick Pillars massy proof,
> And storied Windows richly dight,
> Casting a dimm religious light.
> There let the pealing Organ blow
> To the full voic'd Quire below,
> In Service high and Anthems cleer
> As may, with sweetnes, through mine ear
> Dissolve me into extasies
> And bring all Heav'n before mine eyes. . . .

Nor again (I suggest) is it wayward criticism that when in *L'Allegro* Milton bids us

> to the well-trod stage anon,
> If *Jonson's* learnèd sock be on,
> Or sweetest *Shakespear*, fancies childe,
> Warble his native Wood-notes wilde.

—the invitation is a reader's rather than a playgoer's. Descriptive as this 'warbling,' these 'native wood-notes,' may be of *A Midsummer-Night's Dream* or of *As You Like It*, read and remurmured and tasted over in the library—where, we are told, he loved to sit somewhat aslant in an elbow chair with a leg thrown over one of its arms—they seem to me as little reminiscent of the actual playhouse as those correspondent ones in *Il Penseroso*, wherein reading, and no more than reading, is plainly intended.

> Som time let Gorgeous Tragedy
> In scepter'd Pall com sweeping by,

Presenting *Thebs*, or *Pelops* line,
Or the tale of *Troy* divine;
Or what (though rare) of later age
Ennobled hath the Buskind Stage.

I ask you to consider well that Milton's father allowed him perfect freedom on these London visits—as indeed, if he had not, the youth would have claimed it for himself. In Mr. Birrell's good phrase 'Milton was always determined, whatever else he was or might become, to be his own man.' Over a chastity sensitive as a girl's he had buckled the harness of a strong purpose, and so was doubly proof. But I want you to understand that this was the same John Milton who wrote later, in *Areopagitica*:

He that can apprehend and consider vice with all her baits and seeming pleasures, and yet abstain, and yet distinguish, and yet prefer that which is truly better, he is the true wayfaring Christian. I cannot praise a fugitive and cloistered virtue, unexercised and unbreathed, that never sallies out and seeks her adversary, but slinks out of the race, where that immortal garland is to be run for, not without dust and heat. Assuredly we bring not innocence into the world, we bring impurity much rather; that which purifies us is trial, and trial is by what is contrary. That virtue therefore which is but a youngling in the contemplation of evil, and knows not the utmost that vice promises to her followers, and rejects it, is but a blank virtue, not a pure.

Forgive me that I dwell so much on this self-dedicated youth; and bear with me while I continue (as I shall) to lay stress on Milton's isolation: for indeed, if you will wait, I am piling up material against my later argument. But I have elected, having a general theory to unfold later, to choose a subject of which every personal detail may speciously tell against me.

Let us have it, all fair and square. No man can charge idleness upon this youth who in these years wrote *L'Allegro*, *Il Penseroso*, *Arcades*, *Comus*, *Lycidas*, and the rest. His noble sonnet on *Shakespeare*:

What needs my *Shakespear* for his honour'd Bones . . .

had appeared anonymously in the second or 1632 edition of the Shakespeare Folio as a commendatory verse. His *Comus* had been performed and had won deserved applause on the greensward by Ludlow Castle. *Lycidas* had seen print in 1638, signed 'J. M.' at the end of a collection of obituary poems contributed by thirty-two friends and published by the Cambridge University Press in memory of Edward King. But the most of his poems remained in manuscript: and we have to lay our account with the cold fact that up to the age of thirty-two (and, it may be, later) Milton had not earned a penny for himself.

We need not make very much of this: as we need not, when we come to it, waste our emotion over the more notorious fact that *Paradise Lost* brought just ten pounds to its author during his lifetime, and eight additional pounds to his widow, who parted with the copyright. *Et sunt commercia coeli!* Tears over that will do more credit to our hearts than to our historical sense: for authors did not look, in those days, to earn a living by their books. They published for fame, or in contentiousness, or to authenticate their writings against piratical printers and garbling copyists, or for a variety of reasons which you may trace for yourselves by following the bibliography (say) of Donne's Poems, of Bacon's Essays, of Burton's *Anatomy*, or of Sir Thomas Browne's *Religio Medici*. They did not write for a competence. Shakespeare, as we know, was a good man of business: he never found it possible to collect his plays for publication or bothered the players for leave to collect them. If we go back a century or a couple of centuries from Milton, we find that mere copying of MSS. commanded far higher prices than authorship ever obtained for some hundreds of years under the printing press. If we go forward a century and read of the eighteenth century men commemorated in Johnson's *Lives of the Poets*, we may trace how the patron and the jail between them were still coping with an economic theory that literature, being priceless, would be insulted by a decent payment.

So, you see, when we have accepted Milton's consecration to the high calling of poetry, we need not be astonished that at thirty-two he had not earned a penny. Still for you and me that cold fact, as I have called it, naturally raises the question how Milton's father took it.

He took it very well; and for this and another reason I am glad to pause on a few words about him.

He was, as we have seen, a scrivener; prosperous, and now retired out of London. But, like Ruskin's father, he was a man of liberal and cultivated taste. 'For one thing,' says Masson of the household in Bread Street, and the description may travel to Horton, 'music was perpetual in it'—

> The scrivener was not only passionately fond of music, but even of such note himself as a musical composer, that, apart altogether from the fame of his great son, some memory of him might have lingered among us to this day. Madrigals, songs, and psalm tunes of his composition are to be seen yet in music-books published before his son was born, or while he was but in his boyhood, and not in mere inferior music-books, but in collections in which Morley, Wilbye, Bull, Dowland, Ellis Gibbons, Orlando Gibbons, and others of the best artists of his day were his fellow contributors.

In particular one may name Ravenscroft's *Whole Book of Psalms*, a rather famous compendium of church music published in 1621, in which two tunes called 'Norwich' and 'York' are by John Milton the elder. 'York' tune remains a favourite to this day, and is (I believe) the one to which we yet sing Tate and Brady's 'O God of Hosts, the mighty Lord' (No. 237 in *Hymns Ancient and Modern*).

I shall have something to say by and by about these old song books, and about Milton as an eminently musical poet. Just here I content myself with stressing the fact that music conditioned all his youth, and specially that his father taught him to sing tunably and to play upon the organ—an accomplishment to which he returned for solace in his blind old age.

Experience and observation have both taught me that parents desire their children to be like themselves, only better; and that Providence usually and beneficently frustrates the first part of that desire. It appears evident that the elder Milton, seeing that his son declined to be a bishop and (even more firmly) to become a lawyer, longed to make a musician of him. But I quoted Mr. Birrell just now to the effect that our poet was always determined, whatever else he was or might become, to be his own man. Let me append to this Masson's most probable conjecture, that he had at Horton, 'learnt to be master, and more, in his father's house'—his father, let me remind you, being well over seventy.

Now to his father, sometime in this Horton period, Milton addressed a poem, *Ad Patrem*, in Latin hexameters; and the decent obscurity of a dead language has to some extent veiled their importance in the story of John Milton's life. But listen to these few lines.

> Nec tu perge, precor, sacras contemnere Musas,
> Nec vanas inopesque puta, quarum ipse peritus
> Munere mille sonos numeros componis ad aptos,
> Millibus et vocem modulis variare canoram
> Doctus Arionii meritò sis nominis haeres.
> Nunc tibi quid mirum si me genuisse poëtam
> Contigerit, charo si tam propè sanguine juncti
> Cognatas artes studiumque affine sequamur? . . .
>   At tibi, chare pater, postquam non aequa merenti
> Posse referre datur, nec dona rependere factis,
> Sit memorâsse satis, repetitaque munera grato
> Percensere animo, fidaeque reponere menti.
>   Et vos, O nostri, juvenilia carmina, lusus,
> Si modò perpetuos sperare audebitis annos,
> Et domini superesse rogo, lucemque tueri,
> Nec spisso rapient oblivia nigra sub Orco,
> Forsitan has laudes, decantatumque parentis
> Nomen, ad exemplum, sero servabitis aevo.

Here it is in Masson's rendering: which deserves, in my opinion, more praise than it has ever received.

Do not thou, I beseech, persist in contemning the Muses,
Thinking them vain and poor, thyself the while to their bounty
Owing thy skill in composing thousands of sounds to the verses
Matching them best, and thy cunning to vary the voice of the singer
Thousands of trilling ways, acknowledged heir of Arion.
Why shouldst thou wonder now if so it has chanced that a poet
Comes to be son of thine, and if, joined in such loving relation,
Each of us follows an art that is kin to the art of the other? . . .
So my father dear, since the perfect sum of your merits

Baffles equal return, and your kindness all real repayment,
Be the mere record enough, and the fact that my grateful remem-
     brance
Treasures the itemed account of debt and will keep it for ever.
Ye too my youthful verses, my pastime and play for the present,
Should you sometimes dare to hope for eternal existence,
Lasting and seeing the light when your master's body has mouldered
Not whirled down in oblivion deep in the darkness of Orcus,
Mayhap this tribute of praise and the thus sung name of my parent
Ye shall preserve, an example, for ages yet in the future.

But one thing remained for this vowed youth, as for Ruskin,
to be cope and crown in his preparation. In the month of
April 1638—his mother having died a year before, and his old
father at length giving consent—Milton set out with a man-
servant upon that journey which should be the dream of every
young Englishman who aspires to be an artist; and passed
through Paris; thence, by the Mediterranean coast, to Italy—
to Florence, to Rome.

IV

I started by reading the immortal Invocation to Light
which opens the Third Book of *Paradise Lost,* and by drawing
your attention to four points on which Milton would seem
expressly to justify himself through his Epic, and his Epic
through the man. They were:

1. Prophetic Sublimity ⎫ these two justifying the
2. Music   ⎭   work
3. His loneliness   ⎫ these justifying the
4. His physical blindness   ⎭   workman

this last—the poignant physical affliction of blindness—giving
the stab which releases the whole personal, passionate outburst.

Now I grant that Milton's blindness so far causes and conditions his loneliness that to keep the two at all separate in our
minds is not easy, as to keep them strictly separate would be
pedantic. Still I would have you keep the two so far distinct
in your minds as not to attribute all his loneliness to his later
blindness. For his was an isolated youth from the start,

through his parents' ambition: and inner pride and outer circumstance isolated the farther his middle life, long before blindness overtook him.

May I employ here a figure of the sort that used to be dear to Ruskin's heart? Some of you may remember (from the notes to your Aristophanes) that the Greeks were used to brand certain breeds of their race-horses with this or that letter of their ancient alphabet; and that in particular there was a certain Corinthian strain marked with a Koppa (or φ) and claiming, for original sire, no less a stallion than Pegasus. Now Pegasus, as you also know, was the winged horse of Song. He had slaked his thirst in Pirene: Pallas, goddess of Wisdom, had caught him, bridled him, broken him (for the which meed the Corinthians stamped the figures of the pair on their coinage: the goddess on the obverse, the winged horse on the reverse; with a Koppa, their City's initial letter). He had saved Helicon for the Muses, and by impact of his hoof, upspringing toward heaven, had released their own fountain Hippocrene— the Horse's Well—to gush perpetually down the mountain-side. So now, if only for a fancy and to help our memory, let us harness up these four scions of Pegasus (κοππατίοι) in our minds; three at first—Prophecy, Music, Loneliness; afterwards, in due time, tracing up Blindness to complete our four-in-hand. This, at any rate, is the team I am attempting to drive through our study of Milton: and since my words must be so far less swift than the charioteer's eye, you will forgive me for directing your notice by dull successions from one to another of the team, when the plunges of their gallop are almost actually—nay to appearance quite actually and vividly —simultaneous.

V

We left Milton in his thirtieth year, on the road to Italy. 'It has been remarked,' I read, 'that Milton's chief enthusiasm in Italy was not art but music.' I have not remarked this, and I find no evidence for it unless by 'art' we are to understand painting alone.   Certainly he is silent, so far as we know, about pictures; and as certainly he attended a concert in the palace of Cardinal Francesco Barberini, at which he heard the famous Leonora Baroni sing.   For the rest, the lines which I read you from the epistle *To his Father* leave us in no doubt that Milton had made definite choice of Poetry for his first interest.   He always, as we say, knew his own mind, and the names of the men with whom he consorted at Florence, in the chief Academies or Literary Clubs, are the names of men of letters.   Beyond a doubt he was already determined upon a great Poem, though undecided upon his theme, and whether to build an Epic or a Tragedy.   Certainly he was so determined, and still so undecided, a year later.

Undoubtedly Milton revelled in Music, then and until the close of his days.   You remember my quoting Masson's words; his father's house, at Horton, as in Bread Street, was always 'full of music'—fuller than most houses, I grant you (being the house of an old composer), but not thereby, nor by any means, so sharply different from its neighbours as such a house would be in our own days.   I will not say that we have utterly lost the art of chamber music.   But if you consider the mass of the old music books preserved to us and dating from the late sixteenth and early seventeenth centuries, you will sigh for a delicate domestic joy almost, if not quite, departed. Take up one of the old four-part song books; spread it open upon the table: see how it falls apart, with two scores reading this way and the other two that way.   Then call up the picture of your four singers standing up to it after supper—say hostess and daughter, host and guest—or four jolly men laying down tobacco pipes, facing two-and-two, and trolling 'There is a Lady sweet and kind,' or 'Since first I saw your face I resolved to honour and renown ye,' or 'There was a Frog jumped into a Well,' or solemnly:

> The man of life upright
>   Whose guiltless heart is free
> From all dishonest deeds
>   Or thought of vanity . . .

''Twas merry in hall.' Can you not hear it, picture it? the hearty yet mutually corrective pitch and pause of those choristers, who knew one another's foibles so well in their day; the intermittent touch of lute or virginal or *viol da gamba*; the candle-light on the board, the decanters and glasses pushed out of the way of the late-opened book; the lifted chins and those our forefathers' beards wagging in rhythm or in fugue:

> My true love hath my heart, and I have his,
>   By just exchange one for another given. . . .

Yes, Milton had grown up attuned

> To hear the lute well toucht, or artfull voice
> Warble immortal Notes and *Tuskan* Ayre.

But it is surely with organ-music, rather, that our thoughts instinctively associate him: and this as well through his masterly command of speech, to make it suggest the full range of eloquent sound—from clear flute-note to diapason open and thundering —as because it was, as we know, his favourite instrument, taught him by his father. You all remember Tennyson's alcaics:

> O mighty-mouth'd inventor of harmonies,
> O skill'd to sing of Time or Eternity,
>   God-gifted organ-voice of England,
>   Milton, a name to resound for ages.

Now the poem of Milton's which earliest translates his passion for actual organ-music into poetry that really resembles it; not merely confessing the passion as *Il Penseroso* confesses it, in the lines:

> There let the pealing Organ blow
> To the full voic'd Quire below,
> In Service high and Anthems cleer
> As may, with sweetnes, through mine ear
> Dissolve me into extasies
> And bring all Heav'n before mine eyes . . .

but infusing it, as by throbbing pulse of the organ itself, is, of course, the short one entitled *At a Solemn Musick*; which I invite you to consider for this reason and for another to which, after reading the lines, I shall presently come.

* H 974

Conjecture assigns them to 1634 or thereabouts — say four years before Milton started on his Italian tour.　They probably followed soon upon *Arcades*: for they come next after *Arcades* in the volume of Milton MSS. preserved in the Library of Trinity College here; and the volume contains no fewer than four drafts of this piece, 'exhibiting,' says Masson, 'in perhaps a more extraordinary manner than any other extant specimen of Milton's autograph, his extreme fastidiousness in composition, his habit of altering, correcting, rejecting, erasing and enlarging, till he had brought a piece to some satisfactory perfection of form.'　But now take the lines themselves—observe how the flute note begins, and how, gradually, the pipes open and swell to their power:

At a Solemn Musick

Blest pair of *Sirens*, pledges of Heav'ns joy,
Sphear-born harmonious Sisters, Voice and Vers,
Wed your divine sounds, and mixt power employ,
Dead things with inbreath'd sense able to pierce,
And to our high-rais'd phantasie present
That undisturbèd Song of pure concent,
Ay sung before the saphire-colour'd throne,
To him that sits theron,
With Saintly shout and solemn Jubily,
Where the bright Seraphim in burning row
Their loud uplifted Angel trumpets blow,
And the Cherubick host in thousand quires
Touch their immortal Harps of golden wires,
With those just Spirits that wear victorious Palms,
Hymns devout and holy Psalms
Singing everlastingly;
That we on Earth with undiscording voice
May rightly answer that melodious noise;
As once we did, till disproportion'd sin
Jarr'd against natures chime, and with harsh din
Broke the fair musick that all creatures made
To their great Lord, whose love their motion sway'd
In perfect Diapason, whilst they stood
In first obedience, and their state of good.
O may we soon again renew that Song,
And keep in tune with Heav'n, till God ere long
To his celestial consort us unite,
To live with him, and sing in endles morn of light.

I said that I held, in brief reserve, another reason for quoting these lines. But surely you see it? Surely you perceive that here, four years before his Italian tours; that here and in such lines as these of *Lycidas*:

> So *Lycidas* sunk low, but mounted high,
> Through the dear might of him that has walk'd **the waves** . . .
> And hears the unexpressive nuptiall Song,
> In the blest Kingdoms meek of joy and love,
> There entertain him all the Saints above,
> In solemn troops, and sweet Societies
> That sing, and singing in their glory move,
> And wipe the tears for ever from his eyes.

—surely (I say) you perceive that Milton, before his Italian journey, had fairly mastered his style, fairly mastered the organ-music of speech? What occupied him now was architectonic—the *structure* of his great poem, whether in form of Tragedy or of Epic: and what he sought earnestly now, to decide his choice between these two consecrated forms, was a worthy Subject.

VI

But here we must pause for a minute or so, to fetch him back from Italy. From Rome he travelled to Naples, with the intent to cross thence to Sicily, and extend his tour to Greece. At Naples, however, news overtook him of political troubles at home; troubles in Scotland, and civil war in England imminent thereupon, if not inevitable. He turned back. The decision was prompt, but the retreat leisurable. He spent another two months at Rome, a second two months in Florence: made an excursion to Lucca, crossed the Apennines, passed through Bologna and Ferrara to Venice, where again he lingered a month. [Here, by the way, let me interpose that Milton not only acquainted himself with the outward aspect of these cities, but consorted with many of the most distinguished Europeans of that day.]

From Venice, after despatching to England by sea the books he had collected in his wanderings, he proceeded to Verona and Milan; thence, over the Pennine Alps, to Geneva; rested there a week or two; and thence (again through Paris) pushed home for England and Horton, which he reached early in August 1639, to find all well and rejoicing over his return.

Now actually he arrived close under the fore-cast shadow of an event—the outbreak of the Great Civil War—which was to postpone the grand purpose for another twenty years: and he knew its stroke to be overhanging. But there is evidence that Milton behaved as so many men do under the last fatal hurry of an uncontrollable event. Restlessly, and as though time were now all-important after long indecision, he fell to choosing the Subject of his projected masterpiece, scribbling and covering sheets of paper with lists of possible themes and titles.

I spoke casually, just now, of certain Cambridge papers in Milton's autograph. If you will go to Trinity College Library, you may see with your own eyes even such a paper as I have just mentioned, in Milton's own handwriting—a list of projected Subjects, ninety-nine in all, with notes here and there on their possibilities. They are mainly Biblical Subjects, and the Fall of Man in various forms of presentment has clearly a dominant hold in his mind. But here are some others. *Naboth falsely witnessed against; Elijah bringing the Rain; Hezekiah Besieged; Herod Massacring*, or *Rachel Weeping, Christus Patiens; Christ Risen; Hardiknute Dying in his Cups; Athelstan Exposing his Brother to the Sea and Repenting; Macbeth*— 'beginning at the arrival of Malcolm at Macduff. The matter of Duncan may be expressed by the appearing of his ghost.'

Macbeth! Some reasons which explain Milton's design, and even in part excuse his audacity in proposing a theme handled by Shakespeare thirty years before, were discussed in *The Nineteenth Century* for December 1891, by that most learned scholar Mr. John W. Hales, and you may find the paper reprinted in his volume entitled *Folia Litteraria*. To-day, however, we are not concerned with speculation on Milton's *Macbeth*. The point I ask you to note in all these entries is that he indexes all these themes as subjects for *tragedy*, and, where he annotates, is obviously considering them as dramatic themes. There is no doubt at all that, at this time—say about 1639—Milton intended his great poem to be a Tragedy, not an Epic.

Soon after his return to England the household at Horton was broken up; his brother and his brother's wife, with one child, removing to Reading, the aged father accompanying them. Some little while before this removal Milton himself had taken lodgings in London, over a tailor's shop in St. Bride's Churchyard, Fleet Street. A little later, wanting more room for his books, he moved to a 'garden house' in Aldersgate Street. In one or other of these lodgings he made out the list now in Trinity Library; and so we see him, waiting on the Muse, seated alone, in the loneliness of London. Yet that loneliness was not so complete as he might well have wished: for besides his brother at Reading (who later took the Royalist side, in time turned Roman Catholic under James II, and lived to become Sir Christopher Milton and a Judge) he had a surviving sister, Anne, who had married one Edward Phillips of the Crown Office in 1624, had been left a widow in 1631 with two young sons, had married again, and was now dwelling near Charing Cross. It was considered that the boys Edward and John might well go to their uncle to be schooled. The younger, aged nine, boarded with him: Edward, aged ten, came daily. Now Milton held strong theories about Education, and subsequently printed them in a Tract addressed to Master Samuel Hartlib: but he seems to have enjoyed it in operation only a little more than his pupils. He could scarcely have enjoyed it less than they. He was a strong flogger.

So we come back to his loneliness, which now heavily deepens, and continues to deepen, creeping about him like a darkness before ever the actual darkness descended. We mistake if we think of Milton as naturally morose, or as ungenial, unsociable, ascetic. He ate and drank delicately, being fastidious and temperate in all things (until he took to pamphleteering, and hooked his boarding-irons alongside

Salmasius and other controversialists, when his language became such as—well, such as we should hardly look for from the
sort of gentleman that Christ's College had called a lady). But
he loved good wine, and the good converse that befits it—as
witness his sonnet:

To Mr. Lawrence

Lawrence, of vertuous Father vertuous Son,
   Now that the Fields are dank, and ways are mire,
   Where shall we sometimes meet, and by the fire
Help wast a sullen day; what may be won
From the hard Season gaining: time will run
   On smoother, till *Favonius* re-inspire
   The frozen earth; and cloth in fresh attire
The Lillie and the Rose, that neither sow'd nor spun.
What neat repast shall feast us, light and choice,
   Of Attick tast, with Wine, whence we may rise
To hear the Lute well toucht, or artfull voice
   Warble immortal Notes and Tuskan Ayre?
   He who of these delights can judge, and spare
To interpose them oft, is not unwise.

He had had friends; not many; but two young and dear ones:
of whom one, Edward King, had died early, to live eternally
in *Lycidas*. Of the death of the other, Charles Deodati, he
had heard a rumour abroad, but did not learn the particulars
until he reached England. Deodati was son of an Italian
physician naturalized in London and (one gathers) an old
friend and neighbour of the Milton household. The youth
had taken his medical degree; and had started in practice in the
north of England—near Chester, it is believed. He had been
Milton's one confidant, mainly by letter, during the Horton
days. He had died in London, little more than four months
after Milton's start upon his tour: but no news of this would
seem to have reached Milton until he was homing back with a
heart (as he himself tells us) impatient to rejoin his friend and
pour out his soul in talk of Italy—so dear to the one through
ancestry, and to the other, now, by acquaintance. 'Knowst
thou that Land? . . .' But not only was Deodati dead: he had
died under tragic circumstances to which a few letters and a
cluster of burial entries in the registers of St. Anne's, Black-

friars, give some faint clue. The old father, Dr. Theodore
Deodati, had married, at sixty-four, a second wife. A step-
motherly war had broken out. It drove Philadelphia, a
daughter by the first marriage, from the house; and with
Charles, newly returned from the north, she took refuge in
lodgings; where a fever, or the plague in some form, destroyed
them both, in August 1635, but a few weeks after the wife of
an elder brother, also concerned in the quarrel, had died in
childbirth.

Every one knows *Lycidas*: few read the Latin *Epitaphium
Damonis* in which Milton commemorated this other friend,
Charles Deodati. A good Latinist would, I think, condemn
its Latin; which, scorning the unscholarly vulgate and seeming
to aspire even to the Virgilian of the Eclogues, can truly be
beaten for Virgilian by any clever sixth-form boy of our day.
I suppose it to be of a seventeenth century quasi-Augustan
pattern in Latin composition. I quote a few lines only:

> Ite domum impasti; domino jam non vacat, agni.
> Pectora cui credam? quis me lenire docebit
> Mordaces curas, quis longam fallere noctem
> Dulcibus alloquiis, grato cum sibilat igni
> Molle pirum, et nucibus strepitat focus, at malus Auster
> Miscet cuncta foris, et desuper intonat ulmo?

But here again I have recourse to Masson's hexameter rendering:

> *Go unpastured, my lambs: your master now heeds not your bleating*·

—that is the refrain—

Whom shall I trust with my thoughts? Or who will teach me to
  deaden
Heart-hid pains? Or who will cheat away the long evening
Sweetly with chat by the fire, where hissing hot on the ashes
Roasts the ripe pear, and the chestnuts crackle beneath, while the
  South-Wind
Hurls confusion without, and thunders down on the elm-tops?

There is nothing, of course, in the *Epitaphium* comparable
with the grace of *Lycidas*: and yet the Latin, helped by its
refrain (though that be borrowed from the Eclogues), has a

sob in it which somehow is not felt in *Lycidas*: a στοργή of friendship which *Lycidas* in its perfection either misses or— more likely—classically avoids.

So, at thirty-one, Milton had lost his only two coaeval and intimate friends, and both shockingly. And so he comes to the edge of the year 1640—the year of the Long Parliament— which, as I suppose, tore across the personal affections of Englishmen a rent more fatal than England had known before or has known since. Whatever else Civil War may mean, it must mean that you feel a possible half of your fellow-country- men to be your direct enemies, hot and embittered: that for social amenity you substitute hatred toward that possible half; and worse—that you live in guardful suspicion; that, of any man you meet on the public thoroughfare you know not, though he smile, if he be a friend or conceal a dagger under his cloak. Every day increases suspicion, and all suspicion isolates.

VII

The Civil War broke out; and on top of its outbreak Milton took a step which intensified the misery of isolation at least tenfold: for you cannot marry a wife for comfort and be left by her with no worse loss than lack of the comfort you sought. Every one knows the story of poor Mary Powell; perhaps because no one has quite solved the mystery of it. The War had opened in 1642. About Whitsuntide, 1643, Milton made a sudden dash into leafy Oxfordshire, and returned to Aldersgate with a bride of seventeen, he being then thirty-five. As his nephew Phillips put it, 'he took a journey into the country, nobody about him certainly knowing the reason, or that it was any more than a journey of recreation: but home he returns a married man, that went forth a bachelor.' Con- sidered merely as a raid, or (to borrow one of his own phrases) a 'brief model' of marriage by capture, this might pass for an exploit, the more gallant because he had taken his spoil in the very heart of the enemy's camp—Mary's father being a Royalist

Oxfordshire squire, with an old estate, a mansion, 'a carriage and what not' (Masson) and a considerable quantity of debts. Research, I regret to say, has discovered that among these was one of £500 to Mr. John Milton; and if this at all explains the mystery—if the poor girl went for better or worse in discharge or in consideration of that debt—why then silence is best.

But of marriage, even though it be effected by capture, the delicate problem of translating passion into companionship remains invariable. Of Milton we are told that 'though keenly alive to the subtle charm of a woman's personality, [he] was unpractised in the arts of daily companionship. He had an ideal. . . . One of his complaints was that his wife was mute and insensate, and sat silent at his board.' But later, of another wife, this exacting man complained because she *wouldn't* sit silent. She sang: and, as he remarked, 'she had a good voice, but no ear.' So, we may conjecture, when the third Mrs. Milton tuned her nocturnal note, her lord sat darkling or in shadiest covert hid. 'It must'—I resume the quotation from Mr. Birrell—'have been deadly dull, that house in Aldersgate Street. Silence reigned, save when broken by the cries of the younger Phillips sustaining chastisement.'

After a month Mary left him. In the violence of his indignation he penned his famous tract—*The Doctrine and Discipline of Divorce restored to the good of both sexes*; and this doctrine being abhorrent to friends and foes alike, he lived for two years the loneliest man, perhaps, in London. Then his wife came back, knelt at his feet and was forgiven—nobly, generously forgiven—and very soon his roof was sheltering the whole family of Powells, ruined in the King's cause. Mary died in childbed, in 1652.

Had he any friends—friends in the true sense—during the years that followed? Yes, certainly Andrew Marvell, his assistant in the Latin Secretaryship, was one. Both were essentially men of high thought, and men of style. Men of style abounded in that seventeenth century, but Marvell was remarkable among them. As I shall show later, a like problem in poetry occupied the minds of both, and both were experimenting upon it. And Milton had recommended Marvell for his post. Yes, Wordsworth is right: Marvell was one of those who 'called Milton friend.'

But how came Milton on the 21st of February, 1653, to ask that Mr. Andrew Marvell might be appointed to assist him?

Because he himself was by this time blind.

Blindness—total blindness: and upon that, in 1660, loss of place, exile, persecution, hiding. . . . Think of it all!

Ah, but what of the great work that we saw him—so long ago and after so long a preparation—on the eve of writing? Almost twenty years have passed: Milton has now turned fifty: and not a line of it is written. Is that also lost, then?—since for a man conscious of power, dedicated to use it so as ever in his 'great task Master's eye,' to be robbed of his work, or to know *that* lost through default, is a worse hell than blindness. Then is that also lost?

No: for see! This man—sans light, sans friends, sans hope, sans everything: this man—

> though fall'n on evil dayes
> On evil dayes though fall'n, and evil tongues,
> In darkness, and with dangers compast round,
> And solitude—

this indomitable man seats himself in his shabby leathern chair as in a throne, throws a leg over its arm in the old negligent boyish attitude, and begins to speak our great English epic.

VIII

In his pamphlet entitled *The Reason of Church Government*, published in 1641 (that is, when he was nearing thirty-three), Milton avows to the world that he has for some time been minded by encouragement of his friends, 'and not less by an inward prompting which now grew daily upon me, that by labour and intense study (which I take to be my portion in this life) joined with the strong propensity of nature, I might perhaps leave something to aftertimes as they should not willingly let it die. These thoughts at once possessed me and these other: that if I were certain to write, as men buy leases, for three lives and downward, there ought no regard be sooner had than to God's glory by the honour and instruction of my country.' He dwells upon the patriotic motive: he intends not hardly 'to arrive at the second rank among the Latins' but

to fix all the industry and art I could unite to the adorning of my native tongue . . . to be an interpreter and relater of the best and sagest things among mine own citizens throughout this Island in the mother-dialect; that what the greatest and choicest wits of Athens, Rome, or modern Italy, and those Hebrews of old, did for *their* country, I, in my proportion, with this over and above of being a Christian, might do for mine; not caring to be once named abroad, though perhaps I could attain to that, but content with these British Islands as my world, whose fortune hath hitherto been that, if the Athenians, as some say, made their small deeds great and renowned by their eloquent writers, England hath had *her* noble achievements made small by the unskilful handling of monks and mechanicks.

He goes on to say that he has been dubious in what form to shape his grand theme—whether in Epic or Tragedy or Lyric. I ask your forgiveness for extracting a few sentences only from a passage which Milton himself makes apology for having condensed.

Time serves not now [he says], and perhaps I might seem too profuse, to give any certain account of what the mind, at home in the spacious circuits of her musing, hath liberty to propose to herself through highest hope and hardest attempting; whether the *Epick* form whereof the two poems of Homer, and those other two of Virgil and Tasso are a diffuse, and the Book of Job a brief model. . . . Or whether those *Dramatick* Constitutions, wherein Sophocles and Euripides reign, shall be found more doctrinal and exemplary to a nation. . . . Or if occasion shall lead to imitate those magnific *Odes* and *Hymns* wherein Pindarus and Callimachus are in most things worthy, some others in their frame judicious, in their matter most and end faulty; but those frequent Songs throughout the Law and the Prophets beyond all these, not in their divine argument alone, but in the very critical art of composition, may be easily made appear over all the kinds of *Lyrick* Poetry to be incomparable.

Thus Milton reports himself to be hesitating whether to choose Epic, Tragedy or Lyric for his form. But the MS. in Trinity College Library (written about this time or a little earlier) tells us that, for the form, he had actually chosen

Tragedy; and that for his subject, *The Fall of Man* had laid compelling hold on him, superseding the theme of *King Arthur*, which, as his Latin poem *Manso* and the *Epitaphium Damonis* plainly tell, had engaged his thought during his Italian tour. *Paradise Lost* not only heads the list in the Trinity MS., it is twice repeated: and each time a draft of the dramatic scheme follows the title.   The first is brief; it runs:

The Persons: Michael; Heavenly Love; Chorus of Angels; Lucifer; Adam, Eve with the Serpent; Conscience; Death, Labour, Sickness, Discontent, Ignorance, with others, Mutes, Faith; Hope; Charity.

He scores this out and writes another parallel with it.

The Persons: Moses [Michael or Moses was first set down, then Michael deleted]; Justice, Mercy, Wisdom; Heavenly Love; the Evening Star, Hesperus; Lucifer; Adam; Eve; Conscience; Labour, Sickness, Discontent, Ignorance, Fear, Death, Mutes; Faith, Hope, Charity.

This again is scored out, and a third draft follows, almost a *scenario*:

Paradise Lost; The Persons; Moses prologises, recounting how he assumed his true body; that it corrupts not because of his [having been] with God in the Mount; declares the like of Enoch and Eliah, besides the purity of the [place] that certain pure winds, dews and clouds preserve it from corruption; whence [ex]horts to the sight of God; tells they cannot see Adam in the state of innocence by reason of their sin.—[Act 1] Justice, Mercy, Wisdom, debating what should become of Man if he fall.   Chorus of Angels sing a Hymn of the Creation.—(Act 2) Heavenly Love; Evening Star; Chorus sing the Marriage Song and describe Paradise.—(Act 3) Lucifer contriving Adam's ruin.   Chorus fears for Adam, and relates Lucifer's rebellion and fall.—(Act 4) Adam, Eve, fallen; Conscience cites them to God's examination.   Chorus bewails and tells the good Adam hath lost.—(Act 5) Adam and Eve, driven out of Paradise. presented by an Angel with Labour, Grief, Hatred, Envy, War, Famine, Pestilence, Sickness, Discontent, Ignorance, Fear, Death entered into the world: mutes to whom he gives their names, likewise Winter, Heat, Tempest etc.; Faith, Hope, Charity comfort him and instruct him.
Chorus briefly concludes.

This draft—in which, as you perceive, each Act ends on a grand chorus—is left standing.   Later, we come on a fourth and yet more elaborate one, with the Acts similarly ending in choruses. To read it through would take more time than we can spare here. It does little beyond elaborating or altering details, and it concludes, 'Compare this with the former Draft.'

VIII

Having now established that Milton first cast *Paradise Lost* in the form of a Tragedy, I ask you to examine it with me upon three points:

(1) The first: What persuaded him to alter his mind and make an Epic? This, being capable of a personal and adventitious answer, will be found (I foresee) comparatively unimportant.

(2) The second—and for us, as students of literature, touching the heart of the argument: How did that change of form affect the poem? this again raising the question, Is the Epic form alive to-day or effete?

(3) The third: How far has *Paradise Lost* triumphed over omens apparently against it, and by what sleight or skill?

First, then, for the reasons that persuaded Milton to turn his planned Tragedy to Epic.

I think I can convince you that he did so unwillingly. To begin with, he had his Aristotle's *Poetics* by heart, and believed in the scheme of old Greek tragedy as the only true pattern. For not only have we the drafts in the Trinity MS. all scaled to this pattern: not only have we the prejudice implicit, yet earlier, in a significant grudging parenthesis in *Il Penseroso*.

> Som time let Gorgeous Tragedy
> In Scepter'd Pall com sweeping by,
> Presenting *Thebs*, or *Pelops* line,
> Or the tale of *Troy* divine;
> Or what (though rare) of later age
> Ennobled hath the Buskind Stage.

We have it—after more than thirty years—exhibited in practice by *Samson Agonistes*, and in theory confirmed by the preface to that drama. A quotation from Aristotle's famous definition of Tragedy underscores the title of *Samson*;[1] and

[1] *Samson*, we may note, is twice entered on the Trinity list of projected dramas.

the preface, after premising that, of the plot 'they only will best judge who are not unacquainted with Aeschylus, Sophocles and Euripides, the three tragic poets unequalled yet by any, and the best rule to all who endeavour to write Tragedy,' goes on boldly to accept as a precept that Unity of Time which can with difficulty be read into a casual observation which Aristotle certainly never meant to be a rule.[1] 'The circumscription of time,' adds Milton, 'wherein the whole drama begins and ends, is, according to ancient rule and best example, within the space of twenty-four hours.'

We have here, then, an Aristotelian 'more loyal than the king': and those of you, Gentlemen, who have done me the pleasure to read the *Poetics* through with me in private class, remembering the comparison between Epic and Tragedy with which that treatise (as we have it) concludes, will not doubt that Milton consented with Aristotle in preferring Tragedy as the higher of the two great serious forms of verse.

'But,' you may ask, 'what does it matter?' adding, 'Surely Milton never designed these dramas for actual presentation on the stage?'

My retort is that he certainly did; and that therefore it matters a great deal.

For consider. In the first place, two of his earlier compositions, dramatic in form, had already been staged and acted —*Arcades*, in 1633 (?), as 'part of an Entertainment presented to the Countess Dowager of Derby at Harefield by some Noble Persons of her Family,' and *Comus* on Michaelmas Night, 1634, as a masque at Ludlow Castle before the Earl of Bridgewater, son-in-law of the aforesaid Countess of Derby, and then Lord President of Wales: the parts of the Two Brothers being taken by two of his sons, Lord Brackley and young Mr. Thomas Egerton, that of the lady by his fourteen-year-old

---

[1] *Poetics*, c. 5, ἡ μὲν ὅτι μάλιστα πειρᾶται ὑπὸ μίαν περίοδον ἡλίου εἶναι ἢ μικρὸν ἐξαλλάττειν = 'Tragedy endeavours to keep as nearly as possible within one circuit of the sun or something near that.' Aristotle lays down no law here, but is merely (as Bywater puts it) dealing with the practice of the theatre in his time.

daughter Lady Alice Egerton, whose pure girlish voice, acknowledged to have been exquisite, we can, with a little imagination, hear singing Lawes' music (Lawes himself enacted the Attendant Spirit) in the lovely Echo song:

> Sweet Echo, sweetest Nymph that liv'st unseen
>   Within thy airy shell
> By slow *Meander's* margent green,
> And in the violet imbroider'd vale
> Where the love-lorn nightingale
> Nightly to thee her sad Song mourneth well;
> Canst thou not tell me of a gentle Pair
> That likest thy *Narcissus* are?
>   O if thou have
> Hid them in some flowry cave,
>   Tell me but where,
> Sweet Queen of Parly, daughter of the Sphear,
> So maist thou be translated to the skies,
> And give resounding grace to all Heav'ns Harmonies!

—'strains' says the listening Thyrsis

> that might create a soul
> Under the ribs of Death.

Milton, then, had written two dramatic pieces; both of which had been acted, and acceptably.

You may urge that it is a far cry from a masque such as *Comus* (even when we have allowed that *Comus* differed from other masques of its time, and differed successfully) to a set drama presenting, on a classical model, Heaven and Hell, with the story of Adam's fall.   Then next I pray you remember: first, that the masque, just then, was superseding the kind of play we summarize in our minds as Elizabethan: that the Elizabethan or (if you will) the Shakespearian type had pretty well worn itself threadbare in the hands of Tourneur, Shirley, and far worse practitioners: that a new form was wanted; and that if the new form attempted to present even Heaven and Hell, the masque, which quite commonly coped with Olympus and all its gods, magniloquent in speech and floating in movement, had—with a little daring—the whole theatrical apparatus ready to hand.

Further, will you remind yourselves that Milton in 1640 was scarcely fifty years removed from the old morality play, and by only a little more from the miracle play? To think of harking back and taking a fresh start from these may seem absurd enough to us, who live almost three hundred years later. But let us put ourselves back in his time, and suppose ourselves debating how to replace an outworn dramatic convention with something at once different and yet faithful to artistic tradition. Supposing this, will you deem it an extravagant conjecture that Milton's mind seriously harked back over a short half-century? Does it even strike you—reminding yourselves how much more diffident of itself English literature was then than it is now, how much humbler before the authority of the classics —as a hope only possible of occurrence to a thoroughly impracticable mind? Well then, even so, let us recall our knowledge of the man; that he had lived a dedicated and self-cloistered life, that he was always a somewhat impracticable fellow, proud and more than conscious of his powers; that he came to the drama as a mere scholar, without any of the apprenticeship through which, day in and day out, the easy natured Shakespeare, always willing to learn, had learned to beat the University wits, and even Ben Jonson, at their own game; that he was so signally throughout life a *sic volo sic jubeo* fellow, and that he had already two amateur successes in the classical style to encourage him. Recollecting all this, can we, with positive evidence before us of his having planned *Paradise Lost* as a drama, pronounce it inconceivable, or even less than probable, that Milton meant to achieve on the actual stage something of the sort that Handel afterwards achieved in oratorio?

Then why did he change his mind?

I give you the answer to that in a dozen words. *In 1642 Parliament closed the Theatres: which remained shut until the Restoration.*

A Puritanical religion always strikes *first* upon the theatre.

As it had been under the fathers of the Church from Tertullian to Augustine, so it happened again when Milton was a young man. 'The unlawfulness of dramatic entertainments,' says Masson, 'had always been a tenet of those stricter English Puritans with whom Milton even then felt a political sympathy'; and Prynne's famous *Histriomastix*, in which he denounced stage-plays and all connected with them through a thousand quarto pages (1632), had helped to confirm Puritanism in this tenet.

Say that Milton remained true to his belief in the drama. From the 2nd of September, 1642, when the Long Parliament passed its ordinance suppressing stage-plays, down to the very eve of the Restoration—that is, for close upon eighteen years —his dream of recreating our national drama had come to naught and remained at naught, for the simple reason that the door of every theatre stood closed and locked by law. There-fore, I say, Milton turned from Tragedy to Epic. Years after —in 1667 or thereabouts—when those doors had been re-opened as sluices to the reactionary discharge of Restoration Drama, the old man gallantly accinged himself to his old task and wrote *Samson Agonistes*; not *Samson Pursophorus* ('Sam-son the Firebrand-bringer') as projected in the old Trinity list, but Samson the Champion in bonds; blind as himself was blind.

IX

Meantime we have *Paradise Lost*, a tragedy turned into epic. Here, for a specimen, we have, inserted in Book IV, the ten lines which Milton had once shown to his nephew Edward Phillips 'as designed for the very beginning of the sayd tragedy' —the lines in which Satan, first setting foot on earth, addresses the Sun, 'high in his meridian tower,' fell blazing over Eden.

> O thou that with surpassing Glory crownd,
> Look'st from thy sole Dominion like the God
> Of this new World; at whose sight all the Starrs
> Hide their diminisht heads; to thee I call,
> But with no friendly voice, and add thy name,
> O Sun, to tell thee how I hate thy beams,
> That bring to my remembrance from what state
> I fell, how glorious once above thy Sphaere,
> Till Pride and worse Ambition threw me down,
> Warring in Heav'n against Heav'ns matchless King.

So we come to the question, What effect had Milton's change of design upon *Paradise Lost*, for good or evil? And with that question we touch the heart of the argument by which for seven years now, from this desk, I have tried and proved your powers of endurance. In season, and often (I fear me) out of season, still my plea has been that *we cannot separate art, and specially the literary art, from life—from daily life—even from this passing hour—and get the best out of either.*

The moral of this is, that you may have great artists, great poets, great painters and sculptors: but you will never have a great era of art; you will never have the excellent joys of painting, sculpture, music, poetry 'in widest commonalty spread'; as you will ever keep your man of genius constricted and tortured; so long as you treat him as a freak, as a pet, as anything but an honest workman supplying a social demand. If he be a high master, he will yet be proud, as every high master deserves to be. God himself cannot make the best violins save by employing Stradivarius. Let me quote here a passage written by Mr. Charles Marriott on the art of a great modern sculptor, Rodin. He says, and most truly:

Because he was a great artist, Rodin suffered in an exaggerated form the disadvantage suffered by every artist since the Middle Ages. He is cut off from his base. In a sense it would be true to say that the disadvantage began when 'artist' came to mean anything but a supremely gifted workman. Lack of general recognition is a symptom rather than a cause of it. The great artist must always work in moral and intellectual isolation, and it does not hurt him to do so any more than it hurts the saint. What hurts him, what hurt Rodin, and what the artist of the Middle Ages never knew, is material isolation; to live and work without some definite relation to the everyday lives of his fellow creatures. The pecuniary relation, however satisfactory in itself, is not enough. Even when it takes the form of an important public commission, it suffers from exactly the same disadvantage as 'diplomatic relations.' *It does not represent the unconscious will of the people.* As for the relation established by what is called 'intelligent appreciation,' it might be said fairly that there is nothing worse for an artist. Unless he is inhumanly arrogant, it makes him an opportunist. One had only to see the sidelong glance of the great old man, as he exposed a piece to some cultured visitor, to recognize how eagerly he waited upon suggestion.

If those words be true—as I believe them to be true—do they not shed a most illuminating ray into our great Epic? There was a time in England when England demanded a theatre and London crossed over from the stairs to Southwark to behold it. Of that common demand was begotten a Shakespeare to satisfy it. Shakespeare was an artist working to be equal (and more, but first equal) to a vivid demand, as Burke afterwards wrought to be equal to an audience which he could visualize as the British Senate and address with a consciousness that every word spoken there carried sonorous echoes upon material weight. But with Milton we have a man, in Mr. Marriott's words, 'cut off from his base.' He would reform the theatre, and behold! of a sudden there was no theatre to reform.

I have been at pains, trying to be fair, to heap every circumstance of Milton's circumstantial loneliness upon you. Yet here, I assert, lies the secret of the solitude in which we feel ourselves—so to say—marooned as we meditate the wonderful poem, and listen to that exquisite music—as it were

> Breaking the silence of the seas
> Among the farthest Hebrides.

I challenge you, at any rate, to deny that when we listen to Shakespeare, even at his greatest, it is always to a fellow speaker intimate and winning, sure of an affectionate ear: that on the contrary, when we read *Paradise Lost* we feel no such genial fellowship: we yield rather to the wand in the grasp of a high compelling master. Nay, I am sure that most of you will concede this: and still, the point being so important, I ask your leave to stress it with help of a few admirable sentences printed anonymously, some years ago, in *The Times Literary Supplement.*

A fit comparison with the state of mind induced by reading Milton's poetry may be found in one of the paintings on the ceiling of the Sistine Chapel—the *Creation of Adam.* Like Michaelangelo's Adam we have been touched to life by an immortal finger, and wake

to find ourselves on the dizzy edge of a mountain: like the figure
that shelters under the arm of the Most High, we are caught up and
whirled by an irresistible power.   The predominant feeling is one
of awe.   We are mastered by something so great that we cannot
question, and think of complaint almost as of blasphemy.   Our
admiration is not asked, our adherence is not claimed; both are
imposed upon us by a purpose too strong for common humanity
to resist.   We have not been appealed to by a friend; we have been
commanded by a master.

I believe that I have blinked nothing of the share which
Milton's individual character—with its 'honest haughtiness
and self-esteem' as he himself puts it—with, as we may add, its
intellectual purity, its obstinacy, its lofty arrogance—contributed to produce that effect.   But that this does not wholly
account for it, and possibly accounts for less than one-half,
we may convince ourselves in a minute by taking almost any
passage from Shakespeare, almost any passage from Milton,
and setting them side by side.   Listen first to Cordelia, comforting old Lear:

> O my dear father!   Restoration hang
> Thy medicine on my lips: and let this kiss
> Repair those violent harms that my two sisters
> Have in thy reverence made! . . .
> Had you not been their father, these white flakes
> Had challenged pity of them.   Was this a face
> To be opposed against the warring winds?
> To stand against the deep dread-bolted thunder?
> In the most terrible and nimble stroke
> Of quick, cross lightning? to watch—poor perdu!—
> With this thin helm?   Mine enemy's dog,
> Though he had bit me, should have stood that night
> Against my fire.

Now hear Michael to Adam:

> 'So maist thou live, till like ripe Fruit thou drop
> Into thy Mother's lap, or be with ease
> Gatherd, not harshly pluckt, for death mature:
> This is old age; but then thou must outlive
> Thy youth, thy strength, thy beauty, which will change
> To withered weak and gray; thy Senses then
> Obtuse, all taste of pleasure must forgoe
> To what thou hast; and, for the Aire of youth

> Hopeful and cheerful, in thy blood will reigne
> A melancholly damp of cold and dry
> To waigh thy spirits down and last consume
> The Balme of Life.'
>   To whom our Ancestor:
> 'Henceforth I flie not Death, nor would prolong
> Life much, bent rather how I may be quit
> Fairest and easiest of this combrous charge,
> Which I must keep till my appointed day
> Of rendring up, and patiently attend
> My dissolution.'

>   *Michael* replied:

> 'Nor love thy Life. nor hate; but what thou livst
> Live well: how long or short permit to Heav'n.'

Solemn, most noble lines, and altogether majestic! Yet at once we note how much more vividly—and poignantly, because vividly—Cordelia speaks. And next we note that the difference is not only difference between Shakespeare and Milton; that much of it lies in *the form of Art chosen*: that Cordelia speaks vividly because that form compels us to see every accessory gesture, to witness the kiss, to watch her fingers as they lift Lear's white locks, as they piteously trace the furrows down the worn cheek, pause when a criss-cross suggests the cross double cut of lightning, stray back to the thin helm, recoil to clench themselves in the cry:

>   Mine enemy's dog,
>   Though he had bit me, should have stood that night
>   Against my fire.

Lastly we see how the form of the art, being so much more vivid; and the subject, being so much more human and intense upon the human heart; force the speech to utter those strange, unexpected, yet most befitting words—'poor perdu!'—force Cordelia to seek back and snatch, as it were out of girlhood, out of lost days of kindness, familiar tender images to coo them over that great head brought low.

When Aristotle—worshipping Homer yet not overawed by Homer's authority—declared, in the last chapter of the *Poetics*, for Tragedy as a higher art on the whole than Epic, he had

much to back his daring. Tragedy, even as Epic, dealt with
gods, demi-gods, a few ancient and royal houses. Its human
characters all owned something of divine descent and were by
consequence exalted in dignity and passion as, circumstantially,
by the spectacle of their deeds and downfalls. Tragedy, moreover, came straight out of religious observance and worked
upon higher solemnities than Epic, which was a strain sung
to the feast in a chieftain's hall, convivial rather than cere-
monial; of the dais and the high table. Tragedy moved still
around an altar. Yet even Aristotle, in his day, has to start
with a defence against those who prefer Epic on the ground
that it appeals to a more refined audience; their objection being
o the intrusion of actors with their capers and gestures, intended to help out the meaning for common wits. Aristotle's
answer amounts to this; that, if it be bad, we must curse the
histrions and attach the blame neither upon the tragic writer
nor upon the tragic form. And the answer is all very well and
sufficient, so far as it goes. But there were two things Aristotle
could not possibly foresee. The first was the social degradation
of the theatre. I pass its spectacular decline in Rome, its fatal
loss there of all religious and ancestral honour, its not unpro-
voked persecution by the Fathers of the Church, its exile from
society for a thousand years. But I ask you to note that when
at length the hussy returned to take men's hearts by storm again,
she came back a vagrant, in tawdry finery soiled with her dis-
creditable past. The practitioners of drama were still, by legal
definition, 'vagabonds' and liable to whipping; it offered in a
furtive way allurements that no effrontery could pass off as
religious; it trafficked neither with gods nor with demi-gods,
but in human passions; it commanded neither temple nor
municipal stage and chorus; it put up for the day in inn-court-
yards, or found lodging among the disorderly houses of the
Bankside, itself scarcely less disorderly. Not even a Shakespeare could efface the stigma of its old trade, or quite exempt
even a *Hamlet* or a *Lear* from association in men's minds with
cat-calls, nuts and oranges.

Aristotle could as little foresee all this as he could foresee that Epic, continuing respectable under tradition, keeping its proud trailing robe aloof from contact with the skirt of its royal sister turned drab, would increase in estimation by her decrease. But so it happened. Dryden (though himself a prolific writer of drama and critic enough to beware of touching the *Poetics* otherwise than gingerly) has to write—'The most perfect work of Poetry, says our master Aristotle, is Tragedy. . . . But . . . an heroick poem is certainly the greatest work of human nature.' And to the first *édition de luxe* of *Paradise Lost* (published in 1688) he contributed the famous 'pinchbeck epigram'—as Mark Pattison calls it—

> Three Poets, in three distant Ages born . . . etc.

—in which the Epic poet is assumed to stand above all others.

Again, in Addison's famous pages which he devoted to criticizing *Paradise Lost* you will find it tacitly assumed that Epic is the highest form of poetry. When we reach Dr. Johnson—who comes to *Paradise Lost* with no disposition to do it justice, we find him admitting hardly that

> By the general consent of criticks the first praise of genius is due to the writer of an epick poem, as it requires an assemblage of all the powers which are singly sufficient for other compositions.

In short—and partly no doubt through the success of *Paradise Lost*—it became the tradition of the penniless literary aspirant to set out for London (as Crabbe did) with an Epic in his pocket. What he found there was not a public who needed him, but, with luck, a patron who patronized him because in that age the role of Maecenas consorted with a British nobleman's ideal construction of himself. Yet there is evidence in plenty that the great man's languid demand for Epic Poetry (*with* a Dedication) not seldom turned into a brisk defensive movement against the number of clients ready to supply it: and if you study the 'poetical remains' of the eighteenth century preserved for us in volume after volume of Chalmers's monumental collection, I doubt not your exclaiming 'Small blame to him!' or your sympathizing with Horace Walpole—an eminent victim—who, suffering from gout in addition, calls out upon

Epic as 'that most senseless of all the species of poetic composition, and which'—his testiness, you perceive, penetrating
to the relative clause—'and which pedants call the *chef d'œuvre*
of the human mind. . . . When nothing has been impossible
to genius in every other walk, why has everybody failed in this
but the inventor, Homer? . . . Milton, all imagination, and a
thousand times more sublime and spirited than even Virgil,
has produced a monster.'

Where is the literature owning more than one Epic poet
unmistakably of the first rank?

Here let me in parenthesis, Gentlemen, stress that word
'unmistakably.' A deal of stupid moralizing has been written
at one time and another around the fact that Milton in his lifetime received but ten pounds in money, and his widow but
eight additional pounds, for the copyright of *Paradise Lost*.
Let none of it get in our way between us and the equal certainty
that *Paradise Lost*, published in 1667 (the year after the Great
Fire), stepped easily and at a stride to its place in men's estimation as one of the world's great Epics. Some might decry
it, others might exalt: but it was *that*, and admittedly, and from
the first. The fame of it at once collected about his lodgings in
Artillery Walk a conflux of visitors; 'much more' reports
Aubrey, 'than he did desire.' The story goes that Dryden laid
the book down and exclaimed 'This man cuts us all out and
the ancients too!' and the anecdote may or may not be vera-
cious. But whether or not Dryden said it, *Paradise Lost* was
reprinted in 1674 (the year of Milton's death); in 1688 appeared
the first *édition de luxe*, published on a subscription started by
Lord Somers; and for this edition, to be printed under its
engraved portrait of Milton, Dryden wrote his famous lines:

> Three Poets, in three distant Ages born,
> Greece, Italy, and England did adorn.
> The first in Loftiness of Thought surpass'd,
> The next in Majesty, in both the last:
> The Force of Nature could no farther go;
> To make a third she join'd the former two.

—a 'pinchbeck epigram.' But what concerns us is that Dryden

wrote it, and that so eminent a critic could sound so confident a note of applause within a few years of Milton's death: as, when Mark Pattison proceeds to tell us that the Whigs cried up *Paradise Lost*, and the Tories had therefore to cry it down, it only concerns *us* that the applause and the detraction alike based themselves upon admission of its greatness. Here, at any rate, Addison and Dr. Johnson find common ground. I suppose no honest critic ever put greater pressure on the forgiveness of his conscience than did Johnson when he shared in the campaign of writing down Milton. But what does Johnson write in a postscript to Lauder's dishonest attack, *An Essay in Milton's Use and Imitation of the Moderns in his 'Paradise Lost*,' published in 1750? Newton's great edition had just been published, and Johnson had noted, in the memoir prefixed, that Milton's granddaughter, Elizabeth Foster, was still alive and in poor circumstances, keeping a small chandler's shop in Cock Lane, Shoreditch. He writes promptly and generously:

That this relation is true cannot be questioned: but, surely, the honour of letters, the dignity of sacred poetry, the spirit of the English nation, and the glory of human nature, require—that it should be true no longer. In an age, in which statues are erected to the honour of this great writer, in which his effigy has been diffused on medals, and his work propagated by translations, and illustrated by commentaries; in an age, which amidst all its vices, and all its follies, has not become infamous for want of charity: it may be, surely, allowed to hope that the living remains of Milton will be no longer suffered to languish in distress. It is yet in the power of a great people, to reward the poet whose name they boast, and from their alliance to whose genius, they claim some kind of superiority to every nation of the earth; that poet, whose works may possibly be read when every other monument of British greatness shall be obliterated; to reward him—not with pictures, or with medals which, if he sees, he sees with contempt, but—with tokens of gratitude, which he, perhaps, may even now consider as not unworthy the regard of an immortal spirit.

That is talking. That is how great men should salute great antagonists as they pass.

But, to return to Aristotle: though he found no significance in the fact that Homer had remained without successor to the Epic mantle, yet he might (one thinks) have surmised a warning in the argument he was at pains to counter—the argument that Epic in his day had come to address an intellectual public and must therefore be of an order superior to Drama, which addresses any and every one and thereby makes itself vulgar (φορτική). For a form of art which has arrived at catering for intellectuals only—and Homer certainly addressed no such audience—is an art for the few in any nation of men. We should not therefore condemn it, perhaps. But the truth remains, history certifying, that great Epic writers tend, in modern times, to be lonely men. There is nothing in the least lonely about Homer: you can, with a very small amount of imagination, hear the fed men-at-arms 'having put from themselves the desire of meat and drink,' murmuring response to him all adown the long hall. But surely when we picture Virgil to ourselves, it is as a lonely scholarly man, refining his verse with interminable secret pains. The Middle Ages, anyhow, chose to regard him as a wizard, and you will find it difficult to reconcile that conception with sociability or with any service of Epic to the wine-cup. To Dante Virgil was a companion, indeed, and a guide; but austere, tall beyond all ordinary height, not flesh and blood. And Dante was even a lonelier man than Virgil; and Milton loneliest of the three. High, rarefied intellectuals all, and in progression less and less sensitive in their verse to human passion, human frailty!

We find ourselves here on the edge of a difficult question. 'Can Epic be written again in these days? Or has it rarefied itself away into a lost art?—lost, albeit though so grand, so tremendously imposing.'

I decline the speculation. Poetry for me has always been the stuff the poets have written—just that and no more: and criticism the business of examining that, of sifting out (if one can) gold from dross. But with rules and definitions I take leave to have no concern at all, nor curiosity concerning any such commerce. Rules are made to be broken, by the artist who can; definitions to be valued by any critic who cares.

And in these animadversions of mine upon Milton and *Paradise Lost* I beg you not for a moment to suppose me as regretting that he did not make a Tragedy of it.   Here it is—our grandest Epic—and a poem for which, however late we come to a full appreciation, every one of us who speak in English ought to be proudly thankful.

I will not even say that a man attempting Epic in our days *must* be a lonely man, although I think that he must, and although I note that the grandest Epic effort of this generation has been made by Mr. Charles Doughty; and that of writers now living you will with difficulty name one lonelier or one whose fame is less commensurate with his worth.   But I will say that, while finding it happily impossible to imagine a time when delight in the *Iliad*, the *Odyssey*, the *Aeneid*, the *Divine Comedy* shall have perished among men, I cannot persuade myself but that the manufacture of great Epic must become harder and harder yet, and its rare visitations diminish out and pass into a tale that is told—that is, unless some genius shall arise to bow and bend its grand manner to narrate the nobler deeds of men conspicuous for virtue among their fellow-men of which our own later age has supplied examples, say in Lee, Lincoln, Gordon.   At present its own nobility obliges it; and our very reverence binds the tradition upon it that it must traffic with the gods, or with the heroic origins of a nation, or with both.   Our civilization has reduced the multitudinous, warm-breathing companionable gods of Greece and Rome— *tot circum unum caput volitantes deos*—to one God; a God removed beyond vision and far out of reach of those tender intimate railleries which a Greek might use as a lover towards *his* Olympians; an Almighty, moreover; and by that almightiness capable of nullifying any scientific process from cause to effect, and nullifying thereby any human story concerning Him: while, as for national origins and antique heroes, science steadily dissipates the romantic aura about them, to substitute a fog of its own.   The mythology—or what there ever was of a mythology—behind *Beowulf* is not only no longer ours; it has so far faded out of the mind of our race that, in comparison with Greek fable, it awakes little curiosity and can scarcely, for any length of time, keep a hold on our interest.

Let us take this matter of national origins first, and remember that we are dealing with Milton. Milton at first proposed King Arthur for the hero of his *magnum opus*: and I would in passing remind those foolish people who run themselves down as Anglo-Saxon, that if they claim (as, if they do, I am sure they mistake themselves) to belong to that very old fiasco, they cannot at any rate claim the heroic shade of Arthur for a kinsman's, or his Table Round as recording any compliment to their ancestry. Well, Milton at first intended to commemorate King Arthur. But actually and although he wrote a history of Britain, Milton, with his classical propensity and Italianate upbringing, had no local sense of England at all. He was a Londoner whose travel in this country reached just so far north of London as Cambridge, and just so far west as Horton in Buckinghamshire. In intimacy with the *genius loci* of any spot in rural England—which, after all, remains the true England—with the palimpsest, the characters, faint but indelible, which her true lover traces on Berkshire or Sussex downs, along the edge of Cambridgeshire fens, over Dartmoor or the wild Yorkshire country, or up the great roads to the Roman Wall—in this knowledge a page of Drayton, or even a half-line of Shakespeare, will put Milton down. One recalls the magniloquent use he makes of place-names:

> City of old or modern Fame, the seat
> Of mightiest Empire, from the destined walls
> Of *Cambalu*, seat of *Cathaian Can*,
> And *Samarchand* by *Oxus*, *Temirs* throne,
> To *Paquin*, of *Sinaean* kings, and thence
> To *Agra* and *Lahore* of great *Mogul*
> Down to the golden *Chersonese*, or where
> The *Persian* in *Ecbatan* sat, or since
> In *Hispahan*, or where the *Russian Ksar*
> In *Mosco*, or the Sultan in *Bizance*,
> *Turchestan*-born . . .

or

> From *Arachosia*, from *Candaor* east,
> And *Margian* to the *Hyrcanian* cliffs

> Of *Caucasus*, and dark *Iberian* dales,
> From *Atropatria* and the neighbouring plains
> Of *Adiabene*, *Media* and the south
> Of *Susiana* to *Balsara's* hav'n . . .

with the rest of it. But of homelier English place-names, as
ancient as the most of these and as delicately syllabled, he will
not condescend to make one single catalogue. Of the epic
origins they enwrap by the thousand I suppose this fastidiously
Italianate Englishman to have been either unaware, or, if
aware, disdainful. For him the Mount of St. Michael,
Caragluz, is not nameworthy in itself. Its vision in *Lycidas*
looks seaward and southward

> toward *Namancos* and *Bayona's* hold;
> Look homeward Angel now, and melt with ruth.

but he does his wafting with dolphins!

X

On the theological story of *Paradise Lost* I shall be very
brief. If our English springs could boast of Naiads; or Newmarket Heath had ever, in legend, been scoured by Centaurs;
if our dim past (into which Milton sought in youth for a theme)
had possessed a tolerable theogony for its background; I
dare say he would not have had recourse to Judaic suggestion
or, if you will, to Judaic inspiration, for his theme. But, as
it happened, he did; and the result is curious.

Men of the eighteenth century praised him for the grandeur
of his conception; and his detractors, too, of that century took
him on that ground. Neither Addison nor Johnson can ever
get far away from the prepossession that here, whatever we
may think of him, was a tremendous fellow who took hold of
the pillars of heaven and hell. Encomiast and detractor alike
have always this at the back of their criticism.

It has been said that miracles, like curses, come home to
roost. We pass to another century, and find Mark Pattison
writing thus:

There is an element of decay and death in poems which we vainly style immortal. Some of the sources of Milton's power are already in process of drying up. I do not speak of the ordinary caducity of language, in virtue of which every effusion of the human spirit is lodged in a body of death. Milton suffers little as yet from this cause. There are few lines in his poems which are less intelligible now than they were at the time they were written. This is partly to be ascribed to his limited vocabulary, Milton, in his verse, using not more than eight thousand words, or about half the number used by Shakespeare.

(And one remembers that *Paradise Lost* is easily the most learned poem in our language, and that Shakespeare by repute was an indifferently learned man!)

Pattison goes on:

The defects of English for purposes of rhythm and harmony are as great now as they ever were, but the space that our speech fills in the world is vastly increased, and this increase of consideration is reflected back upon our older writers.

But if, as a treasury of poetic speech, *Paradise Lost* has gained by time, it has lost far more as a storehouse of divine truth. We at this day are better able than ever to appreciate its form of expression, its grace of phrase, its harmony of rhythmical movement, *but it is losing its hold over our imagination.*

And thereupon Pattison, as a thoughtful nineteenth century agnostic, proceeds to tell us that, while it would have been a thing incredible to Milton that the hold of Jewish scriptures over the imagination of English men and women could ever be weakened, 'this process . . . has already commenced.' But years pass and with their passing men shift their point of judgment. As we look at the matter to-day, who cares a penny that Milton's theory of the Creation was right or was wrong? We are no more concerned to believe in it than to believe that Pallas Athene sprang to birth in full armour through a crack in the skull of Zeus. For us, as a reported tale, *Paradise Lost* has surely receded as far back into fiction as anything in the *Odyssey*. We grant all its premisses. We ask only if, those premisses granted, our artist be sincere and true to his art. I will put the question to you in this way—such questions being always raised best on a definite illustration—Does it in the least alter the effect of *Paradise Lost* upon our minds whether we believe or not that God made the world in six days and rested on the seventh, when Milton can command us up from the perfected work in the train of imagined Deity by lines such as these?—

> So Ev'n and Morn accomplish't the Sixt day:
> Yet not till the Creator from his work
> Desisting, though unwearied, up returnd;
> Up to the Heav'n of Heav'ns, his high abode,
> Thence to behold this new created World
> Th' addition of his Empire, how it shew'd
> In prospect from his Throne, how good, how faire,
> Answering his great Idea.   Up he rode
> Follow'd with acclamation . . .
> the Earth, the Aire
> Resounded, (thou remember'st for thou heardst)
> The Heav'ns and all the Constellations rung,
> The Planets in their stations list'ning stood,
> While the bright Pomp ascended jubilant.
> *Open, ye everlasting Gates, they sung,*
> *Open, ye Heav'ns your living dores; let in*
> *The great Creator from his work returnd*
> *Magnificent, his Six days' work, a World!*

We come back to the old objection that, while Milton masters us, he does not win us: he over-awes, he astounds, but he does not charm.   The young, they say, do not easily come to like him.

But let us examine.   I think we all—but especially the young —love spirituality in a poem, and rightly love it.   Now to be intensely spiritual a man must first be humble: and Milton was not a humble man.   He greets us in an attitude uncompromisingly, if not quite affectedly, stiff and classical; as who should say 'Though I tell of Heaven and of Paradise, and though I speak with the tongues of men and of angels, I propose to do it in the Greek formula because that is the only right way—"Sing, Heavenly Muse!"'   Moreover, Milton himself so distinctly visualizes 'things invisible to mortal sight' that when he comes to communicate these mysteries he tells us all—the geography of Paradise, the construction of the bridge over Chaos, the measurement of Mulciber's fall—in terms of our own days and seasons.   But he who accurately describes a sublime thing tends thereby to lessen it in our minds. Immensity cannot be measured and remain immense; in poetical dealing with mystery the part is, and must be, greater than the whole.

XI

A critic, hitherto anonymous, has said:

Shakespeare had other methods. Edgar's purely fictitious description of the cliff at Dover begins with details—the crows and choughs no bigger than beetles, and so forth. They leave us cold, until the last sentence comes:

> I 'll look no more,
> Lest my brain turn and the deficient sight
> Topple down headlong.

And at that we shudder. 'For all beneath the moon,' he adds, 'would I not leap upright'; and though we know there is no cliff, we crouch with him, dizzy. Humanity recognizes and admits the limitations of its speech, and of its common weakness; and humanity replies to the admission with a thrill. It will strive to soar to unimaginable heights with Shelley, because it knows that Shelley is struggling, groping, yearning himself. Milton, the master, sweeping us along on his mighty pinion, seems sometimes to block the prospect with his own knowledge.

An illustration might be taken from painting. There are pictures so masterly, so complete, that they are like commands. 'I will show you,' the artist seems to say, 'what you could never see for yourself, There it is; and there is nothing more to see.' And from the mighty, masterly work we turn aside to some modest picture by a lesser man, and find in it nothing, perhaps, of the splendour we have just left, but an outlet, a loophole of escape, in which the artist seems to say: 'I could see no further. I do not know what is beyond.' Thus he gives us not only the dear touch of bounded humanity, but the sense of mystery, of the immanence of the unknown and the unknowable, which bounded humanity, for all its greed of knowledge, hugs close in secret. In poetry the same effect is obtained not only by such direct means as Shakespeare used in the passage quoted, but by the reticences, the phrases which admit, as it were, that speech cannot express what is meant, the half-words, half-sighs, like 'The rest is silence,' or 'She should have died hereafter.

> There would have been a time for such a word.
> To-morrow, and to-morrow, and to-morrow
> Creeps in this petty pace from day to day

> To the last syllable of recorded time,
> And all our yesterdays have lighted fools
> The way to dusty death. . . .'

lines which do no more than point to the infinite, and leave it infinite still. In Milton, bent as he was upon mapping out the infinite, explaining the strange, there are no such phrases. There are few, even, of those lines, of which there are many in Shakespeare, in Keats, in Wordsworth, which seem, as if by direct inspiration, to mean far more than the words say, to open the doors and set the mind wandering in ways not realized.

> No motion has she now, no force;
>   She neither hears nor sees;
> Rolled round in earth's diurnal course,
>   With rocks, and stones, and trees.

The actual meaning of these words is as nothing compared with their effect upon the mind of the reader. It is not a verse as Abt Vogler might say, but a star.

But after all, these are questions of literary tact. And who will brutally blame some uncertainty of tact upon a blind man, who speaks, but can read no response, no sympathy, no quick answer in the eyes of his fellows: to whom returns not

> Day, or the sweet approach of Ev'n or Morn,
> Or sight of vernal bloom or Summer's Rose,
> Or flocks, or herds, or human face divine?

The redemption after all, and last high vindication of this most magnificent poem are not to be sought in its conception or in its framing, grand but imperfect as Titanic work always has been and ever will be. To find *them* you must lean your ear closely to its angelic language, to its cadenced music. Once grant that we have risen—as Milton commands us to rise—above humankind and the clogging of human passion, where will you find, but in *Paradise Lost*, language fit for seraphs, speaking in the quiet of dawn in sentry before the gates of Heaven?

And the secret of it?

I believe the grand secret to be very simple. I believe you may convince yourself where it lies by watching the hands of any good organist as he plays.

It lies—Milton's had other secrets of course—but the main
  * I 974

secret lies in the movement, the exquisitely modulated slide, of his caesura. Listen to it:

> Father, thy word is past, man shall find grace;
> And shall grace not find means, that finds her way,
> The speediest of thy wingèd messengers,
> To visit all thy creatures, and to all
> Comes unprevented, unimplor'd, unsought,
> Happie for man, so coming; he her aide
> Can never seek, once dead in sins and lost;
> Attonement for himself or offering meet,
> Indebted and undon, hath none to bring:
> Behold mee then, mee for him, life for life
> I offer, on mee let thine anger fall;
> Account mee man; I for his sake will leave
> Thy bosom, and this glorie next to thee
> Freely put off, and for him lastly die
> Well pleas'd;

or

> The Birds thir quire apply; aires, vernal aires,
> Breathing the smell of field and grove, attune
> The trembling leaves, while Universal *Pan*
> Knit with the *Graces* and the *Hours* in dance
> Led on th' Eternal Spring. Not that faire field
> Of *Enna*, where Proserpin gathering flours
> Her self a fairer Floure by gloomie *Dis*
> Was gatherd, which cost *Ceres* all that pain
> To seek her through the world; nor that sweet Grove
> Of *Daphne* by *Orontes*, and th' inspir'd
> *Castalian* Spring might with this Paradise
> Of *Eden* strive;

or

> Som natural tears they drop'd, but wip'd them soon;
> The World was all before them, where to choose
> Thir place of rest, and Providence thir guide;
> They hand in hand with wandring steps and slow,
> Through *Eden* took thir solitarie way.

That is how I see Milton, and that is the portrait I would leave with you—of an old man, lonely and musical, seated at his chamber organ, sliding upon the keyboard a pair of hands pale as its ivory in the twilight of a shabby lodging of which the shabbiness and the gloom molest not him; for he is blind —and yet he sees.

THE POETRY OF GEORGE MEREDITH

I

FOR some years I have foreseen a generation—and it may be facing me to-day on these benches—likely to turn with distaste from George Meredith's prose writings, to neglect or to decry. Nor, apart from my love of the man, can I on my conscience deplore this, seeing that from the first I have insisted, as I shall go on insisting while I speak from this place, that an educated Englishman shoúld write English as cleanly, pellucidly as the average educated Frenchman writes French: that he owes that to the dignity of his country as well as to his private self-respect. Therefore I would warn you against taking Meredith's prose for a model only less earnestly than against Carlyle's because it happens to be less tempting. Any one past that temptation will find sampling or—to use an old-fashioned word—degusting either a recreation for his riper years.

The ordinary educated Englishman, however, stands in small danger of writing poetry in face of the discouragement those riper years are sure to provide, and therefore I can exhort him freely to apply himself to Meredith's verse: for it speaks to youth with the voice of one who encourages, trusts its manhood, and believes in it.

II

Now, for the first point, you must forgive me that I, who had the honour to know him enough to hear him talk frankly, can scarcely think of him as old.

I suppose [he admitted once] I should regard myself as getting old—I am seventy-four. But I do not feel to be growing old, either in heart or mind. I still look on life with a young man's eye. I have always hoped I should not grow old as some do—with a palsied intellect, living backwards, regarding other people as anachronisms because they themselves have lived on into other times and left their sympathies behind them with the years.

He never did. You must understand that while in conversation and bearing he played with innocent extravagancies which, in a smaller man, might be mistaken for affectations— in particular with a high Spanish courtesy which was equally at the service of his cook and of his king—you soon perceived all this to be genuine; the ingrained manner of the man. It did not pretend a false sprightliness of

> Days, when the ball of our vision
>   Had eagles that flew unabash'd to sun;
> When the grasp on the bow was decision,
>   And arrow and hand and eye were one.

But he recognized that this had been, and was irrecoverable; that while the time lasted it had been priceless. No poet, no thinker, growing old, had ever a more fearless trust in youth; none has ever had a truer sense of our duty to it:

> Keep the young generations in hail,
>   And bequeath them no tumbled house.

None has ever been more scornful of the asserted wisdom of our seniors, who,

> on their last plank,
> Pass mumbling it as nature's final page . . .

and would petrify the young with rules of wisdom, lest—as he says scornfully—

> Lest dreaded Change, long damm'd by dull decay,
> Should bring the world a vessel steer'd by brain,
> And ancients musical at close of day.

'Earth loves her young,' begins his next sonnet:

> Her gabbling grey she eyes askant, nor treads
> The ways they walk; by what they speak oppress'd.

III

I have a more difficult defence to put up against his alleged and, in places, undeniable obscurity. Rather, it would be more difficult if I proposed to put up any. But I do not.

Let us separate obscurity from ugliness. Let us take, for example, Shakespeare's *King Lear*, which contains somewhat of both; and I put it to you that our sense of tremendous beauty as we read that play is twin with a sense of the bestial lurking in humankind. Or I ask you to consider Shakespeare's *Pericles* and say 'Is it or is it not the test of the brothel scenes that passes Marina for adorable?'—to consider *The Tempest* and answer 'Where would be Ariel or where even Miranda, or where the whole lovely magic, with Caliban left out?' But obscurity is failure. It may be a partial failure; it may be an entirely honourable failure, born of bravery to face truths for which, because they are difficult or rugged, the writer can hardly find expressive words, while smooth mellifluous words sin against truth. Still it is a disability, albeit (let me add) with this compensation, that when the fuliginous clouds are rifted, when, as often with Donne, with Browning, with Meredith, we stand and gaze into a sudden vista of clear beauty, the surprise is strangely effective: it has an awe of its own and a reward not illegitimate. I might quote you from Meredith separate lines or very short passages by the score to illustrate this. Take one example only, summarizing that love of Earth which we shall find to be the master secret of his teaching:

> Until at last this love of Earth reveals
> A soul beside our own, to quicken, quell,
> Irradiate, and through ruinous floods uplift.

'Irradiate, and through ruinous floods uplift.' Milton taught that line: but for Milton it had never been written: and yet it could never have been written, after Milton, by any but an authentic poet.

IV

Fortunately, however, Meredith has left some poems, un-challengeably beautiful, in which a reader impatient of obscurity will discover little or nothing to tease him. And since—and although my practice this morning may seem to contradict it

—no small part of a teacher's duty consists in saving other people's time, let me indicate a few of Meredith's poems which, if you like them, will lead you to persevere with more difficult ones in which, if my experience be of use, you will find much delight: for there is a pleasure in critical pains as well as in poetic. If you like them not, why then you will be in a position to decide on saving further time, though you lose something else.

The first—*Phoebus with Admetus*—I will read in full. You know the legend: how Phoebus Apollo—lord of the sun, of music, of archery, of medicine—was exiled by his father Zeus for having slain the Cyclops, and condemned to serve a term on earth, tending the flocks of king Admetus of Thessaly. This is the tale of the shepherds and herdsmen who had known the divine guest and the wondrous great season of plenty he brought: [1]

> When by Zeus relenting the mandate was revoked,
>   Sentencing to exile the bright Sun-God,
> Mindful were the ploughmen of who the steer had yoked,
>   Who: and what a track show'd the upturn'd sod!
> Mindful were the shepherds as now the noon severe
>   Beat a burning eyebrow to brown evetide,
> How the rustic flute drew the silver to the sphere,
>   Sister of his own, till her rays fell wide.
>   God! of whom music
>   And song and blood are pure,
>   The day is never darken'd
>   That had thee here obscure.
>
> Chirping none the scarlet cicalas crouch'd in ranks:
>   Slack the thistle-head piled its down-silk grey:
> Scarce the stony lizard suck'd hollows in his flanks;
>   Thick on spots of umbrage our drowsed flocks lay.
> Sudden bow'd the chestnuts beneath a wind unheard,
>   Lengthen'd ran the grasses, the sky grew slate:
> Then amid a swift flight of wing'd seed white as curd,
>   Clear of limb a Youth smote the master's gate.

---

[1] Mark the triple hammer-beat, closing the 2nd, 4th, 6th, 8th stanzaic lines throughout. It is one of Meredith's master-tricks.

Water, first of singers, o'er rocky mount and mead,
  First of earthly singers, the sun-loved rill,
Sang of him, and flooded the ripples on the reed,
  Seeking whom to waken, and what ear fill.
Water, sweetest soother to kiss a wound and cool,
  Sweetest and divinest, the sky-born brook,
Chuckled, with a whimper, and made a mirror-pool
  Round the guest we welcomed, the strange hand shook.

Many swarms of wild bees descended on our fields:
  Stately stood the wheatstalk with head bent high:
Big of heart we labour'd at storing mighty yields,
  Wool and corn, and clusters to make men cry!
Hand-like rushed the vintage; we strung the bellied skins,
  Plump, and at the sealing the Youth's voice rose:
Maidens clung in circle, on little fists their chins;
  Gentle beasties through pushed a cold long nose.

Foot to fire in snowtime we trimm'd the slender shaft:
  Often down the pit spied the lean wolf's teeth
Grin against his will, trapp'd by masterstrokes of craft;
  Helpless in his froth-wrath as green logs seethe!
Safe the tender lambs tugg'd the teats, and winter sped
  Whirl'd before the crocus, the year's new gold.
Hung the hooky beak up aloft, the arrowhead
Redden'd through his feathers for our dear fold.

Tales we drank of giants at war with Gods above:
  Rocks were they to look on, and earth climb'd air!
Tales of search for simples, and those who sought of love
  Ease because the creature was all too fair.
Pleasant ran our thinking that while our work was good,
  Sure as fruits for sweat would the praise come fast.
He that wrestled stoutest and tamed the billow-brood
  Danced in rings with girls, like a sail-flapp'd mast.

Now of medicine and song, of both of which Apollo is God.
Song—good poetry is always linked with medicine in Meredith's
mind: twin restoratives of human sanity:

Lo, the herb of healing, when once the herb is known,
  Shines in shady woods bright as new-sprung flame.
Ere, the string was tighten'd we heard the mellow tone,
  After he had taught how the sweet sounds came.

Stretch'd about his feet, labour done, 'twas as you see
  Red pomegranates tumble and burst hard rind.
So began contention to give delight and be
  Excellent in things aim'd to make life kind.

Last, the invocation to all beasts, leaves, trees, to join in
remembering him:

You with shelly horns, rams! and promontory goats,
  You whose browsing beards dip in coldest dew!
Bulls, that walk the pastures in kingly-flashing coats!
  Laurel, ivy, vine, wreath'd for feasts not few!
You that build the shade-roof, and you that court the rays,
  You that leap besprinkling the rock stream-rent:
He has been our fellow, the morning of our days!
  Us he chose for housemates, and this way went.
        God! of whom music
        And song and blood are pure,
        The day is never darken'd
        That had thee here obscure.

                                V

  Begin with that, or begin with its fellow, the exquisite gentle
tale of Melampus the good physician to whom the woodland
creatures in reward that he

                    loving them all,
    Among them walk'd, as a scholar who reads a book,

taught their love of medicine, and where to find the herbs of
healing: and from *Melampus* go on to the ringing ballad *The
Nuptials of Attila*, or that favourite of mine *The Day of the
Daughter of Hades* which tells how Persephone (ravished wife
of dark Hades, released by him on a day to revisit earth and
embrace her mother Demeter) takes with her in the chariot
her daughter Skiageneia, child of Shadow; and how this girl-
goddess, slipping from the car, confronts a mortal youth,
Callistes:

                She did not fly,
      Nor started at his advance: . . .

for all the wonder and beauty of this upper earth were running through her blood, quickening love and memories half surmised in every drop from her mother inherited—'the blood of her a lighted dew':

> She did not fly,
> Nor started at his advance:
> She looked, as when infinite thirst
> Pants pausing to bless the springs,
> Refreshed, unsated.   Then first
> He trembled with awe of the things
> He had seen; and he did transfer,
> Divining and doubting in turn,
> His reverence unto her;
> Nor asked what he crouched to learn:
> The whence of her, whither, and why
> Her presence there, and her name,
> Her parentage: under which sky
> Her birth, and how hither she came,
> So young, a virgin, alone,
> Unfriended, having no fear,
> As Oreads have; no moan,
> Like the lost upon earth; no tear;
> Not a sign of the torch in the blood,
> Though her stature had reached the height
> When mantles a tender rud
> In maids that of youths have sight,
> If maids of our seed they be:
> For he said: A glad vision art thou!
> And she answered him: Thou to me!
> As men utter a vow.

Classical to me it seems; and clasically radiant, as if painted by Titian, the Sicilian day that followed for these two: she grandly innocent in his company, recognizing and naming the fruits of earth:

> Pear, apple, almond, plum . . .
> And she touch'd them with finger and thumb,
> As the vine-hook closes: she smiled,
> Recounting again and again,
> Corn, wine, fruit, oil! like a child,
> With the meaning known to men.

Read this poem carefully and (I dare to say) you will read in this girl-goddess not only what is the secret of the heroines in many of Meredith's novels — Lucy Desborough, Sandra Belloni, Clara Middleton—but also the secret of Shakespeare's later heroines — Perdita, Imogen, Miranda: and will not wonder how the youth Callistes, when at evening her father's awful chariot rapt her from him, was left with no future but to crave for her until his life's end:

> And to join her, or have her brought back,
> In his frenzy the singer would call,
> Till he followed where never was track,
> On the path trod of all.

There are those who would counsel you to begin your study of Meredith with *Modern Love* rather than with the poems I have chosen: and here their counsel may easily be wiser than mine, personal taste interfering to make me wayward. As a poetic form, the sonnet-sequence—even when turned as Meredith turns it, from quatorzain to seizain—is about the last to allure me. I should add, however, that Meredith's use of the sixteen-line stanza in *Modern Love* is exceedingly strong and individual: and that in the past hundred years few quatorzains, or sonnets proper, will match his *Lucifer in Starlight*. As a subject, the relations of the husband, the wife and the other man, especially when rehearsed by the husband, have usually (I state it merely as a private confession) the same physical effect on me as a drawing-room recitation. I want to get under a table and howl. From the outset the recital makes me shy as a stranger pounced upon and called in to settle a delicate domestic difference; and as it goes on I start protesting inwardly, 'My dear sir—delighted to do my best . . . man of the world . . . quite understand . . . sympathetic, and all that sort of thing. . . . But really, if you insist on all this getting into the newspapers. . . . And where did I put my hat, by the way?' In short—take the confession—with the intricacies and self-scourgings of *Modern Love* I find myself less at home than with the franker temptations of St. Anthony, and far less than with the larger, liberally careless, amours of the early gods.

Nevertheless, and by all means, try both ways and choose which you will, provided it coax you on to search the real heart of Meredith's muse in *The Woods of Westermain*, *Earth and Man*, *A Faith on Trial*, *The Empty Purse*, *Night of Frost in May*, and the like.   You will find many thorned thickets by the way; and some out of which, however hard you beat them, you will start no bird.   The juvenile poems will but poorly reward you, until you come to be interested in them historically, as Pre-Raphaelite essays which Meredith outgrew.   The later Odes celebrating French history—*The Revolution*; *Napoléon*; *France, 1870*; *Alsace-Lorraine*—should be deferred (I think) till you are fairly possessed by the Meredithian fervour. They have their splendid passages; but they are undeniably difficult.   Moreover I hold you must acquire a thorough trust in a bard before trusting him at an Ode, which is of all forms of poetry the most pontifical, before you compose your spirit to a proper humility while he indues his robes, strikes attitude and harp, and starts telling France what he thinks of her, or anything so great as France what he thinks of it, albeit he may sift out approval and end on a note of encouragement.   After reading odes in this strain I, for one, always feel that I hear France—or whatever it is—murmuring politely at the close, 'Thank you—*so* much!'

VI

But it is in the poems I named just now, and in others collected under the two general titles *A Reading of Earth* and *A Reading of Life*, that you will find the essential Meredith: and, as these titles hint, he is a teacher, an expositor.   Now why many of our English poets should be teachers is a dark question—to be attempted perhaps though probably not resolved, in some later lecture: as why an expositor, of all men, should be obscure and even succeed in giving us enlightenment by means of obscurity, is an even darker question—although I make no doubt that the genius of this university, sometime

adorned by the late and great Dr. Westcott, can somehow
provide it with an answer. But the philosophy of Meredith,
when you come to it, cannot be denied for strong, for arresting,
for athletic, lean, hard, wiry. It is not comfortable: Stoical,
rather; even strongly Stoical, as we use the epithet. But it
differs by the whole heaven from ancient Stoicism, being
reared on two pillars of Faith and Love. And, yet again, the
Faith differs utterly from the Faith which supports the most
of our religions—it can and, as a fact does, consist with agnos-
ticism, and the Love differs utterly from the Love which so
often infects so much of saintliness with eroticism and even
with slyness in daily life. Let me try to outline his belief, using
his own words where I may.

The man is a modern man, lost in doubt, forlorn in a forest
of doubt, but resolved to win through by help of the monitor,
the lantern within him.

> I am in deep woods,
>   Between the two twilights.
>
> Whatever I am and may be,
> Write it down to the light in me;
> I am I, and it is my deed;
> For I know that the paths are dark
>   Between the two twilights.
>
> .   .   .   .   .
>
> I have made my choice to proceed
> By the light I have within;
> And the issue rests with me,
> Who might sleep in a chrysalis,
> In the fold of a simple prayer,
>   Between the two twilights.
>
> .   .   .   .   .
>
> Having nought but the light in me,
> Which I take for my soul in arms,
> Resolv'd to go unto the wells
> For water, rejecting spells,
> And mouthings of magic for charms,
> And the cup that does not flow.
>
> I am in deep woods
>   Between the two twilights:

> Over valley and hill
> I hear the woodland wave,
> Like the voice of Time, as slow,
> The voice of Life, as grave,
> The voice of Death, as still.

He finds there is no true promise (I am but trying to interpret) in religious promises of a compensating life beyond this one. *Those* are the

> spells,
> And mouthings of magic for charms.

He is not appalled by the prospect of sinking back and dissolving into the earth of which we all are created:

> Into the breast that gave the rose
> Shall I with shuddering fall?

More and more deeply as he contemplates Earth he feels that —from her as we spring, to her as we return—so man is only strong by constantly reading her lesson, falling back to refresh himself from her mother-springs, her mother-milk. Even of prayer he writes in one of his last novels, *Lord Ormont and His Aminta*:

> Prayer is power within us to communicate with the desired beyond our thirsts. . . . And let the prayer be as a little fountain. Rising on a spout, from dread of the hollow below, the prayer may be prolonged in words begetting words, and have a pulse of fervour: the spirit of it has fallen after the first jet. *That* is the delirious energy of our craving, which has no life in our souls. We do not get to any heaven by renouncing the Mother we spring from; and when there is an eternal secret for us, it is best to believe that Earth knows, to keep near her, even in our utmost aspirations.

To be true sons of Earth, our Mother: to learn of our dependence on her, her lesson: to be frugal of self-consciousness and of all other forms of selfishness; to live near the bare ground, and finally to return to it without whining: that is the first article of his creed. Earth never whines, and looks for no son of hers to whine:

> For love we Earth, then serve we all;
>   Her mystic secret then is ours:
> We fall, or view our treasures fall,
>   Unclouded, as beholds her flowers
>
> Earth, from a night of frosty wreck,
>   Enrobed in morning's mounted fire,
> When lowly, with a broken neck,
>   The crocus lays her cheek to mire.

To set up your hope on a world beyond this one is (according to Meredith) but lust for life prolonged — 'a bloodthirsty clinging to life' in Matthew Arnold's phrase—demanding a passport beyond our natural term:

> The lover of life knows his labour divine,
>   And therein is at peace.
> The lust after life craves a touch and a sign
>   That the life shall increase.
>
> The lust after life, in the chills of its lust,
>   Claims a passport of death.
> The lover of life sees the flame in the dust
>   And a gift in our breath.

Transience?—yes, and to be gratefully accepted, like human love, for transience!   Earth, the Stoic mother, looks on while her son learns the lesson; she will not coddle:

> He may entreat, aspire,
> He may despair, and she has never heed:
> She, drinking his warm sweat, will soothe his need,
>   Not his desire.

To this extent, then, he is one with the beasts that perish. To this extent he is like Walt Whitman's animals.   Says Whitman:

> I think I could turn and live with animals . . .
> They do not sweat and whine about their condition,
> They do not lie awake in the dark and weep for their sins,
> They do not make me sick discussing their duty to God.

But the difference is that man *understands*: understands that as in his mother Earth,

> deepest at her springs,
> Most filial, is an eye to love her young . . .

so he, seeing how in life the love of boy and maid leads to the nourishing and love of children, must see further that his first duty in life is to love and care for the young. For himself, he must curb our 'distempered devil of self,' gluttonous of its own enjoyments. Meredith promises nothing—nothing beyond the grave, nothing on this side of it but love sweetening hard fare:

> The sense of large charity over the land,
> Earth's wheaten of wisdom dispensed in the rough,
> And a bell giving thanks for a sustenance meal.

VII

Well, there it is, Gentlemen, for you to take or to leave. I am here to talk about literature to you, not about doctrine. But I think that, after the mystics we discussed last term, you may find the herb of Meredith medicinal, invigorating: a philosophy austere though suffused with love; mistaken, if you will, but certainly not less than high, stern, noble, meet for men.

I have indicated some of his poems through which you may arrive at it. But he wrote one poem which stands apart from these and might (you may say) conceivably have been written by another man. If I allowed this, which I cannot, I should still hold that no one short of a genius could have invented it; as I hold that, with Spenser's *Epithalamion*, it shares claim to be the greatest song of human love in our language, as it is certainly the topmost of its age: all that Swinburne or Rossetti ever wrote fading out like fireworks or sick tapers before its sunshine. I mean *Love in the Valley*, with a number of stanzas from which I shall this morning conclude, feeling all the while that I have no gift to read them as they deserve.

Love in the Valley

Under yonder beech-tree single on the green-sward,
  Couched with her arms behind her golden head,
Knees and tresses folded to slip and ripple idly,
  Lies my young love sleeping in the shade.
Had I the heart to slide an arm beneath her,
  Press her parting lips as her waist I gather slow,
Waking in amazement she could not but embrace me:
  Then would she hold me and never let me go?

Shy as the squirrel and wayward as the swallow,
  Swift as the swallow along the river's light
Circleting the surface to meet his mirrored winglets,
  Fleeter she seems in her stay than in her flight.
Shy as the squirrel that leaps among the pine-tops,
  Wayward as the swallow overhead at set of sun,
She whom I love is hard to catch and conquer,
  Hard, but O the glory of the winning were she won!

When her mother tends her before the laughing mirror,
  Tying up her laces, looping up her hair,
Often she thinks, were this wild thing wedded,
  More love should I have, and much less care.
When her mother tends her before the lighted mirror,
  Loosening her laces, combing down her curls,
Often she thinks, were this wild thing wedded,
  I should miss but one for the many boys and girls.

.   .   .   .   .

Lovely are the curves of the white owl sweeping
  Wavy in the dusk lit by one large star.
Lone on the fir-branch, his rattle-note unvaried,
  Brooding o'er the gloom, spins the brown eve-jar.
Darker grows the valley, more and more forgetting:
  So were it with me if forgetting could be willed.
Tell the grassy hollow that holds the bubbling well-spring,
  Tell it to forget the source that keeps it filled

Stepping down the hill with her fair companions,
  Arm in arm, all against the raying West,
Boldly she sings, to the merry tune she marches,
  Brave in her shape, and sweeter unpossessed.
Sweeter, for she is what my heart first awaking

Whispered the world was; morning light is she.
Love that so desires would fain keep her changeless;
Fain would fling the net, and fain have her free.

.   .   .   .   .

Hither she comes; she comes to me; she lingers,
   Deepens her brown eyebrows, while in new surprise
High rise the lashes in wonder of a stranger;
   Yet am I the light and living of her eyes.
Something friends have told her fills her heart to brimming,
   Nets her in her blushes, and wounds her, and tames.—
Sure of her haven, O like a dove alighting,
   Arms up, she dropped: our souls were in our names.

A Song of Songs, which is Meredith's!

THE POETRY OF THOMAS HARDY

I

WE elders—from among whom, for various reasons, your professors are chosen as a rule—may hope to help you in understanding poets long since dead. For Chaucer, Shakespeare, Milton, Dryden, Wordsworth, Byron, Shelley, are removed almost as far from us as from you. They have passed definitely into the ward of Time. What was corrupt or corruptible in them is now dust, though we embalm it in myrrh, sandal-wood, cassia: dust equally for us and for you: what was incorruptible flowers as freshly for you as for us. We have but the sad advantage of having studied it a little longer.

But when we come to poets of the time of Tennyson, Browning, Matthew Arnold, our difference of age asserts itself; middle-aged men of the 'sixties, young men of the 'nineties, children of this century, read them at correspondent removes, perceptible removes. And, though you may like it not, it is (I believe) good that we seniors should testify to you concerning these men who were our seniors, yet alive when we were young, and gave us in youth, believe me, even such thrills, such awed surmises, such wonders and wild desires, as you catch in your turn from their successors. Nay, it is salutary, I believe; for the reason that it appears to be the rule for each new generation to turn iconoclast on its father's poetic gods. You will scarcely deny that on some of you the term 'Victorian' acts as a red rag upon a young bull of the pasture: that, to some of you, Tennyson is 'that sort of stuff your uncle read.' Well, bethink you that the children of yet another generation will deal so and not otherwise with your heroes: that it is all a part of the continuous process of criticism through which our roseate raptures and our lurid antipathies pass, if not into the light of common day, into that of serener judgment. Blame

not your uncle that at the age of fourteen or earlier, in the
walled garden screened from the windows of the house, he
charged among the vegetables chanting:

> A bow-shot from her bower-eaves,
> He rode between the barley-sheaves . . .

or

> Strew no more red roses, maidens,
>   Leave the lilies in their dew:
> Pluck, pluck cypress, O pale maidens!
>   Dusk, O dusk the hall with yew! . . .

or

> I forgot, thou comest from thy voyage—
>   Yes, the spray is on thy cloak and hair.
> But thy dark eyes are not dimm'd, proud Iseult!
>   And thy beauty never was more fair . . .

or

And the tent shook, for mighty Saul shuddered: and sparkles 'gan
  dart
From the jewels that woke in his turban, at once with a start,
All its lordly male-sapphires, and rubies courageous at heart.

For to dream of these things, and to awake and find oneself
an uncle—that is the common lot.   Nor blame him that he
continues loyal to them.   It keeps him human: it may set you
pondering, reconsidering a little; and so may help to advance
the true business of criticism.   I come down a little further;
past Morris and Swinburne to Yeats (say) or Francis Thompson.   We admired and admire them as generously as, I hope,
you admire them; but I think not quite in the same way.   To
us, their almost exact contemporaries, their first poems appealed
as youth to youth; with none of the authority they exercise, I
dare to say, upon you.   To us they carried no authority at all.
They carried hope, they bred ardour: but we criticized them
freely as poems written by the best of *us*.   They have to wait a
few years for the race to deify them.   You and we possess
them by a different line of approach.

Now take the young poets who are your contemporaries.
Of them I say sadly, resignedly, that a man even of my years
has no right to speak, or very little power to speak usefully.

Young poets write not for antiquity, nor for middle-age.
They write for *you*: their appeal is to *you*.   All that *we* can do
is to keep our hearts as fresh as we may; to bear ever in mind
that a father can guide a son but some distance on the road,
and the more wisely he guides the sooner (alas!) must he lose
the fair companionship and watch the boy run on.   It may
sound a hard saying, but we can only keep him admiring the
things we admire at the cost of pauperizing his mind.   It may
sound another hard saying, that the younger poets do not
write for us old men; yet it is the right course of nature.   I
hope William Cory's apophthegm is not strictly true:

> One's feelings lose poetic flow
> Soon after twenty-seven or so;
> Professionizing modern men
> Thenceforth admire what pleased them then.

But if it be (though I plead for some rise in the age-limit), then
poetry but consents with the rule of Nature whose highest
interpreter she is.   Deepest in her too—in Meredith's phrase—

> Deepest at *her* springs
> Most filial, is an eye to love her young.

II

After this somewhat wistful opening, let me claim an exception for my subject this morning.   Thomas Hardy—
I cannot call him Doctor Hardy even in a University which
not long ago did itself honour in complimenting him—Thomas
Hardy is my elder, and so much my elder that for thirty years
I have reverenced him as a master: that is, as a master of
the Novel.   His first novel *Desperate Remedies* dates back
to 1871: his first artistic triumph *Under the Greenwood Tree*,
to 1872.   Pass intervening years and come to the grand
close in *Tess of the D'Urbervilles* (1891), *Jude the Obscure*
(1895): on that last date his career as a novelist ceases, and at
the age of fifty-five.   Three years later, in 1898, he publishes
his first book of verse.   Now any pettifogging fellow can point

out that this volume, entitled *Wessex Poems*, contains many poems composed long before 1898—some so far back as 1865; and the more easily because Hardy is careful to print the dates.[1] So for that matter do some of Hardy's later volumes contain early poems, either printed as first written, or as revised. But this little affects the plain fact that in 1895, or a little later, Hardy definitely turned his back on prose fiction and started to appeal to a new generation as a writer of high poetical verse if the gods should allow. To this purpose he has held. A second volume, *Poems of the Past and the Present* followed in 1901; *The Dynasts*, Part I in 1903, Part II in 1906, Part III in 1908, *Time's Laughing-stocks* in 1909. *Satires of Circumstance* were collected in 1914. His latest volume *Moments of Vision* appeared but the other day, and bears 1917 on its title-page. So, seeing that all this, including that great epical drama, *The Dynasts*, falls within the ken of the last twenty years, you may allow perhaps that it concerns men of your age and mine, equally if not similarly.

III

You may answer, 'By all means let it concern you. The point is, can a man of Thomas Hardy's age write what appeals to *us*?' Well, yes, I think his poetry may appeal to you, as it certainly concerns you. That his Muse is predominantly melancholy I brush aside as no bar at all. If youth do not understand melancholy, why then the most of Shelley, the most of Byron, a great part of Keats, or—to come to later instances—a great, if not the greater, part of Francis Thompson and Yeats and most of the young poets of the Irish school, is closed to it: which is absurd. 'No, no! go not to Lethe' for Melancholy. She dwells neither there nor with middle-age:

---

[1] So that, as Whistler said of an art-critic who judged a water-colour for an oil-painting, 'it was accurately described in the catalogue and he had not even to rely on his sense of smell.'

> She dwells with Beauty—Beauty that must die;
>   And Joy, whose hand is ever at his lips
> Bidding adieu; and aching Pleasure nigh,
>   Turning to poison while the bee-mouth sips:
> Ay, in the very temple of Delight
>   Veil'd Melancholy has her sovran shrine,
>   Though seen of none save him whose strenuous tongue
> Can burst Joy's grape against his palate fine;
>   His soul shall taste the sadness of her might,
>   And be among her cloudy trophies hung.

No, indeed: it is proper to youth to know melancholy as it is to have raptures. Only to middle-age is it granted to be properly cheerful. Yes, there are compensations! Let us assure you that only towards middle-age will you burst upon a palate fine the true juice of Chaucer's *Prologue*, written in *his* middle-age, or of Montaigne, or of Molière: as in youth you will choose Rossetti, but later transfer your choice to William Morris, least sick or sorry, best of cheer, among the poets of his time.

As for Hardy's pessimism, that, to be sure, does not consort well with youth. But, as I shall hope to show, it always challenges youth; it is never faded, jejune, effete; it never plays —or, to be accurate, it seldom plays—with old mere sentimentalities. Even when it plays with commonplaces it leaves them unconventional. In his depths the man is always thinking, and his perplexities, being all-important and yet unsolved, are by your generation to be faced, whether you solve them or not.

IV

For another point, close beside and yet more important, we have talked of insensibility to poetry and how with the years it may steal upon the reader. Now most of you remember, I daresay, Matthew Arnold's late and mournful lines on the drying up of poesy in the writer:

> Youth rambles on life's arid mount,
>   And strikes the rock, and finds the vein,
> And brings the water from the fount,
>   The fount which shall not flow again.

> The man mature with labour chops
> 　For the bright stream a channel grand,
> And sees not that the sacred drops
> 　Ran off and vanish'd out of hand.

> And then the old man totters nigh
> 　And feebly rakes among the stones,
> The mount is mute, the channel dry;
> 　And down he lays his weary bones.

Well, at any rate Thomas Hardy contradicts, and in practice, *that* rather cheap kind of pessimism. (There was always, I think, in Matthew Arnold a tendency to be Wordsworth's widow, and to fall rather exasperatingly 'a-thinking of the old 'un.'

I am aware that to support this theory of desiccation in poets many startling instances may be cited. But without saying yea or nay, or supposing it symptomatic of our age, I cannot think it quite accidental that out of the small number of poets I have been privileged to know personally, two should have tapped, quite late in life, a well of poetry abundant, fresh, pure; of *lyrical* poetry, too, fresher, purer and far more abundant than ever they found as young men. It happened so, at all events, with an old schoolmaster of mine, the late T. E. Brown, whose quality and whose performance are now generally admitted. It has happened so with Thomas Hardy. His first poems—or, to say it more accurately, the poems in his first-published volume—were stiff, awkward. They often achieved a curious, haunting, countrified lilt; they worked always true to pattern: you felt about them, too, that the verses held the daemon of poetry, constricted, struggling for expression. But in form they resembled the drawings with which the author illustrated that first volume. These were architectural draughts (Hardy had been an architect). When they told a story, you wondered why he, so well able to do it, had not written this particular story in prose. The poetic thought was there: but the words were hard and precise, sometimes scientifically pedantic. For instance, in the last poem I shall read to-day he drags in the word 'stillicide,' which means the drip of water

in a cavern, or from eaves. Stevenson has recorded his
mingled feelings on discovering, in the process of his scientific
studies, that 'stillicide' was not a crime. The early poems
faceted no rays, they melted into none of those magical,
chemical combinations out of which words became poetry
and a new thing, 'half angel and half bird.'

Years pass, with their efforts; and then in his latest volume,
published by this man at the age of seventy-seven, he discovers
a lyrical note which I shall quote to you, not at all because its
theme is characteristic—for it is not—as not at all because it is
deep and wonted—for it is not. It is, if you will, 'silly sooth,
and dallies with the innocence of love.' Yes, just for that
reason I quote it, and because in a poet of ordinary evolution
it would fall naturally among the *Juvenilia*:

> Lalage 's coming:
> Where is she now, O?
> Turning to bow, O,
> And smile, is she,
> Just at parting,
> Parting, parting,
> As she is starting
> To come to me?
>
> Lalage 's coming,
> Nearer is she now, O,
> End anyhow, O,
> To-day's husbandry!
> Would a gilt chair were mine,
> Slippers of vair were mine,
> Brushes for hair were mine
> Of ivory!
>
> What will she think, O,
> She who 's so comely,
> Viewing how homely
> A sort are we!
> Nought here 's enough for her,
> All is too rough for her,
> Even my love for her
> Poor in degree.

Lalage 's come; aye,
Come is she now, O!
Does Heaven allow, O,
A meeting to be?
Yes, she is here now,
Here now, here now,
Nothing to fear now,
Here 's Lalage!

If that be too trivial, take another—remembering that I give them only as metrical specimens, merely to show how this poet, whose metrical muscles were stiff and hard at fifty-odd has at seventy-odd (the date is 1913) worked them supple, so that now the verse cadences to the feeling:

Out of the past there rises a week—
    Who shall read the years O!
In that week there was heard a singing—
    Who shall spell the years O!—
In that week there was heard a singing,
    And the white owl wondered why.
In that week there was heard a singing,
    And forth from the casement were candles flinging
Radiance that fell on the deodar and lit up the path thereby.

Or take him on a lower note:

I need not go
Through sleet and snow
To where I know
She waits for me;
She will wait me there
Till I find it fair,
And have time to spare
From company . . .

                .   .   .

What—not upbraid me
That I delayed me,
Nor ask what stayed me
So long?   Ah, no!—
New cares may claim me,
New loves inflame me,
She will not blame me,
But suffer it so.

I reserve for the while the most individual quality in Hardy's versifying (to me an individual excellence) which has given it character from the first—I mean his country lilt; because I must approach it, and the man, and his philosophy of life, all three by one path.

V

First of all, and last of all, he is a countryman. And the first meaning of this is that his mind works like most country minds in this great little island. They are introspective *because* insular: and their soil is cumbered, piled with history and local tradition: a land of arable inveterately and deeply ploughed; of pastures close-webbed at the root by rain and sun persistently reviving the blade which the teeth of sheep and cattle persistently crop; of its heaths—such as Newmarket—where racehorses in training gallops beat their hoofs in the very footprints of Boadicea's mares and stallions; of mines, working yet, that paid their first-fruits to Sidon and Carthage, choked harbours, dead empires. In this land of ours, I say, the mind of a native must dig vertically down through strata. Though it be the mind of a farm labourer, it knows its acres intimately; not only their rotation of crops, and slant to wind or sun, but their several humours, caprices, obstinacies of soil; and, always with an eye to windward, hopes for the weather it knows likeliest to profit them. So when, as with Hardy, a countryman has the further knowledge that comes of book-learning, and acquires with it the historical sense, that sense still feels vertically downwards, through soil and subsoil, through the mould of Norman, Dane, Saxon, Celt, Iber, and of tribes beyond history, to the geological formations layered over by this accumulated dust.

Further, you know that the tales of old time which haunt a true countryman's imagination are tales of violence, of lonely houses where suppressed passions inhabit, to flame out in murder or suicide, to make a legend, to haunt a cross-road or a mile-post: fierce, primitive deeds breaking up through the slow crust of custom: unaccountable, but not unnatural —along the king's highway, a gibbet where sheepstealers used to swing: in such and such a copse a tree, on that tree such and such a branch where a poor girl hanged herself for love: at the three roads by the blacksmith's a triangle of turf still called 'Betsy Beneath' because there they buried her uncoffined and drove a stake through·her.

Further, if you know your rural England, you will know that every village in it is a small shop of gossip. 'Have you heard? Young Peter Hodge is at upsides with his wife? yes, already, and her only expectin'.' 'They tell me Farmer So-and-so have a mortgage, if you 'll believe, on the Lower Barton Farm.' 'So, that girl Jenny is in trouble as I always foretold.' Vengeance o' Jenny's case!

Well as I interpret this most genuine, most autochthonous of living writers, I see him leaning over the gate of a field with a wood's edge bordering it. He knows the wood so intimately that his ear detects and separates the notes of the wind as it soughs in oak, hornbeam, pine (see the opening of *Under the Greenwood Tree*, or *The Woodlanders, passim*). Of the sheep on the pasture he knows when their lambs will fall. He judges the grass, if it be sufficient. He knows that breast-shaped knob on the knap of the hill and how many centuries have worn to this what was the high burial mound of a British chieftain: he knows the lias beneath the chief's grave, and the layered rock still deeper—that is, he knows as near as geologists can tell. He knows, having a boy's eye for this, where a nest is likeliest to be, and of what bird. But what more intrigues him than any of these things—still as he follows the line of the hedge—is that under one innocent-looking thorn such and such a parish tragedy was enacted. Just here, they tell, two brothers quarrelled and one smote the other with a reaping-hook; just there was lovers' bliss and just there, a brief while later, the woman's heart broke.

For (you must know) though a gossip's, this countryman's heart is strangely tender. Let me pause for proof, by one short poem, that even Blake's heart was not tenderer than Hardy's. It is called

The Blinded Bird

So zestfully canst thou sing?
And all this indignity,
With God's consent, on thee!
Blinded ere yet a-wing
By the red-hot needle thou,
I stand and wonder how
So zestfully thou canst sing!

Resenting not such wrong,
Thy grievous pain forgot,
Eternal dark thy lot,
Groping thy whole life long,
After that stab of fire;
Enjailed in pitiless wire;
Resenting not such wrong!

Who hath charity? This bird.
Who suffereth long and is kind,
Is not provoked, though blind
And alive ensepulchred?
Who hopeth, endureth all things?
Who thinketh no evil, but sings?
Who is divine? This bird.

Above all, his pity is for women, partly for the fate that condemns their bloom to be brief and evanescent (unless written in time on a man's heart where it never grows old)— so brief the chance, with no term to the after-pain! But he pities them more because he sees the increase of our race to rest on an unfair game, in which, nine throws out of ten, the dice are loaded against the woman; a duel of sex, almost at times an internecine duel, which his soul grows to abhor: for

Victrix causa deis placuit, sed victa Catoni,

and, looking up, he sees God, or whatever gods may be, deriding the victim. We are all flies to these gods who tease us for their sport. Even if man labour and profit his fellows with an idea, yet, in Milton's phrase (as quoted by Hardy)

> Truth like a bastard comes into the world
> Never without ill-fame to him who gives her birth.

But, for women, who, nine times out of ten, pay the price of the great jest, Hardy feels most acutely. 'Poor wounded name,' he quotes and inscribes on the title-page of *Tess*,

> Poor wounded name! my bosom as a bed
> Shall lodge thee . . .

and in the last sentence of his most sorrowful tale he flings his now famous taunt up at 'the President of the Immortals,' even as passionately as did Cleopatra for her own loss:

Iras.	Madam!
Charmian.	O madam, madam, madam!
Iras.	Royal Egypt!
	Empress!
Charmian,	Peace, peace, Iras!
Cleopatra.	No more, but e'en a woman, and commanded
	By such poor passion as the maid that milks

(Tess was a dairy-maid)

> And does the meanest chares. It were for me
> To throw my sceptre at the injurious gods;
> To tell them that this world did equal theirs
> Till they had stol'n our jewel.

VI

Say what you will, this indignation in Hardy is noble, is chivalrous, and, as the world is worked, it has much reason at the back of its furious 'Why?—Why?—Why?' It has great excuse when it sours down to bitterest irony, as in this early ditty of two country-bred girls meeting in London—and you will note how the old market-jog of rhythm and rhyme *ache* themselves into the irony:

> 'O 'Melia, my dear, this does everything crown!
> Who could have supposed I should meet you in Town?
> And whence such fair garments, such prosperi-ty?'—
> 'O didn't you know I'd been ruined?' said she.

—'You left us in tatters, without shoes or socks,
Tired of digging potatoes, and spudding up docks;
And now you 've gay bracelets and bright feathers three!'—
'Yes: that 's how we dress when we 're ruined,' said she. ...

.   .   .   .   .

—'I wish I had feathers, a fine sweeping gown,
And a delicate face, and could strut about Town!'—
'My dear—a raw country girl, such as you be,
Isn't equal to that.   You ain't ruined,' said she.

Women (I think) are more impatient of irony than men: and
when Hardy turns his irony upon them—as he often does in
his novels—I have observed that they eye it suspiciously,
restively; they would be undetected in their devices, hate instinctively that which shows their secret ways of power at
work under show of servility.   Hardy, their champion, would
break down the servility: and they distrust him for it.

Well—and though they be ungrateful—perhaps their instinct
is true and his is a childless creed: and for men, though it be
manly to face and test it, an unhopeful creed.   For women it
must be certainly unpromising to read the doctrine of *Jude
the Obscure*, which works out to this, that man's aspirations
to make the world better are chiefly clogged by the flesh,
and that flesh is woman.   To man it can scarcely be less
heartening to be barred with the question

Has some Vast Imbecility,
    Mighty to build and blend,
    But impotent to tend,
Framed us in jest, and left us now to hazardry?

Or come we of an Automaton
    Unconscious of our pains?
    Or are we live remains
Of Godhead dying downwards, brain and eye now gone?

Well, when it comes to this, I for one can only answer that,
if it were, we must yet carry on somehow, sing a song on the
raft we cannot steer, keep a heart of sorts, and share out the
rations to the women and children.   But that word recalls me.

It is a *childless* creed.   It has no more evidence than Meredith's: intellectually viewed, I find them equal: but Meredith has hope, hope for the young: and I must put my money on hope.

VII

Further, when I consider, these poems—as those novels—crowd the sardonic laughter of the gods too thickly.   There is irony enough in life, God knows: but here is a man possessed with it.   All men, all stories, tramp with him to his titles, *Life's Little Ironies, Satires of Circumstance, Time's Laughing-stocks.*   So one hesitates and asks: Is life, after all, a parish full of bad practical jokes?   *Is* our life framed like *this*?   No: as we take up poem after poem in which human loves and aspirations find themselves thwarted, set astray, or butting against some door that, having opened a glimpse of paradise, shuts by some power idiotically mischievous if not malignant —shuts with a click of the latch and a chuckle of mocking laughter—we tell ourselves, 'These things happen: but rarely save by our own fault.'   And while we debate this, Hardy spreads out his theme upon one grand ironic drama, *The Dynasts.*

I suppose *The Dynasts* to be—and I shall not allow for rival Doughty's noble but remote, morose, almost Chinese, epic, *The Dawn in Britain* (this, too, a product of a man well past meridian)—I suppose *The Dynasts* to be the grandest poetic structure planned and raised in England in our time.   In the soar and sweep of that drama the poet—whom, a moment ago, we were on the point of accusing for provincial, lays Europe beneath us 'flat, as to an eagle's eye': a map with little things in multitudes, ants in armies, scurrying along the threads which are roads, violently agitated in nodules which are cities.   But let me quote one or two of Hardy's own stage directions and thereby not only save myself the vain effort to do what has been perfectly done for me, but send you, if you would practise the art of condensed and vivid description, to models as good as can be found in English prose. Imagine yourselves, then, an audience aloft and listening to the talk of such Spirits as watch over human destinies.

The nether sky opens, and Europe is disclosed as a prone and emaciated figure, the Alps shaping like a backbone, and the branching mountain-chains like ribs, the peninsular plateau of Spain forming a head. Broad and lengthy lowlands stretch from the north of France across Russia like a grey-green garment hemmed by the Ural mountains and the glistening Arctic Ocean.

The point of view then sinks downward through space, and draws near to the surface of the perturbed countries, where the people . . . are seen writhing, crawling, heaving, and vibrating, in their various cities and nationalities.

A new and penetrating light descends on the spectacle, enduing men and things with a seeming transparency, and exhibiting as one organism the anatomy of life and movement in all humanity and vitalized matter included in the display.

So the focus slides down and up; and again down: it narrows on the British House of Commons, or on a village green, or on a bedroom in a palace: it expands to sweep the field of Auster-litz. I ask you to turn for yourselves to one marvellous scene of a cellar, full of drunken deserters, looking out on the snow-tormented road along which straggles the army of Sir John Moore and struggles for Coruña. But here is a passage in the retreat from Moscow:

What has floated down from the sky upon the Army is a flake of snow. Then come another and another, till natural features, hitherto varied with the tints of autumn, are confounded, and all is phantasmal grey and white.

The caterpillar shape still creeps laboriously nearer: but instead of increasing in size by the rules of perspective, it gets more attenuated, and there are left upon the ground behind it minute parts of itself, which are speedily flaked over, and remain as white pimples by the wayside.

Pines rise mournfully on each side of the nearing object. . . . En-dowed with enlarged powers of audition as of vision, we are struck by the mournful taciturnity that prevails. Nature is mute. Save for the incessant flogging of the wind-broken and lacerated horses there are no sounds.

The reader s excitement, thus cunningly maintained, tempts

him to hurry over many poetic faults and not a few imbecilities: the most constant fault lying (with few breaks, as when the Empress Josephine pleads against her brutal divorce) in such blank verse as the characters are forced to employ throughout. Whatever may be thought of Hardy's lyrical gift, over blank verse he had little command. Probably he had never practised this, the easiest of all metres in which to write, the hardest in which to write expertly: and *The Dynasts* as a whole suggests that he had no ear for it, no sense even that it required an ear. He can put across a Parliamentary debate by sawing the speeches into flat lengths of decasyllables. Even to Josephine he allows:

> But are you *really* going to part from me?

and to the Tsar Alexander in distress:

> The principle in this case anyhow
> Is shattered by the facts . . .

The poetic use of supernatural beings, set above human strife as spectators of it, dates back at least as far as Homer, who goes farther and lets them interfere with it. Their use as choric commentators on life, to assure us from time to time what fools we mortals be, and to convey the poet's own notion of a Supreme Being (whether of what he is or of what he ought to be), has the full licence of tradition. But without echoing those critics who hold that *The Dynasts* would be the better if the whole spiritual apparatus were cut out, one may suggest that these choruses, with their 'aerial music,' would have served Hardy's purpose better had he confined them to a Prologue or an Epilogue or both. As they stand they are tremendously lyrical, but seldom good: the dithyramb that did well enough for a Wessex lilt too often thins to something perilously like a 'right butter-woman's rank to market' when intoned through mouths supposed as celestial: while, when Hardy attempts an intricate stanza, he falls into a trap our seventeenth century lyricists too often set for themselves—a surprisingly clever opening on a pattern set, without inspiration in reserve to keep it up. Further, these choruses are given to employ and exaggerate a quasi-philosophic lingo which had already tempted Hardy to spoil many a fine passage of his prose; a lingo suggestive of immature psycho-analysis mixed up with home-made products such as 'to not-be' for 'to die.'

At rare intervals the spirits rise to real poetry, as when the small wild creatures of nature protest under the wheels and trampling of our troops falling back from Quatre-Bras upon Waterloo.

> Yea, the coneys are scared by the thud of hoofs,
> And their white scuts flash at their vanishing heels,
> And swallows abandon the hamlet-roofs.
>
> The mole's tunnelled chambers are crushed by wheels,
> The lark's eggs scattered, their owners fled,
> And the hare 's hid litter the sapper unseals.
>
> The snail draws in at the terrible tread,
> But in vain; he is crushed by the felloe-rim;
> The worm asks what can be overhead . . .

although, when one comes to reflect, this pother in the animal kingdom needs no Waterloo: any steam-plough breaking a pasture can stir up like protests, to scale.

The main trouble, however, with these Phantom Intelligences —to be frank about it—is that they *bore*. They keep harping upon one string; or rather, keep plucking out their several strings to one monotonous chord—that the world is fatally directed by a Something that cannot be Providence while witless of what it is doing. Nor can it be conceived as an Immanent Will if, after making a general mess of things through aeons of Time, it can be awakened by Consciousness and resolve to do better—the only hope promised us by the final Chorus:

But—a stirring thrills the air
Like to sounds of joyance there
     That the rages
     Of the ages
Shall be cancelled, and deliverance offered from the darts that were
Consciousness the Will informing, till it fashion all things fair.

In sum, Hardy had a most tender sense of the miseries and waste of all this unintelligible world, but neither a faith nor a philosophy to help him beyond indignant protest: for which reason I am one with those who hold that *The Dynasts* would have been better without these Phantom Intelligences, the drama itself being so majestically effective, upon a theme as ancient as its truth is salutary—that the gods allure to destroy any overweening mortal, be he Titan or tyrant.

For the rest, and should anything in these reservations appear too captious, let me quote from one of Hardy's own letters— 'I prefer late Wagner, as I prefer late Turner, to early . . . when a man not contented with the grounds of his success goes on and on, and tries to achieve the impossible, then he gets profoundly interesting to me.'

So, whatever verdict Time may pass upon it, *The Dynasts* will remain profoundly interesting as the last Testament of a great writer who had profoundly interested, and influenced, a generation.

VIII

I fall back, to conclude, upon Wessex; appropriately, I think, upon a churchyard in a corner there, where kinsmen, friends, neighbours, mingle their dust; where, as Hardy's friend and homelier predecessor put it,

> The zummer aïr o' theäs green hill
> 'V a-heav'd in bosoms now all still.

Faithful to this dust, to ancestry, old associations, the

> Nescio quâ natale solum dulcedine cunctos
> Ducit, et immemores non sinit esse sui . . .

the native returns: and the dead whisper, and this is what they tell:

> William Dewy, Tranter Reuben, Farmer Ledlow late at
>   plough,
>   Robert's kin, and John's, and Ned's,
> And the Squire, and Lady Susan, lie in Mellstock churchyard
>   now!

'Gone,' I call them, gone for good, that group of local hearts
and heads;
    Yet at mothy curfew-tide,
And at midnight when the noon-heat breathes it back from
walls and leads,

They've a way of whispering to me—fellow-wight who yet
abide—
    In the muted measured note
Of a ripple under archways, or a lone cave's stillicide:

'We have triumphed: this achievement turns the bane to
antidote,
    Unsuccesses to success,
Many thought-worn eves and morrows to a morrow free of
thought.

'No more need we corn and clothing, feel of old terrestrial
stress;
    Chill detraction stirs no sigh;
Fear of death has even bygone us: death gave all that we
possess.'

W. D. 'Ye mid burn the wold bass-viol that I set such vallie by.'
Squire.   'You may hold the manse in fee,
You may wed my spouse, my children's memory of me may
decry.'

Lady. 'You may have my rich brocades, my laces; take each household key;
    Ransack coffer, desk, bureau;
Quiz the few poor treasures hid there, con the letters kept by
me.'

Far. 'Ye mid zell my favourite heifer, ye mid let the charlock grow,
    Foul the grinterns, give up thrift.'
Wife. 'If ye break my best blue china, children, I shan't care or ho.'

All. 'We've no wish to hear the tidings, how the people's fortunes
shift;
    What your daily doings are;
Who are wedded, born, divided; if your lives beat slow or
swift.

'Curious not the least are we if our intents you make or mar,
    If you quire to our old tune,
If the City stage still passes, if the weirs still roar afar.'

—Thus, with very gods' composure, freed those crosses late
    and soon
    Which, in life, the Trine allow
(Why, none witteth), and ignoring all that haps beneath the
    moon,

William Dewy, Tranter Reuben, Farmer Ledlow late at
    plough,
    Robert's kin, and John's, and Ned's,
And the Squire, and Lady Susan, murmur mildly to me now.

W. S. GILBERT

I

I HAD parted, at the Cambridge Post Office, with a young friend of parts who 'deplores' (as he puts it) our whole heritage of English poetry and holds with reason that it ought to make a fresh start. Musing on this assurance of his, on my way to the Botanic Garden, and resigning myself, as my custom is, to grieving

> when even the Shade
> Of that which once was great is passed away,

I encountered two long lines of men on opposite sides of the thoroughfare; the one drawing, or seeking to draw, Unemployment Pay; the other taking, or seeking to take, tickets for Gilbert-and-Sullivan Opera.

'Ah, there,' thought I, 'after all, the last enchantment of the Victorian age has captured you, my lads, and holds you by the Achilles' tendon!' For I recognize your faces. You are the same that, the other day, were affecting to despise

> Come down, O maid, from yonder mountain height—

or

> O lyric love, half angel and half bird!

But as soon as it comes to 'Tit-willow!' or 'The Policeman's lot is not a happy one,' you are held and 'laid by the heel.'

Now I wish to inquire into this and the reason of it; and, believe me, not sardonically. My first introduction to Gilbert-and-Sullivan Opera dates back to an amateur performance of *H.M.S. Pinafore* that enchanted a child. The first play I ever saw in a London theatre was *Patience*, in the course of its first run at the Opéra Comique. As an undergraduate I have taken as much trouble as any of you to listen to *The Sorcerer*, *Princess Ida*, *The Mikado*; and my own two favourites, *Iolanthe* and *The Gondoliers*, still conjure up by

association all manner of happy memories. I yet can surrender myself (at intervals) to Gilbert-and-Sullivan with an
abandon you may ascribe to the natural gaiety of declining
years, or to sentimentality—which you. will. Let that pass:
for, with your leave, the question affects not *me* but *you*. Why
do you who expend so much cleverness in deriding the more
serious contemporaries of W. S. Gilbert and Arthur Sullivan,
yet experimentally confess to this one most typically late-
Victorian enthusiasm which binds your spiritual contemporaries
with your fathers and grandfathers?

You at any rate will not plead—you, who follow so eagerly
all the many experiments of our Festival Theatre in sub-
stituting mechanics for drama—that you cling to a tradition
of the provinces. That provincial audiences flock to these
Operas even as you do; that amateurs throughout England
spend their winters in rehearsing one and another of them; that
regularly, in the week following Easter, the railways convey
down baskets of regulation wigs and costumes from Covent
Garden to remote towns and Village Institutes—all this is
certain

II

Now this, when we consider how typically late-Victorian these
Operas are—how limited in range of idea, even of invention—
how much of their quiddity (in *Patience*, for example) belongs
to its hour in a past era; may well give us a shock. It might
also give me occasion to ask, why some of you, and those not
the least intelligent, haunt these Operas, although in clever
debate you think it not unseemly to deride Meredith for a
mountebank and Tennyson for a maiden aunt?

But I seem to know you too well to believe that in your heart
of hearts you cherish any such foolish opinions, at any rate
ineradicably, or truly believe Gilbert and Sullivan to be the
lone Dioscuri of our late-Victorian night. Let us start on the
plain common ground that, after fifty years or so, their work
continues to delight young and old, and try to account for it.

III

The appeal of Music being, by virtue of its indefiniteness, so
much more elusive of date than the spoken or written word,
and especially if the subject be at all 'topical,' shall we hold
that Gilbert survives mainly through Sullivan's music? Vaguely
we may feel Sullivan's melody to be as Victorian as are Gilbert's
plots and tricks and whole theatrical concept; but these, having
to be framed in words and on lines of logic—and topsy-turvy
logic is yet logic and the basis of Gilbert's wit—can be brought
to tests which music airily eludes. They are written in words
and can be attacked in words; and must continue to suffer
this comparative disadvantage until critics of music find
a method of expressing their likes and dislikes by musical
notation.

But no; this explanation will not serve. For Gilbert, very
much of his period and exposed to all the perils which must
beset any man who would attract a theatrical audience by wit
and song, was yet (if you will search his *libretti*) extremely wary
of topical allusions that might date him. In *Patience*, to be
sure (one of his earliest), he shot at, and winged, a passing
mode. But save for a passing allusion to the late Captain
Shaw of London's Fire Brigade and a somewhat pointed one
in *Utopia, Limited* to the light refreshment provided for *débu-
tantes* at Queen Victoria's Drawing-Rooms, you will seek his
work in vain for topical references. To be sure, in *H.M.S.
Pinafore* (his earliest success) he poked obvious fun at Mr.
W. H. Smith, First Lord of the Admiralty: but there exists a
most illuminating letter of his in which he hopes he has removed
all suspicion of personal offence by indicating that the victim
was a Liberal!—a letter which should be a *locus classicus* for
research into the ultimate obtuseness of wit. Dealing with
his times as he knew them, he could not of course foresee that
events would in time blunt the application of one of his neatest
shafts—the Sentry's song in *Iolanthe*. But I think we may
agree that in this slow-moving country of ours Gilbert's raillery
has worn as well as the absurd institutions against which he

not too seriously aimed at. They are accustomed to that sort of thing, and have allowed him to wear just as well as they have worn.

I suggest that if you mark and note this avoidance of topical allusion in Gilbert, you will come to the conclusion with me that the man considered himself as one writing for posterity, as carefully at least as Horace Walpole did in composing his familiar letters to Horace Mann. But on this point I shall presently have more evidence to bring. For the moment let his many years' survival stand for presumptive evidence that Gilbert wrote with intent to last.

This intention apart, it were unjust to hold that Gilbert lives by the grace of Sullivan. Offenbach's music was as tunable as Sullivan's and belonged to its age as closely. But Offenbach lacked good librettists, and for this reason you do not stand in long files to buy tickets for Offenbach. You may say that you do not for the more obvious reason that his Operas are never presented in England nowadays; but the true reason, if you search for it, is that Offenbach never found his Poet, his twin mind. Now Gilbert and Sullivan lived each by the grace of the other. Habitually, in actual practice, Gilbert wrote first, plot and lyric, and Sullivan followed; which is the only right order in the making of an Opera, and was convincingly the right order in the making of these men's Operas. For the contribution which Sullivan brought was not only his genius for melody, nor a wit that jumped with Gilbert's, nor a separate and musical wit which revelled in parody. Priceless as these gifts undoubtedly were, above them all (I think) we must reckon the quite marvellous sense of *words* in all his musical settings. You may examine number after number of his, and the more closely you examine the more will you be convinced that no composer ever lived with an exacter appreciation of words, their meaning, their due emphasis, their right articulation. A singer must be a fool indeed if you do not hear through Sullivan's notes the exact language of any song. Take, for example, the well-known Sentry song in *Iolanthe* and attempt to unwed the wit of the air from the wit of the thought and words; or take the Lord Chancellor's song in the same play:

> The law is the true embodiment
> Of everything that 's excellent,
> It has no kind of fault or flaw—
> And I, my Lords, embody the law.

and note how Sullivan subdues the air to something almost commonplace and almost silly, but just so as to bring out the intention of demure absurdity, with allowance for every syllable and room for the gesture in the fourth line. Yet should you think he is subduing himself to anything but his artistry, turn to the great duet in *The Sorcerer,* or to the robust Handelian burlesque that winds up 'He remains an Englishman' in *H.M.S. Pinafore,* and mark how riotously his own wit takes charge when Gilbert's gives it the rein.

IV

Gilbert had the advantage of setting the themes and dominating the stage-management of the Operas. But before we call his the master-spirit (which by no means implies that it was the more valuable) in the combination, let us take a little evidence from the actors and singers they commanded. Remind yourselves that these two men, when they started at the old Opéra Comique, off the Strand, had to work with the cheapest material. The 'brassiness' of the orchestra during the first run of *Pinafore*—the combined incompetence in *Patience* of the vocalists as actors and of the actors as vocalists —would be incredible to-day even if faithfully reproduced to eye and ear. In that first run of *Patience* one or two of the cast could act a little, one or two could sing a little; Miss Rosina Brandram alone, asserting that there would be too much of her in the coming by-and-by, could do both.

But these two men, combining upon an idea, turned even shortness of means to their service. They found themselves in the position long and vainly required by a neighbour of mine, a great gardener—'I want an intelligent fellow ready to plant a cabbage upside down without questioning.' Having at first a stage so inexpensive, a cast which had to listen and obey, they imposed their idea, or ideas, with a tyranny to which countless anecdotes bear witness.

The most of these anecdotes are of Gilbert: but Sullivan, if less irascible in rehearsal, appears to have been almost as ruthless. Here is the musical procedure, as related by George Grossmith—who knew it if any man did:

The music is always learned first. The choruses, finales etc., are composed first in order; then the quartets, the trios; the songs last. Sometimes, owing to changes and re-writing, these are given out to the singers very late (so late that the singer sometimes found less difficulty in learning the new tune than in unlearning the old one). The greatest interest is evinced by all as the new vocal numbers arrive . . . Sullivan will come suddenly, a batch of MS. under his arm, and announce that there is something new. He plays over the new number—the vocal parts only are written. The conductor listens and watches and, after hearing them played over a few times, contrives to pick up all the harmonies, casual accompaniments etc. Sullivan is always strict in wishing that his music shall be sung exactly as he has written it. One of the leading performers was singing an air at rehearsal, not exactly dividing the notes as they were written, giving the general form as it were. 'Bravo!' said Sullivan, 'that is really a very good air of yours. Now, if you have no objection, I will ask you to sing mine.'

But the little finger of Gilbert at rehearsal would be thicker than Sullivan's loins. He kept at home a small model stage, made to scale, and a box or boxes of tiny bricks varying in height and colour. These he would group and re-group in endless patient stage-management until satisfied just where and just how at any given moment any actor should be standing. Then he would come to the theatre and, moving everybody about as on a chessboard, start to bully them into speaking to his exact wish. To quote Grossmith again:

The music rehearsals are child's play in comparison with the stage rehearsals. Mr. Gilbert is a perfect autocrat, insisting that his words shall be delivered, even to an inflexion of the voice, as he dictates. He will stand on the stage and repeat the words, with appropriate action, over and over again until they are delivered as he desires.

Add that Gilbert, on top of a detestable temper, had a tongue like a whip-lash: and—well, you see, as any of you who wish to be artists must learn in some way, sooner or later, that there is not only a pleasure in poetic pains but a tax upon human pains for poetic pleasure.

V

If I have established that Gilbert's is a dominant, even tyrannical brain in these plays which you find so delightful, let us go on to deal with them a little after the manner of Aristotle. Obviously they obey Aristotle in preferring plot to character, even though by inversion: for, his plots being always legal rather than moral in their topsy-turviness (Gilbert, you know, was a barrister and made his first success as a playwright in *Trial by Jury*), his characters behave always on a topsy-turvy legal logic—a logic as mad as Lewis Carroll's or madder; they transfer their affections, or reverse their destinies, by insane rational process:

> Quiet peaceful contemplation
> Disentangles every knot.

A captain in the Royal Navy turns out to have been changed at birth with a common seaman: it follows that, the revelation made, they change places and stations. A promising lad has, by a lapse of terminological exactitude, been apprenticed to a pirate instead of to a pilot; a love-philtre works the wrong way (as it did in *A Midsummer-Night's Dream*); a drummer ascends the throne of Barataria on the affidavit of a foster-mother in eight lines of *recitative*.

Within these limits of absurdity you will notice that all the Operas have limits also in ethic, and are built on an almost rigid convention of design. There is usually an opposition of the Victorian real against the fanciful: of a House of Peers, for example, in robes, against a chorus of fairies under Westminster clock-tower: of a body of Heavy Dragoons against Bunthorne and his lackadaisy maidens. There is almost always a baritone singer, more or less loosely connected with the story, introduced with some sort of patter-song—the First Lord's song in *Pinafore* (which, by the way, started its success), the Major-General's in *The Pirates*, the Lord Chancellor's in *Iolanthe*, and so on. There is also a lady with a contralto voice, who deplores her mature years. The more you examine the Operas to compare them, the closer you will get to a severe and narrow model. And the model in its ethical content is no less straitly laced. It invites you to laugh at the foibles of kings, soldiers, lawyers, artists, and faddists of all sorts. But it touches no universal emotion, no universal instinct even (such as conviviality). Still less does it allow us to think of the base on which Society is built, or admit a thought on it to intrude in any way upon our tomfooling. We all belong to the upper or upper middle class, or to the class which apes these two. We are all conscious of class distinctions, are a little too consciously snobbish even while we enjoy the exposure of snobbery. The general moral, in fact, is that of the song which he characteristically entitled *King Goodheart*:

> There lived a King, as I 've been told,
> In the wonder-working days of old,
> When hearts were twice as good as gold
>   And twenty times as mellow.
> Good temper triumphed in his face,
> And in his heart he found a place
> For all the erring human race
>   And every wretched fellow.
> When he had Rhenish wine to drink
> It made him very sad to think
> That some, at junket or at jink,
>   Must be content with toddy:
> He wished all men as rich as he
> (And he was rich as rich could be),
> So to the top of every tree
>   Promoted everybody. . . .

That King, although no one denies,
His heart was of abnormal size,
Yet he 'd have acted otherwise
    If he had been acuter.
The end is easily foretold,
When every blessed thing you hold
Is made of silver, or of gold,
    You long for simple pewter.
When you have nothing else to wear
But cloth of gold and satins rare,
For cloth of gold you cease to care—
    Up goes the price of shoddy:
In short, whoever you may be,
To this conclusion you 'll agree,
When every one is somebody,
    Then no one 's anybody!

VI

That, you may say, is all very well—or would be well enough
if Gilbert could be cleared as a writer who genuinely sym-
pathized with some things, or with one class, and just happened
not to sympathize with others.   That is common enough with
authors, and especially with comedians and writers of light
verse.   Their business being to apply the touch of common
sense to human affairs, one may even allow a certain hardness
to be a part of their outfit [I am ungrateful enough even to find
a certain hardness of surface in that favourite of us all, C. S.
Calverley].   But Gilbert had a baddish streak or two in him;
and one in particular which was not only baddish but so
thoroughly caddish that no critic can ignore or, in my belief,
extenuate it.   The man, to summarize, was essentially cruel,
and delighted in cruelty.   I lay no heavy stress on his addiction
—already glanced at—to finding fun in every form of torture
and capital punishment.   This indeed persists in his work from
The Bab Ballads right through the plays:

Oh! listen to the tale of little Annie Protheroe;
She kept a small post-office in the neighbourhood of Bow,
She loved a skilled mechanic, who was famous in his day—
A gentle executioner whose name was Gilbert Clay.

I think I hear you say, 'A dreadful subject for your rhymes!'
O reader, do not shrink—he didn't live in modern times!
He lived so long ago (the sketch will show it at a glance)
That all his actions glitter with the limelight of Romance.

In busy times he laboured at his gentle craft all day—
'No doubt you mean his Cal-craft' you amusingly will say—
But, no—he didn't operate with common bits of string,
He was a Public Headsman, which is quite another thing.

And when his work was over, they would ramble o'er the lea,
And sit beneath the frondage of an elderberry tree;
And Annie's simple prattle entertained him on his walk,
For public executions formed the subject of her talk.

And sometimes he 'd explain to her, which charmed her very
    much,
How famous operators vary very much in touch,
And then, perhaps, he 'd show how he himself performed the
    trick,
And illustrate his meaning with a poppy and a stick.

It persists (I repeat) through *The Bab Ballads* and into play
after play; until, if you are tired and seek a *terminus ad quem*,
I suggest this, from *The Mikado*, where an artless maiden sings:

> He shivered and shook as he gave the sign
>   For the stroke he didn't deserve;
> When all of a sudden his eye met mine,
>   And it seemed to brace his nerve.
> For he nodded his head and kissed his hand,
>   And he whistled an air did he,
>   As the sabre true
>   Cut cleanly through
>   His cervical vertebrae!
>   When a man 's afraid
>   A beautiful maid
>   Is a charming sight to see.
>   And it 's O, I 'm glad
>   That moment sad
>   Was soothed by sight of me!

Or—

> To sit in solemn silence, in a dull dark dock,
> In a pestilential prison, with a life-long lock,
> Awaiting the sensation of a short, sharp, shock
> From a cheap and chippy chopper on a big black block.

On this cheap and chippy chopper business I merely observe that Gilbert revelled in it; as any one else may, so long as I am not asked to join the party.

But Gilbert's cruelty took an uglier twist upon one incurable and unforgivable vice—that of exposing women to public derision on the stage just because they are growing old and losing their beauty. We can forgive Horace or Catullus (if hardly) for venom against their cast-off mistresses. We should all think the better of them had they refrained. But the revulsion, even the vituperation, of a wearied amorist—unpleasant as one may think it—consists with our experience of men and women. It is *humanly* vile. What disgusts one in Gilbert, from the beginning to the end, is his insistence on the physical odiousness of any woman growing old. As though, great Heaven! themselves did not find it tragic enough—the very and necessary tragedy of their lives! Gilbert shouts it, mocks it, apes with it, spits upon it. He opens with this dirty trump card in *Trial by Jury*, where the Judge tells how, as a briefless Barrister:

> I soon got tired of third-class journeys,
>   And dinners of bread and water;
> So I fell in love with a rich attorney's
>   Elderly, ugly daughter.
>
> The rich attorney, he wiped his eyes,
>   And replied to my fond professions:
> 'You shall reap the reward of your enterprise,
>   At the Bailey and Middlesex Sessions.
>
> You 'll soon get used to her looks,' said he,
>   'And a very nice girl you 'll find her—
> She may very well pass for forty-three
>   In the dusk, with a light behind her!'

He follows it with 'Little Buttercup' in *Pinafore*, in *Patience* with

> Fading is the taper waist—
>   Shapeless grows the shapely limb.
> And, although securely laced,
>   Spreading is the figure trim!

> Stouter than I used to be,
>   Still more corpulent grow I—
> There will be too much of me
>   In the coming by-and-by!

—in *The Mikado* with

> The flowers that bloom in the Spring, tra la,
>   Have nothing to do with the case:
> I 've got to take under my wing, tra la,
> A most unattractive old thing, tra la,
>   With a caricature of a face.

—and so he proceeds until the end, in *The Mountebanks*, to a scene which almost drove one from the theatre in nausea.

But I dare say the best rebuke of this was the gentle one administered by his favourite actress, Miss Jessie Bond. When she told Gilbert she was going to marry, he burst out, 'Little fool!' 'I have often,' she answered, 'heard you say you don't like old women. I shall be one soon. Will you provide for me? You hesitate. Well, I am going to a man who will.'

VII

Mr. Rudyard Kipling has observed somewhere that in the life of every happily married man there must come a moment when the sight of his wife at the head of the table suggests the appalling thought that this must go on for ever. Without going so far as this, one may say that even in the happiest marriage one or both of the partners has an occasional sense of some ambition missed. So it happened, we know, in the immensely successful partnership of Gilbert and Sullivan, and it led to frequent quarrels, endeavours on Sullivan's part to break away, finally to estrangement, though happily to no such deadly feud as closed the almost equally successful partnership of MM. Erckmann-Chatrian. Sullivan dreamed that he was capable of High Opera; and so perhaps he was, had he attempted it sooner. But few men can usefully resolve to embrace a new and higher career on their silver wedding-day, and when Sullivan produced *Ivanhoe* at the Royal English Opera House in 1891 it was evident that his resolve had come too late.

But Gilbert, who had bound him to his task, in latter days so sorely against his protestations, also cherished a soaring dramatic ambition. Of men so irascible as he it may usually be observed that they have a bee in their bonnet. (I may use that expression because Gilbert once wore a bonnet as officer in the Gordon Highlanders Militia and had a photograph taken—reproduced in his *Biography*—in the full costume of that gay regiment.) And the very queer bee in Gilbert's bonnet was a violent antipathy against the name and fame of Shakespeare, particularly against the public appreciation of *Hamlet*. It sounds incredible, but there it was. He not only lampooned the great tragedy in a play, *Rosencrantz and Guildenstern*: he never could get away from Hamlet and Ophelia; he had to go on and befool their story, as in *The Mountebanks*, in a silly dumb show—and again to drag the very weeds and the mud out of Ophelia's end:

> When she found he wouldn't wed her,
> In a river, in a medder,
> Took a header, and a deader
> Was Oph-e-li-a!

Levity, vulgar and blatant!—Yes, and almost we might call it incredible in the man, even if explicable by that same strain of insensitiveness which deadened him to all charity for women past their first youth. It has indeed a like suggestion of impotence.

But insensitiveness will not cover this fault, which actually lay very near the raw. Reading his 'Life' and his plays together, we perceive that this neat rhymer, neat wit, neat barrister, neat stage-manager, nursed at the back of his head a conception of himself as a great and serious dramatist—even as Sullivan, with better excuse, nursed the conception of himself as a great composer in Oratorio. Nor did Gilbert fail to realize this conception for want of trying. He has left a number of 'serious' dramas behind him—dramas in prose and verse—all more or less unsuccessful on the stage. He even essayed one on the *Faust* theme, fated to allure and defeat all but great souls. He could not see that, whilst genius may be versatile and many-sided, there are certain talents which naturally *exclude* greatness. In his workshop, maybe, he was happy to deem himself possessed of high seriousness. When his efforts came to be produced, the public quite accurately divined that he was not. The discovery cost a not very critical generation of audiences no great effort; but it bit into Gilbert's self-esteem, and he bit upon the wound.

Most of us in ordinary life have known men who, apt to make fun of others' foibles, show extreme anger or sulkiness when the slightest fun is retorted upon their own. Gilbert was such a man: a professional cynic and ruthless (as almost all reported anecdotes attest) in wounding with a jest, but extremely touchy—nay, implacably vindictive—when his own withers were wrung, however lightly.

VIII

But before he turned to *libretto* Gilbert in his lighter plays, unrewarded by applause, did perhaps as much as his friend Robertson, and more than his friend Byron, to break up by solvent the turgid tradition of mid-Victorian drama and expose its theatricalities. It is usual to ascribe the revolution to Robertson. But Robertson, although he showed a glimmering light towards such reality as exists in 'realism,' did not—being himself a sentimentalist—probe the real disease of sentimentality. It was Gilbert who probed it and applied the corrosive; and the corrosive proved too strong at first for the public taste: perhaps because it confined itself to destroying the fatty tissue without any promise of healing. At any rate his satirical comedies, deliberately intended to provoke mirth, fell flat; and this no less to their author's bewilderment than to his exasperation.

Let us take *Engaged*, to my mind the best of these, and anyhow characteristic; and let us select one short typical passage. The heroine (or one of them), Miss Treherne, is speaking:

'Cheviot, I have loved you madly, desperately, as other woman never loved other man. *This* poor inexperienced child'—a second heroine—'who clings to me as the ivy clings to the oak, also loves you as woman never loved before. Even, *that* poor cottage maiden, whose rustic heart you so heedlessly enslaved'—a third heroine—'worships you with a devotion which has no parallel in the annals of the heart. In return for all this unalloyed affection, all we ask of you is that you will recommend us to a respectable solicitor.'

In those few lines we detect the Gilbertian imbroglio, with the Gilbertian treatment which afterwards served him so well. Yet the public took *Engaged* coldly. To its mind the play wanted a 'something.'

What? . . . But already we have the answer. Venables anticipated it when he congratulated Thackeray on the success of the *The Four Georges*, delivered as lectures in Willis's Rooms, 'Capital, my dear Thack! But you ought to have a piano.'

Later on, in Sullivan, Gilbert found his piano, and something more.

But I doubt if, in his own development, he ever progressed an inch deeper in meaning than anything you can find implicit in the passage I have quoted, or (stage-craft apart) any technical skill in lyric or even in plot that he had not anticipated in *The Bab Ballads*. I find—since we talk of pianos—some symbolic truth in the vignette drawn by his own hand and reprinted in successive editions on the title-page of those lays. It represents an infant thumping a piano. You may even read some prophecy in the title of his first real operatic success—*Pinafore*.

IX

At any rate you may assure yourselves, by examination of the *libretti*, that Gilbert, having found his piano, stuck to variations upon a few themes of the *Ballads* and to the end of his career returned to them for his plot. By deft rehandling of their themes, with their originally conceived topsy-turvies and logical reductions to absurdity, he won his success in the partnership; and it is at least some vindication of your elders' intelligence, Gentlemen, that they delighted in this play of mock logic, as they had already fallen to it genially, in their nurseries, over *Alice in Wonderland*, a province of it in which all had been kindly.

For *The Bab Ballads*—if you are wise, you will treat them as wise men treat *Tristram Shandy*. You will not argue, but either like them or leave them alone. I do not compare them as achievements, but simply as they are unsusceptible to criticism; and, however wrong I may be about Gilbert, I have read enough miss-the-mark criticism of Sterne by eminent persons, from Thackeray down, to assert that there are some writings for which criticism has found little guidance between 'I Like It' and 'I Like It Not.'

For my part I rejoice in *The Bab Ballads*, and find them on the whole considerably superior to the lyrics with which Gilbert diversified the Operas. Nor can I easily believe that, being the man he was, he deliberately and artistically keyed down his wit to the requirements of the music and of stage-presentation. He may have done so half consciously. The possibility, however, suggests a question on which we may conclude.

X

An examination of Gilbert's and Sullivan's success in some-times wedding, sometimes alternating, words with music to produce a genuine, if narrow, form of Light Opera may be of some use to those who accept, as to those who on its results feel a little doubtful about accepting, the Wagnerian and post-Wagnerian claims for Grand Opera. I feel some timidity in advancing so much as a foot over this ground; since of all hierophants those of music are the most scornful of intruders who would ally their pet art with others that make life enjoyable. I observe also that the majority of these apostles of harmony are as intense in vendetta as incapable of explaining what it is all about; so that one wavers in amaze between the 'interpretations' in the programme of any Symphony Concert and the Billingsgate in which these critics pursue their sacerdotal loves and hates.

But I suppose that, after all, it works out to this:

(1) Grand Opera, like any other opera, is an artificial thing; a lovely form of art if its components of drama, words and music be intelligently blended, yet always so artificial that the audience's imagination and intelligence must be invited together to assist in their own captivation.

(2) If these three elements (to omit scenery) of drama, words and music could be captured, each at its highest, *and perfectly blended*, we should have perfection in one combined form of art.

(3) But this combination implies that each contributory has its due place, each giving its best and yet subduing it to the others' best, at the right moment: that suppose, for example, one could enlist Shakespeare and Beethoven together for an Opera of *Lear*, or Molière and Mozart for a *Don Giovanni*, still the composing authors must each submit his genius to the total result.

(4) Now the trouble is that such things don't happen in this world.

(5) But suppose the theory sound. Of all men of genius Wagner was perhaps the worst equipped with those concomitants which his theory demanded. Therefore, being one of the most arrogant of men, he put music in supreme command and tortured our divinest of gifts—the modulated speaking voice for which Sophocles and Shakespeare wrote—to speak *through* music; which is to say, largely *against* it. It is not for me to do more than marvel at the genius for orchestration which stunned or mesmerized sensible men into accepting a megalomaniac theory. The temperate voice of the eighteenth century may whisper something salutary at this point: for, after all, Joshua Reynolds *could* paint.

I believe [says Reynolds] it may be considered as a general rule, that no art can be grafted with success on another art. For although they all profess the same origin, and to proceed from the same stock, yet each has its own peculiar mode of imitating nature and of deviating from it, each for the accomplishment of its own particular purpose. These deviations, more especially, will not bear transplantation to another soil.

Now Reynolds may easily be wrong if we apply this observation to opera in general, as presumably Hazlitt would have applied it. 'The opera,' says Hazlitt, 'is the most artificial of all things . . . it is an illusion and a mockery. . . . A headache may be produced by a profusion of sweet smells or sweet sounds; but we do not like the headache the more on that account. Nor are we reconciled to it, even at the opera.'

But the Attic Theatre proved, centuries ago, that speech and music, with dancing and scenery, could be brought together to produce one of the very highest forms of art, *provided that each of the contributories were kept in its proper place.* Aristotle recognized this, of course; and, to use our immediate subject for an illustration, Gilbert and Sullivan prove that the difficulty of bringing together accomplished pedestrian speech and accomplished music can be solved *ambulando*, if the rule of keeping them in their proper places be observed more or less as the Greeks observed it. As I have said, a combination of supreme poetry with supreme music and a variety of the other arts at their very best is not granted by the gods to the generations of men; but it seems evident that in some happy moments the co-operation of poet and musician, neither of the first eminence, may almost chemically produce a new thing which, if not transcendent, is extremely pleasing, at once novel and reasonably permanent in its appeal. Opera is an artificial thing. It is not made less artificial on a theory of 'realism' which disguises nature under a new artificiality such as the *leit-motif,* this *leit-motif* being actually as much of a convention as the labels enclosing words which primitive painters and caricaturists drew as issuing from the mouths of their figures. It is, I suggest, greatly to Sullivan's credit that with his incomparable talent for articulating speech in music, he resisted all temptation of that talent to obscure or deafen by music the spoken words which must be the backbone of all drama since they carry and advance the plot.

And—for a last word—it may even be that your delight in Gilbert and Sullivan testifies to a natural unconscious revolt against the theory of opera so prevalent in our time. We know from the history of the Theatre—from the tyranny, for example, laid upon it so long by the theories of Castelvetro and his followers—that a barbarous mistake can be ferociously enforced by pedantry. Against such pedantry a childlike instinct may sometimes usefully assert itself, insisting 'But the Emperor *has* no clothes!'